500

LETTERS

for

DIFFICULT SITUATIONS

EASY-TO-USE TEMPLATES FOR CHALLENGING COMMUNICATIONS

COREY SANDLER AND JANICE KEEFE

Aadamsmedia

Avon, Massachusetts

Published by Adams Media,
a division of F+W Media, Inc.
57 Littlefield Street, Avon, MA 02322. U.S.A.
www.adamsmedia.com

ISBN 10: 1-4405-0077-0
ISBN 13: 978-1-4405-0077-0
eISBN 10: 1-4405-0714-7
eISBN 13: 978-1-4405-0714-4

Printed in the United States of America.

10 9 8 7 6 5 4 3 2 1

Library of Congress Cataloging-in-Publication Data
is available from the publisher.

This publication is designed to provide accurate and authoritative information with regard to the subject matter covered. It is sold with the understanding that the publisher is not engaged in rendering legal, accounting, or other professional advice. If legal advice or other expert assistance is required, the services of a competent professional person should be sought.
—From a *Declaration of Principles* jointly adopted by a Committee of the American Bar Association and a Committee of Publishers and Associations

Many of the designations used by manufacturers and sellers to distinguish their products are claimed as trademarks. Where those designations appear in this book and Adams Media was aware of a trademark claim, the designations have been printed with initial capital letters.

This book is available at quantity discounts for bulk purchases.
For information, call 1-800-289-0963.

Dedication

To my father, who wrote out a long
analysis and plan before he asked
my mother to marry him.

—*Corey Sandler*

●◆

Contents

Introduction ~ ix

PART 1: Person to Person...1

    Chapter 1: Sympathy and Condolences ~ 3
    Chapter 2: Health Issues ~ 8
    Chapter 3: Final Arrangements ~ 15

PART 2: Family Affairs 21

    Chapter 4: Family Matters ~ 22
    Chapter 5: Money and Possessions ~ 27

PART 3: Friends and Neighbors 35

    Chapter 6: Neighborhood Issues ~ 36
    Chapter 7: Helping Friends ~ 47
    Chapter 8: About the Children ~ 56
    Chapter 9: Social Engagements ~ 62

PART 4: Personal Business.. 71

    Chapter 10: Money, Contracts, and Credit Cards ~ 72
    Chapter 11: Disputes and Complaints ~ 84
    Chapter 12: About the Service We Received ~ 91
    Chapter 13: About the Product ~ 103
    Chapter 14: Dealing with a Store ~ 109
    Chapter 15: Traveling About ~ 114
    Chapter 16: Landlords and Real Estate ~ 121

PART 5: Community Organizations................................**131**

    Chapter 17: Membership Matters and Events ~ 132
    Chapter 18: Fundraising, Donations, and Volunteers ~ 141
    Chapter 19: School Days ~ 153
    Chapter 20: Church Business ~ 165

PART 6: Politics and Government **169**

    Chapter 21: Political Intrigue ~ 170
    Chapter 22: Government Affairs ~ 176

PART 7: Business **183**

    Chapter 23: Dear Boss ~ 184
    Chapter 24: Employee to Employee ~ 189
    Chapter 25: Money Matters ~ 193
    Chapter 26: Customer Service ~ 200
    Chapter 27: Hiring and References ~ 205
    Chapter 28: Employee Affairs ~ 213
    Chapter 29: Workday Matters ~ 223
    Chapter 30: Firings, Layoffs, and Cutbacks ~ 230

    Index ~ 239

Introduction

Dear Reader,

All letters should be difficult to write. That's because you should take your time to lay out your thoughts, wishes, or demands in a careful, considered way.

Think of all the times you have blurted out something (or wished you had said something other than what you did). Wouldn't it have been great to say, "Wait a minute. Let me think about what it is I want and how it would be best for me to respond."

The purpose of this book, the third in a series of collections of letters we have published, is to help you think about difficult communication. There's probably not a letter in this book that exactly matches the situation you face, but as you read through this collection there are many phrases and sentences and strategies you can use.

For our purposes, we're not going to be purists about matters of style. You can choose the form of salutation and thanks you think best. Instead we choose to concentrate on showing you ways to express your thoughts and wants in the clearest and most direct way.

The best way to write a letter is imagine you are speaking directly to the recipient. You have the advantage of being able to think carefully about what you want to say, but in the end the letter should sound very much like the words you would say across a desk or the kitchen table.

Unlike most any other book you might buy, we happily encourage you to make use of our words. Pick up phrases, whole sentences, and long paragraphs and adapt them to your needs.

And although this book uses the word "letters" in its title, that is by no means the only use you can make of the five hundred examples you'll find. Use our examples to construct your own letter, e-mail, or text message. Or read them carefully so that you think about what you plan to say face to face or over the phone.

Here's what you can do,

- Need to write a letter to a friend or a family member on a touchy subject? We've got plenty of examples.
- Got something you need to get off your chest and aimed at a government official, a politician, or someone in the school system? Read on.

- ◆ Are you running a small business or employed by one? We've got basic letters about looking for a job, handling your work assignments, hiring, firing, instituting a layoff or a cutback, and most of the other essential details of the workplace.
- ◆ Getting the runaround from a store or a contractor or someone else with whom you do business? We'll help you stand up for your rights.
- ◆ Does your civic organization need help raising funds, spending money, or fixing all that is wrong in town? We've got some ideas.

Go forth and write difficult letters (and other forms of communication). We hope this book will make the task a bit easier.

—Corey Sandler and Janice Keefe

Part 1

Person
to
Person

CHAPTER 1

Sympathy and Condolences

EXPRESSION OF SYMPATHY TO FRIEND ❧ 4

EXPRESSION OF SYMPATHY FOR DEATH
OF CHILD ❧ 4

THANKS FOR EXPRESSION
OF SYMPATHY ❧ 4

MAKING CONTRIBUTION IN MEMORY
OF FRIEND ❧ 4

THANKS FOR SUPPORT IN TIME
OF MOURNING ❧ 5

SYMPATHY FOR DEATH OF PET ❧ 5

SUPPORT FOR ILL FORMER FRIEND ❧ 5

BEST WISHES ON RETURN
FROM HOSPITALIZATION ❧ 6

SAYING GOODBYE TO NEIGHBOR WHO
IS MOVING ❧ 6

ANNOUNCING DEATH OF EXECUTIVE ❧ 6

NOTICE OF DEATH OF EMPLOYEE ❧ 7

CONDOLENCES TO SPOUSE
OF EMPLOYEE ❧ 7

SYMPATHY TO COMPANY ON DEATH
OF EXECUTIVE ❧ 7

Expression of sympathy to friend

Dear Anne,

I was deeply saddened to learn of the passing of your mother.

I spent many hours with her as a volunteer at the elementary school and the food bank. She was a warm and caring woman, and we are all diminished without her.

I know this is a difficult time for you and your family, but I want you to know that you are in our thoughts.

Please let me know if there is anything I can do to help.

Your mother was an exceptional woman and we will all miss her.

Fondly,
Karen Jenkins

Expression of sympathy for death of child

Dear Natalie,

I can hardly imagine the depth of your loss.

Losing a child is not something any of us can prepare for.

Frank and I and all of your friends are thankful for the brief time we had with Patty. She was an extraordinary young person who carried a little ray of sunshine with her everywhere she went. We will never forget her.

I wanted you to know you and your family are in our thoughts. Please let me know if there is anything we can do to assist you in these difficult times.

Love,
Joan Holly

Thanks for expression of sympathy

Dear Caroline,

Thank you for your kind words about Susan. I know the two of you were really close and had a great friendship.

It helps to know that her memory will be kept alive through the special people who knew and loved her.

I promise to keep in touch after I take a few weeks off to clear my head.

Fondly,
Jack

Making contribution in memory of friend

Dear Susan,

I want to extend my most heartfelt sympathies to you and your family.

The entire community of Rolling Meadow will mourn Don. He was a most generous and giving man, donating his time and support to so many of our important organizations.

Knowing of his special affection for the Junior Little League of Rolling Meadow, I have a set up a memorial fund in his name and made the first contribution; I will be encouraging others to add to the endowment, which will be used to pay for equipment for youngsters in need.

Please do not hesitate to let me know if there is anything I can do for you. I hope when the time is right for you, you will call me and we can get together.

Sincerely,
Ella

Thanks for support in time of mourning

Dear Sarah,

Thank you for your very kind expressions of sympathy after Jim's death.

It is so very difficult to lose a loved one, but when it happens so suddenly and unexpectedly the loss is almost too much to bear. I do know that I could not have gotten through these past few weeks without the help and support of all of my wonderful friends.

I am in the healing stage of grief, but you have all given me the confidence I need to continue living my life the way Jim would have wanted.

Sincerely,
Gina

Sympathy for death of pet

Dear Ray,

I just learned of the death of your beloved Irish setter, Wilson.

I am so sorry for your loss. Wilson was an extraordinary companion. He was highly intelligent and very protective of you and your family, and his love was unconditional.

It was always a pleasure to meet you when you were out for a walk with him. I join you in missing him.

Sincerely,
Marsha

Support for ill former friend

Dear Monica,

I'm sorry we haven't seen each other in such a long time, and even sorrier to hear from a mutual friend that you are battling some health issues.

Please know that my thoughts and prayers will always be with you. If there is anything I can do to help or if it would be a comfort for you to talk—about anything—please call me.

Fondly,
Louise

Best wishes on return from hospitalization

Dear Lori,

I just heard the great news that you're finally out of the hospital.

We're so happy you are home and on the mend.

We hope you will be ready soon for the company of some of your friends. Please let me know when you'd like us to come over, and I hope you will allow us to bring a meal or some snacks or a movie; just let us know.

Love,
Joy

Saying goodbye to neighbor who is moving

Stacy and Martin Goodwin
Rolling Meadow

Dear Stacy and Martin,

As you prepare to complete the sale of your home and begin the next phase of your life in the south of France, I wanted to wish you the very best.

As far as Anne and I are concerned, we could not have had better neighbors for the past twenty years. We've never had reason to complain, and we've very much enjoyed having you as friends.

We wish you the best of luck in the sunshine. We'll think of you all the time, but especially when we are shoveling out the driveway after another snowstorm.

Please keep in touch.

Sincerely,
Jim

Announcing death of executive

To the staff of Rolling Meadow Building Supply,

It is with great sadness that I report the passing of our longtime human resources director, Jim Pierce.

For more than sixteen years we have been so very fortunate to have someone as capable and knowledgeable as Jim working on behalf of our family of employees. His door was always open to any staffer who had a question or a problem, and he always seemed to come up with the right decision.

He leaves a devoted wife, Nora, and four children, Peter, Sam, Allison, and Jean.

We express our deepest sympathies to his family and offer our full support at this difficult time.

Roger Gibson
President
Rolling Meadow Building Supply

Notice of death of employee

To All Employees,
From Human Resources Department

We are deeply saddened to report that Jim Hapner, our senior night watchman and one of our longest-serving employees, passed away at Rolling Meadow Memorial Hospital early this morning.

Jim, known to all of us as "Chief," was stricken while on duty. Emergency aid was performed at the company, and he was quickly removed to the hospital where he died soon after arrival.

He is survived by his wife Barbara and his two sons, James Jr., and Emilio.

Chief began work at Rolling Meadow Lumber Company as a salesman in 1989, moving to the security department five years later. He was a model employee and a good friend to most of us, and he will be greatly missed.

We will pass along details about funeral arrangements as soon as they are available. We will also inform you of plans for a special company observance in his honor.

Condolences to spouse of employee

Dear Nora,

On behalf of all of us at Rolling Meadow Building Supply, I want to express our deep sadness at Jim's passing.

Jim was such an important part of our company; it is hard to imagine the coming years without him.

On a personal note, I was privileged to call him a friend. I will never forget how generous and helpful he was to me and my family when we came to Rolling Meadow three years ago. He was always willing to extend a helping hand to all who needed his help. He will be greatly missed.

If there is anything we can do to be of assistance to you and your family at this time, please do not hesitate to ask. It would be our privilege to help.

Sincerely,
Roger Gibson, President
Rolling Meadow Building Supply

Sympathy to company on death of executive

Charles Fuller, President
Rolling Meadow Bank

Dear Charlie,

I was shocked to hear about the tragic death of your executive vice president, Ron Wheeler.

Please accept my personal condolences and those of all of us at Rolling Meadow Cable Company. We dealt with Ron on a number of issues, and I always came away impressed by his knowledge and willingness to help solve any problem that came his way; he will not be easily replaced.

Please keep me informed of any tribute or memorials you will hold. I would like to attend as a friend and to pay my respects to his family.

Sincerely,
Alan Tierney, President
Rolling Meadow Cable Company

CHAPTER 2

Health Issues

OFFERING SUPPORT IN TIME
OF ILLNESS ❧ 9

THANKS FOR SUPPORT IN TIME
OF ILLNESS ❧ 9

ASKING FRIEND FOR ADVICE ON
MEDICAL ISSUE ❧ 9

SEEKING SPECIAL WHEELCHAIR
ACCOMMODATION ❧ 9

INVITING SPECIAL-NEEDS FAMILY TO JOIN
A GROUP ❧ 10

ASKING ASSIGNMENT OF DIFFERENT
DOCTOR ❧ 10

ASKING MEDICAL RECORDS
BE TRANSFERRED ❧ 11

ASKING MEDICAL RECORDS BE TRANSFERRED
FOR CAUSE ❧ 11

NOTIFICATION OF MEDICAL POWER OF
ATTORNEY OR PROXY ❧ 12

OFFERING TO HELP NEIGHBOR RECOVERING
FROM HOSPITALIZATION ❧ 12

INQUIRING ABOUT HEALTH
OF ACQUAINTANCE ❧ 12

HELPING FRIEND DEALING WITH
ILL SPOUSE ❧ 13

TO FRIENDS ABOUT ACQUAINTANCE IN
GRAVE HEALTH ❧ 13

ABOUT DETERIORATING HEALTH
OF ACQUAINTANCE ❧ 13

CHANGING ADDRESS TO
NURSING HOME ❧ 14

ACKNOWLEDGING DIFFICULTIES IN
PERSONAL LIFE ❧ 14

DECLINING INVITATION BECAUSE
OF MOURNING ❧ 14

Offering support in time of illness

Dear Helen,

I was so sorry to hear that Bill's condition has taken a turn for the worse; I think about the both of you all the time.

From the start I have been so impressed with how the two of you have handled this very difficult diagnosis. You both have been an inspiration to all of us on how to handle a crisis with dignity and respect.

I am sure the emotional and physical demands can be overwhelming. I know you have been so very involved in taking care of Bill, but I hope you are able to keep yourself in good health and spirits.

Please let me help. I am available as a driver, cook, listener, or just about anything else you might need. Please call me.

Sincerely,
Abigail

Thanks for support in time of illness

Dear Laura,

I feel as if I have turned the corner and am starting to feel like my old self again. It has been quite a strain to be ill for so long, but I am hopeful now that I can begin to return to my life and friends.

I cannot tell you how frightening it was when I received the initial diagnosis. But you and other friends were so quick to come to my side.

I could not have come this far without the tremendous support I received from wonderful people like you. I am truly blessed to have friends like you.

Sincerely,
Donna

Asking friend for advice on medical issue

Dear Bill,

I hope you don't mind, but I would appreciate some personal advice.

Beth has just been diagnosed with the early stages of Alzheimer's disease. I have heard you speak with such compassion about your wife Lorraine's struggle with the condition.

We have already joined a support group suggested by our doctor, and we hope to benefit from that.

I am hoping I could meet with you sometime in the coming weeks to learn more about how Beth and I can cope with this difficult news. You are already a role model for me.

Sincerely,
Dave Fairchild

Seeking special wheelchair accommodation

Dear Manager,

For the past twenty years our family has included The Nutcracker at the Rolling Meadow Civic Center as an important part of our holiday tradition.

Three weeks ago my wife had a bad fall and broke both of her legs; she will be in a wheelchair for the next few months.

I bought our tickets for the December 20 production in July and got our usual seats in the second row, right-side balcony. That area is not wheelchair-accessible.

When I called the ticket office to attempt to change them to another location I was informed that no refunds or changes were permitted.

We are willing to visit the theater on another night and to pay any additional charge if necessary.

I would appreciate your assistance in allowing us to continue with our holiday tradition in these changed circumstances. I have to believe there is some way the theater can work with someone with a medical need, and I also hope you can assist your ticket office in coming up with a more flexible policy for the next person faced with this sort of unexpected situation.

I look forward to hearing from you.

Thank you.
John Evans

Inviting special-needs family to join a group

Dear Mrs. Ortiz,

I would like to welcome you and your family to Rolling Meadow. It is a wonderful place to live, and we all try to look after each other as best we can.

The school nurse contacted me to say that you had given her permission to contact some area organizations on your behalf.

I would like to invite you and your son Tim to become part of our informal support group.

We are a group of five mothers and six preschool children. All of our children have been diagnosed with various levels of developmental difficulty.

We meet once a week for one hour. The children are able to socialize and play in a structured and supervised situation; as parents we get to share our experiences and strategies in helping our youngsters succeed in school and in life.

I hope you will call me to discuss the group. We welcome your participation.

Regards,
Sue Miller

Asking assignment of different doctor

Donna Sawyer, medical director
Rolling Meadow Assisted Living Home
Rolling Meadow

Dear Donna,

I am writing to request you arrange for a change of doctors for my mother, Louise Morneau.

In speaking with her, she tells us she is very uncomfortable with Dr. Beckett, the new general practitioner who has taken over Dr. Mauer's practice. As you know, my mother does not often complain about anything, and therefore we believe there is a problem we need to deal with.

We have spoken with acquaintances and done some research on doctors in the area, and I feel she would be more comfortable with a female physician like the one she had been seeing for many years before moving to the assisted-living home.

We have spoken with Dr. Mary Salcetti and she has agreed to take my mother as a new patient. I am enclosing full details about Dr. Salcetti, including some forms her office would like filled out as well as a request to Dr. Beckett for the transfer of records.

Please make an appointment for my mother for a checkup. Thanks again for your help.

Sincerely,
Brenda Coffin

Asking medical records be transferred

Jeffrey Mitchell, MD
Rolling Meadow Pediatric Services

Dear Dr. Mitchell,

Please forward all medical records and charts relating to my daughter, Suzanne Karl, to her new pediatrician, Dr. David Meehan, MD.

Dr. Meehan's address is 68 Evergreen Way, Rolling Meadow Hospital, Rolling Meadow.

Thank you.

Sarah Karl

Asking medical records be transferred for cause

Jeffrey Mitchell, MD
Rolling Meadow Pediatric Services

Dear Dr. Mitchell,

Although we have appreciated your attention to our children, in recent months it has become apparent to us that you have taken on more patients than can be reasonably handled. On our last three visits we have had to wait about an hour before being seen, and the office visits themselves were very rushed.

We have decided to have Suzanne seen by a new doctor here in town; based on our conversations with him and his office manager we believe he intends to provide a higher level of service to his patients.

Please forward all medical records and charts relating to my daughter, Suzanne Karl, to her new pediatrician, Dr. David Meehan, MD.

Dr. Meehan's address is 68 Evergreen Parkway, Rolling Meadow Hospital, Rolling Meadow.

Thank you,
Sarah Karl

Notification of medical power of attorney or proxy

Timothy Logan, MD
Rolling Meadow

In regards to Mary O'Neil

Dear Dr. Logan,

Enclosed please find certified copies of a durable power of attorney and a medical proxy prepared by our lawyer to allow us to assist in the care of my mother, Mary O'Neil. We have also enclosed a notarized copy of a letter, signed by mother, granting permission for you to discuss her medical condition and treatment with me.

We very much appreciate the care my mother has received from you for more than a decade. In her older years, we want to be able to assist her and you in handling medical issues as they arise.

If you have any questions about these forms, please contact me or our attorney; I have enclosed a copy of his business card.

Thank you again for your consideration.

Sincerely,
Marie Connor

Offering to help neighbor recovering from hospitalization

Aaron Philips
Rolling Meadow

Dear Aaron,

I was glad to hear from your wife that you are home from the hospital and recovering from your accident. Please accept my best wishes for a speedy recovery.

One of the sure signs of summer was to go by your house and see you mowing your lawn or tending to your garden. I am sure it is a concern for you that you will not be able to care for your property that well for a while.

Your wife asked me about the lawn service we use. I have two young men who cut my grass and do some maintenance on my garden once a week.

As far as I am concerned they are very dependable and do a good job; even better, their rates are quite reasonable. If you would like, I can ask them to stop by to speak to you.

They are scheduled to be at my house this Friday at 10 a.m.

And also, if it would help in any way, please let me know if there are any errands I can do for you. I would be happy to pick up groceries or other items when we go out on our own trips.

Sincerely,
Janet Mosley

Inquiring about health of acquaintance

Paul Winkler
Rolling Meadow

Dear Paul,

We really miss you around the neighborhood and at the senior center.

Please forgive me for intruding, but I was wondering if everything was okay with you. If there is anything I can do—come and visit, run some errands, or just about anything else—please don't hesitate to call and ask.

Sincerely,
Joe Vance

Helping friend dealing with ill spouse

Dear Friends,

I've just learned that Stan's cancer has progressed to the point that he is now in a hospice. They don't know how long he has, but he is still alert and seeing visitors—I'm headed there later this week.

I'm hoping that all of us can also do what we can for Betty. She doesn't drive and has been taking buses or taxis every day. I'd like to organize a rotating car pool to bring her back and forth to the hospice; there are enough of us who care for both of them to arrange for daily transportation and visits to Stan.

Please let me know if you're able to help and the best days for you. I'll put together a schedule.

Shirley

To friends about acquaintance in grave health

Dear Gene and Betsy,

I wanted to give you an update on my uncle Scott's condition.

As you know, a few months ago he was diagnosed with lung cancer. He has been undergoing treatment and has fought hard, but in the last week his condition took a turn for the worse.

He is now in the Hospice Unit at Mercy Hospital; he has come to peace with his prospects. As close friends of Scott, we thought you would like to know and might appreciate the chance to come and see him one last time.

Mornings seem to be the best for him.

Sincerely,
Marjorie Craig

About deteriorating health of acquaintance

Dear Nancy,

I ran into June and her husband at church last Sunday.

As you are probably aware, she has been under a doctor's care for some time. Until I saw her, though, I did not know how serious her condition has become.

Her husband Will later gave me a call and confirmed that she is suffering from a very serious disease, fighting for her life.

I think it would be a good idea for all of her friends to come together and offer our support to June and Will.

She still has energy to go out occasionally and has always enjoyed being with us. I don't think we should wait too long. I'd welcome your suggestions.

Sincerely,
Marge

Changing address to nursing home

Rajiv Gupta, secretary
Rolling Meadow Historical Association
Rolling Meadow

Dear Rajiv,

My mother, Rose Chambers, has been an active member of your association for many years.
She recently suffered a stroke and is now living at the Rolling Meadow Nursing Home.
Please continue to send her your monthly newsletter at that address as the Historical Association is very important to her.
Because her mobility has been affected, she will not be going to the museum any time soon. If there is a way to see that she does not receive solicitations about benefits or parties she cannot attend it would be appreciated.

Sincerely,
Bruce Chambers

Acknowledging difficulties in personal life

Dear Jack,

We think of Susan often and miss her very much. We treasure the time we had with her, and those beautiful New England, in-the-fall memories are very special.
We fully understand how you might feel uncomfortable traveling with us on your own right now.
Can we make a different suggestion? We would love for you to come visit us at our home in Georgia and spend a few days enjoying the beach; we know we'd enjoy seeing you.
I hope you'll accept. We don't want to miss the chance to see you this fall.

Love,
Gloria

Declining invitation because of mourning

Dear Gloria and Phil,

I'm sorry to say that I have decided to decline your invitation to head up to New England to view the fall colors this year. I really appreciate you thinking of me, but this year I just don't feel up to going.
Since Susan passed away in the spring, I have been trying to get my routine back to normalcy, but I'm not quite there yet.
For many years, this trip was one of our favorite activities. Not only was it a magical time of year, but being in the company of some of our dearest friends created some very special memories.
I hope you understand, and I hope you will invite me again next year. I hope by then I'll be ready.

Fondly,
Jack

CHAPTER 3

Final Arrangements

TELLING FRIENDS OF AN ILLNESS ➥ 16

TELLING FRIENDS OF DEATH
IN FAMILY ➥ 16

NOTIFICATION OF DEATH OF
YOUNG PERSON ➥ 16

INVITING GUESTS TO MEMORIAL
SERVICE ➥ 17

THANKING DOCTOR FOR CARE ➥ 17

MAKING PREARRANGEMENTS
FOR FUNERAL ➥ 17

ASKING COST OF FUNERAL ARRANGEMENTS
BE REDUCED ➥ 18

ACCEPTING PROPOSAL FOR
FUNERAL ARRANGEMENT ➥ 18

ASKING ABOUT SAFEGUARDS OF
PREPAYMENT PLAN ➥ 18

SEEKING CHANGE TO PREPAID
FUNERAL ARRANGEMENTS ➥ 19

CHANGING NAME ON SUBSCRIPTION
BECAUSE OF DEATH ➥ 19

CANCELING SUBSCRIPTION FOR
DECEASED RELATIVE ➥ 19

ASKING PROPERTY OWNED BY SIBLINGS
BE SOLD ➥ 20

OFFERING DONATION OF HOME
TO SOCIETY ➥ 20

Telling friends of an illness

To My Dearest Friends,

I am writing to tell you of some difficult news. I have been diagnosed with stage two breast cancer.

I have suspected there was a problem for a while, but it still came as quite a shock when my doctors finally figured out why I have been so weak lately.

I am determined to fight this battle and win, and I expect to be around for a long time to come.

But I want everyone to know that while I am undergoing treatment I will probably not be quite myself. I may need some TLC and a shoulder to lean on from time to time, and as always, I will treasure your friendship and support.

Love,
Julia

Telling friends of death in family

Dear Betty,

It is with great sadness that I write to tell you of my mother Sarah's death on February 3.

Our whole family was able to be with her at the hospice where she spent her final days.

We will be celebrating her life at a service in a few weeks. I will be sure to let you know the details once they are set.

In the meantime, we hope you will join us in remembering her as the vibrant, gracious, and caring person she was.

Sincerely,
Abby Connor

Notification of death of young person

Dear Ruth,

As you know, Megan's valiant struggle against cancer finally came to an end. Our precious little girl died last week.

I wanted to thank you for being so supportive to our entire family during this extraordinarily emotional year, taking care of our other children while we spent time with Megan at the hospital. It was a great kindness and gift to our family.

We feel so fortunate to have had even so brief a period of time with Megan; she will be part of us for all of our days.

We will share with you our plans for a memorial service and celebration of her life soon and we hope you will join with us then.

With our love and gratitude,

Erica Smith

Inviting guests to memorial service

Simon Keller
Rolling Meadow

As you know, my mother Gloria passed in December. In keeping with her wishes we held only a small funeral service for the immediate family at the time.

With the arrival of summer, her favorite time of the year, we have decided to invite her friends and coworkers to join us in a celebration of her life.

We hope you will join us at my home at 87 Mirror Pond Road in Rolling Meadow at 1 P.M. on Sunday, June 28.

It is our plan to share some stories and offer a toast to a wonderful lady and then fulfill her final wish, releasing her ashes over Mirror Pond.

Sincerely,
Sharon Graves

Thanking doctor for care

Timothy Latham, MD
Rolling Meadow

Dear Dr. Latham,

I want to thank you for the exceptional care you gave my mother, Sylvia Jones, in the final weeks of her life.

My mother's last days were very difficult for all of us, but the respect and dignity you showed to her made it easier for her family to accept and deal with her passing.

Thank you again.
Monica Curtis

Making prearrangements for funeral

David Barrows
Rolling Meadow Funeral Home

Dear Mr. Barrows,

I am writing on behalf of my mother, Sylvia Jones, under power of attorney. She has asked me to make prearrangements for her funeral and burial.

Basically, we would like to have the same sort of services provided for my father at your establishment in May 2009.

Please prepare a proposal and send me information about how prearranged funerals are put under contract and the protections offered clients.

Thank you.
Monica Curtis

Asking cost of funeral arrangements be reduced

David Barrows
Rolling Meadow Funeral Home

Dear Mr. Barrows,

Thank you for your proposal for prearrangement of my mother's funeral and burial in Rolling Meadow Cemetery.

With her approval I have chosen a coffin from those you suggested and have indicated it on the enclosed form.

However, the total cost of the funeral is about $2,000 more than we spent for my father; we would like to keep the expense the same. I would appreciate it if you would examine your proposal and find ways to reduce the cost by $2,000.

We were satisfied with the arrangements you made for my father and would like to continue with your establishment. I look forward to hearing from you soon.

Sincerely,
Monica Curtis

Accepting proposal for funeral arrangement

David Barrows
Rolling Meadow Funeral Home

Dear Mr. Barrows,

Thank you for your revised proposal for prearrangement of burial expenses for my mother. The small modifications you suggested in no way diminish the attention we will be devoting to my mother's memory.

At this time we have decided to accept your bid.

I have signed the contract and have enclosed the first payment. Please forward details of the escrow account when it is established.

Sincerely,
Monica Curtis

Asking about safeguards of prepayment plan

David Barrows
Rolling Meadow Funeral Home

Dear Mr. Barrows,

Thank you for sending your proposal for setting up a prepaid funeral contract for my mother.

I would appreciate it if you would also send me the paperwork associated with the state-guaranteed funeral prepayment account.

As I understand the process, you will be establishing an escrow account to hold the funds and will report to us annually on its value including any accrued interest. Under the state program we are protected against any price increases or financial difficulties at the funeral home.

I look forward to hearing from you soon.

Sincerely,
Monica Curtis

Seeking change to prepaid funeral arrangements

David Barrows
Rolling Meadow Funeral Home

Dear Mr. Barrows,

As you know, last year we made prearrangements for the funeral of my mother through your home. We signed a contract based on her wishes at the time.

While I understand that under terms of the prearrangement contract you are not required to permit cancellation of the arrangements, I would like to find out about the possibility of a change.

My mother has now decided she wishes to be cremated rather than interred.

Based on your original proposal, I believe this would not amount to much of a change in the full price since we would not be paying the expenses of burial. We would leave all other arrangements unchanged.

Could you please let me know how this change would affect our prearranged contract?

Thank you.

Sincerely,
Monica Curtis

Changing name on subscription because of death

Subscription services
Timeweek Magazine

In regards to account 6SJ7-20983092-209083

Please change the name on the above subscription from Eleanor Greenwood to Ronald Greenwood. The address remains the same.

My wife passed away three years ago and it is still a jolt to receive mail addressed in her name.

Thank you.
Ronald Greenwood

Canceling subscription for deceased relative

Subscription services
Quilting News

Dear manager,

My mother, Eleanor Bennett, was a subscriber to Quilting News and her present subscription is due to expire in sixteen months.

She passed away recently and I would like to cancel that subscription.

As executor of her estate, please send refunds to me, her son, at the following address:

Donald Bennett
86 Cross Street
Rolling Meadow

Asking property owned by siblings be sold

William Gardner
Rolling Meadow

Dear Bill,

Now that mom's estate has been fully settled, I would like to discuss how we will deal with her house.

We each received half-ownership in the property, and speaking for myself, I would rather have the cash than the responsibility to maintain the old house as a rental unit. The proceeds from a sale would be an immense help for my family.

I know you wanted to keep the house in the family. If you still feel that way, I would be happy to discuss selling out my half to you. Otherwise, I'd like to arrange to meet with a real estate agent and put the property on the market.

Regards,
Steve Gardner

Offering donation of home to society

James Burns, executive director
Rolling Meadow Historical Society

Dear Mr. Burns,

I have been a member of the Rolling Meadow Historical Society for many years, and it has long been my hope to leave my home to the society as an endowment. As you know, it is one of the original structures in the town, with many of its details unchanged from the way it was first built in 1801.

I would hope you are willing to accept my gift of the home, along with a sustaining endowment to pay for its upkeep.

Once I hear from you I will ask my attorney to work with the society's legal counsel to draw up papers prearranging for the donation of the home upon my death.

I look forward to hearing from you soon.

Sincerely,
David Meyers

Part 2

Family Affairs

CHAPTER 4

Family Matters

SEEKING AN END TO FAMILY
ESTRANGEMENT ❖ 23

WARNING ABOUT COLLEGE GRADES ❖ 23

ASKING FOR REDUCED GIFT GIVING ❖ 23

ASKING FAMILY ASSISTANCE
FOR HOLIDAYS ❖ 24

ENDING FAMILY HOLIDAY PARTY ❖ 24

DEFUSING FAMILY ARGUMENT ❖ 24

ALERTING FAMILY TO AWKWARD SITUATION
AT UPCOMING PARTY ❖ 25

NO GIFTS BECAUSE OF ECONOMY ❖ 25

NO CHILDREN AT ADULT PARTY ❖ 26

Seeking an end to family estrangement

Dear Mom and Dad,

I am so sorry that we have not been speaking to each other for so long; I very much want you both back in my life.

I know we will never agree on everything, but I love you and I know you both love me.

I'm writing to tell you that I plan to call next Wednesday evening. We can talk about what got us to this point, but much more importantly I'd like to talk about how we can reconnect as a family. I miss you both.

Love,
Roger

Warning about college grades

Dear Evan,

I am writing to let you know that your father and I are very concerned about your grades this semester at Rolling Meadow Prep School. We received a notification that you are in danger of failing three out of five of your subjects.

We were very proud of you graduating in the top ten percent of your middle-school class and receiving a scholarship to Rolling Meadow. That is why we know you are more than capable of succeeding.

As you prepare for college, one of your biggest challenges will be to learn how to manage your time. We want you to enjoy your new freedom at school, but studies must come first.

We will always be here for you; please let us know if there is a problem we can help you with or if you want us to seek some guidance from counselors at the school.

Love,
Mom

Asking for reduced gift giving

Dear Betsy,

We are very much looking forward to seeing all of our family again this Christmas.

It's been a tough year for most of us; speaking for myself, we've had more than a few financial hits this year. Brad and I are doing our best to keep spirits up, but the kids have had to learn for the first time what it's like to live on a tight budget.

I hope you don't mind, but I would like to make a suggestion that will make it easier on all of us in these difficult times: I'd like to limit the cost of any one gift to no more than $10. (Actually, if you want to give a bit more to the kids and a candy bar to the adults, that's fine with us.)

As far as we are concerned, it is gift enough to see the family. That's what Christmas is supposed to be all about anyway.

And we can hope that next year will be a better one for us all. Please let me know what you think of my idea.

Love,
Anna

Asking family assistance for holidays

Dear Kerry,

I just got a note from June saying that she and George will not be hosting the holiday party this year; I expect you received a similar note.

They have held the party at their home for many years, and I absolutely agree they deserve a much-needed break. But I would hate to see us miss the chance for a family get-together this year.

Can I suggest we all pitch in to make it a great event? I am not much of a cook, but I do have the space to host the party at my house.

If the cooking is divided up amongst you, Judy, Robin, Andrea, and Frank, I think we could put on a great feast . . . and we'll let June and George attend as our special guests.

I think it will be fun and truly in the tradition of a family event. Please let me know what you think.

Love,
Mary

Ending family holiday party

Dear Cindy,

As always, I am writing to wish all of you the best for the coming year. This time, though, there is a change; we will not be hosting a holiday party at our home.

As I'm sure you all know, George has been undergoing chemotherapy for the past few months—a very difficult time for us—and is just now beginning to regain his strength. Happily, it appears that he is on the road to recovery.

Several months ago we made the decision that as soon as he was able we were going to head somewhere warm and different. And so we have booked a two-week cruise to South America that will leave in mid-December and return after January 1.

We promise to extend a toast to all of you and wish that you and your family enjoy much happiness and good fortune in the New Year.

Fondly,
June

Defusing family argument

Dear Uncle Steve,

I hope you will once more come to our annual New Year's Day party. We very much enjoy having the whole family together for the day.

I would, though, make one special request. For the past several years, you and Uncle Jack have become embroiled in some very loud and sometimes unpleasant disagreements about politics. It has put an edge on what should be a celebration of family togetherness and the New Year.

The last thing anyone wants to do is deny anyone the right to their opinion, but we find the prospect of another party like last year to be rather upsetting.

I have written the same note to Uncle Jack. I could not think of celebrating without the two of you there. I just want this New Year to begin on a positive note. Can I have your word that we'll stick to football, food, and family matters?

Love,
Lilly

Alerting family to awkward situation at upcoming party

Dear Family,

The holidays are just a few weeks away, and I want to make sure all of you know that we hope you will join us at the dinner we plan on Christmas Day.

Obviously, this year will be different from years past. Dad has accepted my invitation, and he will be bringing his new wife, Ella.

This has been a difficult year for all of us, but I don't want to exclude dad from our gathering, and that now means that Ella is part of the family as well.

I have already spoken at great length with mom, and she agrees that it is more important than ever that the family stay in touch. Mom has decided that she will make a brief appearance at the party after dinner; we hope that in later years, with the passage of time, the situation will become a bit less awkward.

I hope you will all join us at the party and that we can all treat mom and dad and Ella with love.

Love,
Susan

No gifts because of economy

To Our Family,

I am writing first to tell you all how happy I am that we will be getting together again this year for our Christmas gathering. Seeing all of you and having our children spend time with their relatives is the essence of the holiday for us.

Unfortunately, though, this year brings difficult times for us. With Tom being laid off and my hours at the museum reduced, we have barely enough money to spend on the mortgage and essentials.

Our family has always made a big deal about gift giving, especially to the children.

Our children already know how things have changed in our household. Actually, they have been very good about finding ways to help us save money. One thing we have decided together is that this year we will not be able to participate in the exchange of presents.

I know we are not the only ones suffering in this economy, and I don't want anyone to feel sorry for us. We are very lucky to have a wonderful family and a great party to go to.

Just as we do not intend to spend money on gifts, we also do not expect you to do so for us. We would be very happy to exchange cards, handmade crafts, and cookies.

Love,
Tina

No children at adult party

Lynn Hutton

Dear Lynn,

I am so pleased that you will be coming to Rolling Meadow to attend Uncle Harold's 80th birthday.

In your letter you said you and Dan would be making a weekend of it and bringing your children. We are looking forward to seeing the kids, but we ask that they not come to the birthday dinner, which will be held at a very adult restaurant here in town.

I am sure there will be time for them to see Uncle Harold and Aunt Abby at some point during your visit.

I am enclosing a list of some excellent babysitters; we know them all and I'm sure one of them can help watch the children when you come to the party.

Looking forward to seeing you.

Sincerely,
Wendy

CHAPTER 5

Money and Possessions

TELLING FAMILY OF DECISION TO SELL
SUMMER HOUSE ➡ 28

ASKING FAMILY INVOLVEMENT IN
FINANCIAL DECISIONS ➡ 28

ASKING FAMILY ASSISTANCE
FOR ELDERS ➡ 28

ASKING FAMILY TO CONSIDER CARE
FOR PARENT ➡ 29

SEEKING FAMILY ASSISTANCE
FOR PARENT ➡ 29

ASKING END TO REQUESTS FOR MONEY
FROM PARENTS ➡ 29

ASKING SIBLINGS TO HELP PARENTS
WITH LANDSCAPING ➡ 30

ASKING FOR FAMILY SUPPORT FOR
TAG SALE ➡ 30

FAMILY CELL PHONE LIMITS ➡ 31

ENDING FINANCIAL SUPPORT TO
FAMILY MEMBER ➡ 31

ASKING RELATIVE FOR MONEY ➡ 31

DECLINING TO OFFER LOAN TO
FAMILY MEMBER ➡ 32

RESPONSE TO OFFER BY RELATIVE TO
PERFORM REPAIRS ➡ 32

DIVORCED PARENT ASKING FOR MORE
MONEY FOR CHILD ➡ 32

ASKING FOR RETURN OF ITEM
AFTER DEATH ➡ 33

DISPOSITION OF POSSESSIONS ➡ 33

PARTIAL DISPOSITION
OF POSSESSION ➡ 34

ASKING TO PURCHASE ITEM
FROM ESTATE ➡ 34

Telling family of decision to sell summer house

Dear Children,

Last week I came across a box of old photographs and spent the rest of the day reminiscing about wonderful times at the cottage on Mirror Pond. Each of us has our own special memories, but I'm sure all of us agree we have been so fortunate to have such an extraordinary place in our lives.

It also got your father and me thinking about our future and the amount of time and money we have to spend to keep up the summer home. Now that all of you have your own families we don't use the cottage all that often any more.

We have decided that it is not practical for us to continue to hold on to the house after this season. We're going to put it on the market and use the proceeds for our retirement expenses.

Before we do that, of course, we would be happy to hear from any of you who might want to buy the house and land and keep it in the family. We have a special price in mind if you do, the appraised value minus the amount we would pay to a real estate agent and lawyer, and we'd throw in all of the furniture and all of the memories.

Please let us know by June 1.

Love,
Mom and Dad

Asking family involvement in financial decisions

To Dan, Ed, Mike, Karen, and Marcia,

As you know, I just returned home from visiting mom and dad. I wanted to tell you some of the things I learned and to share some concerns.

For their age, mom and dad appear to be healthy. It is good to see that they are still active in community affairs and take an interest in politics. And, of course, they wanted to know all about each of us and our families.

They are, though, becoming increasingly frail. They are at the point where they need assistance with some basic tasks like house cleaning, meal preparation, and general household repairs.

We have always made it a point to stay out of their financial matters. They worked hard to earn what they have and we never wanted to interfere. I think, though, that it is our duty now to help with some things that are about to become overwhelming.

I would ask each of you to give some thought to how we can help mom and dad financially and with our time. I'd like to set up a telephone conference call by the end of the month. I'll give each of you a call before then to arrange a time.

Love,
Jane

Asking family assistance for elders

Dear Carol,

It has given me a great deal of happiness all these years to live so close to our mother. I have been fortunate to be able to spend so much time with her and I would not trade that for anything.

But I am writing you now to ask for your help.

Mom's care and welfare require more than I can now give her. The time has come when the two of us must make some decisions about her future.

We both love her very much and want her to be safe and happy. Let's talk soon about ways we can share the joy and the burden of helping her with the next phase of her life.

Love,
Marion

Asking family to consider care for parent

To Barbara, Jim and Ross,

Since I live closest to Dad and have the opportunity to see him most frequently, I feel I can provide the best report on his health and well-being.

At his age he still is mentally as sharp as ever. Physically, though, this is not the case. I don't believe it is safe for him to live alone any longer, and I also don't feel he should be driving.

We all knew that if we were lucky enough to have Dad around for a good long period, the time would come when we as his children would probably have to make some decisions for him.

The bottom line is we want him to be safe and happy. We also don't want him to feel that he has no say in what we all hope is a long future.

I propose we individually make some proposals and then share them with each other. We can then present our ideas to Dad and ask for his thoughts.

Love,
Amelia

Seeking family assistance for parent

To Barbara, Jim, and Ross,

I told you recently about my concerns for Dad's safety.

I visited him again today and I think it is time to take some steps to help him. I'm afraid he is very near the time when he can no longer live alone.

I am enclosing some brochures from assisted-living facilities in the area. This would be my personal choice to give Dad his own place but also provide the services and caretaking he needs.

I can no longer be solely in charge; we must do this together. Please contact me as soon as possible with your ideas.

We all love Dad too much to wait until something happens.

Love,
Amelia

Asking end to requests for money from parents

To Barbara and Ross,

I am writing to both of you because I recently became aware of something concerning Dad.

As you know, I am in the process of getting Dad's financial records in order. We have all agreed that the best and safest option for our father was to hire a live-in caregiver for as long as that is possible and to then consider an assisted-living facility.

While working out the economics of this move I found that every month for the past year Dad has been giving Jim a check for $1,000. We all know Dad means well and that Jim has had a hard time making ends meet in his job as a community organizer.

But, in the end, I hope you will agree with me that Dad's welfare has to take the highest priority. None of us wants to tell Dad how to spend his money, but hiring a caretaker or paying for assisted living is going to be costly.

I'd like for the three of us to come to an agreement on how to handle this, and to then meet with Jim. We need to come up with a budget for Dad, and Jim needs to find a way to support himself without affecting the comfort and safety of our father.

Love,
Amelia

Asking siblings to help parents with landscaping

Dear Gus and Billy,

I think it is finally time for dad to sit on the deck while someone else mows the lawn and tends to the landscaping. He's earned the right.

We have two choices: paying for someone to do the job, or adding it to our own chores. As far as I'm concerned, we all live close enough to do it ourselves, and I think it would be a nice way to combine our visits with some help around the house.

Here's what I'd like to propose. There are three of us and six months of work from April through September. How about we alternate months amongst us?

We're all going to be over at the house for Mother's Day. Can I suggest we inaugurate the plan by arriving with work clothes and gloves?

Sincerely,
Jill

Asking for family support for tag sale

To the Family,

As you may know, my mother and father, Tom and Edna, are going to be moving to an assisted-living facility soon.

Since they are moving into a furnished apartment, we have decided the best way to dispose of their belongings (and raise some money for their rent) is to hold a large tag sale on Saturday, July 30.

I am asking any members of the family who can help us to contact me. We need some assistance in moving furniture, working at the tag sale, and then in cleaning out the house.

Although the main purpose of the sale is to raise money for Tom and Edna's new home, we will also be happy to give special prices to members of the family at the sale.

Please let me know if you are available.

Love,
Tonya

Family cell phone limits

Evan, Barbara, and Emily,

I am sending this letter to all three of you; Evan and Barbara at college and Emily at home.

Your mother and I agreed to pay for your cell phones. We like the security of knowing you can always get in touch with us, and we do understand that you like to speak to your friends.

We are covered by a family plan and share a single pool of minutes. When we gave you the cell phone we agreed to pay for it, but you were to stay within the guidelines of a certain number of minutes each month, no more than 250 minutes per month for each of you.

We just received the bill for May, and we find that each of you went significantly over that amount. The added cost to the family was nearly $100.

If this happens again we will have to curtail your usage or ask that you pay for your own phone. We are not interested in controlling or interfering in your lives, but since we are paying the bills we get to set the rules.

Love,
Dad

Ending financial support to family member

Dear Doreen,

It was nice to receive your Christmas card and letter and learn you are very optimistic about the coming year. We all hope for an improvement over the old one.

Mary and I were very sorry about all of the difficulties you went through in the past few months; we know they were all beyond your control. We were very glad we could help a little bit financially and hope this contributed to getting you back on your feet again.

At this time, though, we will no longer be sending you checks each month. Please consider what we have given you in the past as a gift; we do not expect to be repaid.

Please keep us up to date on what is going on in your life; we wish you all good news from now on.

Love,
Peter

Asking relative for money

Dear Uncle Jack,

It is very difficult for me to be writing this letter, but I don't feel I have any other good choice.

As you know, I was laid off from my job last month when the factory closed down. I have been looking for a decent job ever since, but thus far I have had no luck.

June's job at the library is only part time and does not include any benefits. We have cut back on almost everything we can. We've put the rabbit ears back on the television sets and canceled the cable bill, and the car only moves out of the garage when it's absolutely necessary.

I am, though, very near the point where we will not have enough money to pay our mortgage. I have never had to ask for this kind of help, and I hate doing so now, but I have to find a way to care for my family.

I don't expect a gift. But if you would be able to loan me enough to cover our mortgage and health care premiums for the next five months, I'm convinced this will give us enough time to find a new job and get back to paying our own bills.

As I said, I wouldn't be asking if I thought there was any other option.

Fondly,
John

Declining to offer loan to family member

Dear John,

I got your letter and it broke my heart.

I have always been proud of you and June and the way you were raising your two beautiful children.

But I am afraid that I cannot offer you a loan of the size you are asking. First of all, I don't have that much available cash; in retirement we are living on a very tight fixed income. I cannot tap into our retirement savings.

And then there is this: I can't think of anything that could be more damaging to the fabric of a family than to make a major outstanding loan. What if you have difficulty repaying it?

Without getting into specifics, I did discuss your situation with a friend of mine who is a financial planner. He offered to speak with you on the phone to discuss some possibilities including refinancing your mortgage, restructuring other debts, and budgeting issues.

You will always have our support as a member of the family. I wish you the best in finding a job soon.

Love,
Uncle Jack

Response to offer by relative to perform repairs

Dear Dave,

Thanks for giving me a price for the repairs to my car.

I am not surprised that there is so much body work required. I'm just thankful that no one was hurt (other than the deer).

My surprise is with the price you quoted for parts and labor. While you were working on your estimate, we brought our car to one of the body shops here in town; their total price was about $500 less than yours. The cost of parts is nearly identical.

As my cousin, I certainly don't expect you to lose money on work within the family. But I hope you can also understand that we don't want to spend hundreds of dollars unnecessarily.

I'd be happy to discuss this with you and show you the quote from the body shop. Perhaps you can see something we are missing.

Please let me know how you want to proceed.

Bart

Divorced parent asking for more money for child

Dear Natalie,

Marybeth has just informed me that she would like to go to Paris with her French class this spring. She's all excited about it, and I think it would be good for her to begin to learn how to live away from home for a while.

I am writing to see if we can agree between us to split the costs of the trip; Marybeth says it should be about $2,000.

Under our child support agreement, we are together paying for her education and living expenses. Things like a class trip are not included, and I'm certainly not interested in going back to court for this purpose; I doubt the judge would reopen the agreement in any case.

So, can we come together for Marybeth's sake here? Please let me know and then we can discuss it with her.

Sincerely,
Brad

Asking for return of item after death

Dear Kathleen,

Please accept my deepest sympathies on the death of your mother. She was a wonderful person and I was proud to consider her one of my dearest friends.

When you are sorting through your mother's possessions, I expect you will find a small pearl and ruby pin that was one of my favorite pieces of jewelry.

Your mother asked to borrow the pin a few weeks ago to wear at a family gathering. I would very much appreciate it if I could have it back.

I know you have many other things to do; there is no immediate rush, but I would like to make sure the pin does not go astray.

Please give me a call at your convenience and I can come pick it up.

Sincerely,
Claire Cameron

Disposition of possessions

Dear Monica,

It was good to see you at the services for my mother last week; it was not the happiest time, but it was comforting to be surrounded by family and friends.

At the end of the day you pulled me aside to tell me that my mother had promised you her pearl ring. It was not the appropriate time for me to discuss your request, but I did want to let you know my thoughts now.

That lovely ring is of special meaning in my family; I'm not sure you are aware of its history. My father bought it when he was stationed in the Pacific in World War II. My mother proudly wore it for more than forty years.

After my daughter Tina was born, we used to say that someday when she met and married someone as wonderful as my father it would be hers. My mother never said otherwise, and there is no mention of a bequest to you in her will.

I am sure you will understand that we want this remembrance of my mother to remain in the family.

I know you were a good friend to my mother, and I will find some other memento of hers for you to remember her by.

Sincerely,
Chris Walker

Partial disposition of possession

Dear Dick,

You dropped by last week while I was clearing out my father's house; I apologize if I seemed a bit distracted. In the conversation you told me my father had promised to give you his snow blower as thanks for clearing his driveway this past winter. I told you at the time I would get back to you.

My father was a wonderful and very generous man. Many times, though, his generosity exceeded his ability to follow through.

Here's the story, the snowblower cost about $1,000 and it is not fully paid for. The loan from the hardware store still has about $600 outstanding.

In the spirit of my father's promise to you, I am willing to give you the machine if you will take over the remaining payments or pay it off in full. Otherwise I must sell the machine and give the proceeds to the store.

Again, thanks for your many kindnesses to my father. Please let me know your decision about the snowblower as soon as possible.

Stew Gamble

Asking to purchase item from estate

Beverly Adams
Rolling Meadow

Dear Beverly,

I want to again say how sad I am about the death of your mother. She and I were friends for many years and I will miss her very much.

I know that as executor of her estate you're going to be very busy handling the disposition of her property.

I did, though, want to let you know that I have long admired one of your mother's possessions—the dragonfly Tiffany Lamp that was the centerpiece of her parlor. She and I used to joke about it; I kept trying to buy it from her and she would always say it would be the last thing she would ever sell.

It would mean a great deal to me if I could buy this lamp from the family as a remembrance of your mother. If this is possible, I would be happy to pay its appraised value and keep it in a place of honor in my home.

Sincerely,
Ethel Kramer

Part 3

Friends and
Neighbors

CHAPTER 6

Neighborhood Issues

INTRODUCTION TO NEW NEIGHBOR •◦ 37

ASKING NEIGHBOR TO CUT TREE •◦ 37

DECLINING TO SPLIT COSTS
OF LANDSCAPING •◦ 37

OFFER TO BUY SHARED EQUIPMENT •◦ 38

APOLOGIZING FOR FAMILY ARGUMENT
AT DINNER •◦ 38

ASKING PARENTS TO SUPERVISE DOG •◦ 38

COMPLAINT ABOUT NEIGHBOR'S DOG •◦ 39

ASKING FOR CLEANUP AFTER DOG •◦ 39

COMPLAINING ABOUT TEASING
OF DOG •◦ 40

SECOND LETTER TO PARENTS ABOUT
TEASING DOG •◦ 40

DECLINING REQUEST TO CARE
FOR DOG •◦ 40

DECLINING REQUEST TO HOUSE SIT •◦ 41

OBJECTING TO LOUD PARTIES •◦ 41

WITHDRAWING OFFER TO
HELP MOVE •◦ 41

ASKING FOR RETURN OF LOANED ITEM •◦ 42

ASKING FOR RETURN OR PURCHASE OF
LOANED ITEM •◦ 42

REPORTING DAMAGE TO
LOANED ITEM •◦ 42

COMPLAINT ABOUT CONDITION OF
RETURNED ITEM •◦ 43

ASKING REPLACEMENT OF
DAMAGED ITEM •◦ 43

TELLING OF BREAKAGE OF
LOANED ITEM •◦ 43

APOLOGY FOR DAMAGE AND OFFER
TO PAY •◦ 44

RETURNED ITEM NOT THE
RIGHT ONE •◦ 44

DECLINING TO LEND VEHICLE •◦ 44

ASKING FOR MORE TIME WITH
LOANED ITEM •◦ 45

DECLINING MORE TIME WITH
LOANED ITEM •◦ 45

CANCELLING TRIP BECAUSE OF FINANCIAL
DIFFICULTIES •◦ 45

ASKING FORMER ROOMMATE TO REMOVE
ITEMS FROM APARTMENT •◦ 46

Introduction to new neighbor

Tom and Peggy Thompson

Dear Tom and Peggy,

I want to welcome you to the neighborhood. Jim and I live across the street from you, 68 Spruce Lane. I am sure you will find our little block to be a warm and friendly place.

Jim and I have been here for thirty-five years and there is nowhere else I would rather live. When you are settled in, please give us a call or wave at us—we spend most evenings unwinding on our front porch and we'd be happy to have you over for a cool drink.

Sincerely,
Eleanor Whalen

Asking neighbor to cut tree

Stephen Denton
Rolling Meadow

Dear Steve,

Once again we have had to hire someone to clean our rain gutters, which have become clogged with leaves and pods from the maple tree on your property that hangs over into our yard.

When I mentioned this to you last fall you said you would have the tree pruned; this was not done.

I want to maintain good relations with you as our neighbor, but I also am unhappy at the expense and inconvenience caused by this tree. I have consulted with our attorney and he informs me that we have the right to trim or remove any branches that cross the property line.

Before we make that sort of arrangement, we would like to ask you one more time to do it yourself. It may save the tree, and it would certainly save our friendship.

I look forward to hearing from you soon.

Sincerely,
Craig Hennessy

Declining to split costs of landscaping

Ted and Aileen Egan
Rolling Meadow

Dear Ted and Aileen,

Several weeks ago you asked if Marie and I would like to split the costs of planting some trees and doing some landscaping along the property line between our houses.

We met with your landscaper and he detailed the plans that you were interested in. We certainly liked what we saw, but the cost is much more than we are prepared to spend at this time.

If you'd like to discuss a more modest plan we would be happy to do so.

Sincerely,
Ben Noel

Offer to buy shared equipment

Jim Thompson

Dear Jim,

I wanted to wish you and your family the best of luck in your move south—down where the snow doesn't pile up to the window sills. We will miss you; it's been great having you as neighbors.

Three years ago we purchased a snowblower together, an arrangement that has worked out well. The other day you suggested I buy out your share, and I think this is a good idea.

However, I think the price you placed on the machine is too high. I checked with two dealers here in town about the value of a used snowblower as well as a new model, and they suggested the unit we have is worth no more than $400.

If it is agreeable to you, I will pay you $200 for your share of the machine. Otherwise, I suppose the only other solution is to put the snowblower on the market and see how much we can get for it from someone else.

Sincerely,
John

Apologizing for family argument at dinner

Alex Barrows
Rolling Meadow

Dear Alex,

I want to apologize for subjecting you to a bit of family disharmony at Christmas dinner.

My intentions were good; you are a dear friend and Greg and I did not want you to spend the day alone. I imagine there were a few times when you might have wished you were elsewhere.

In any case, I'm sure you understand that the holidays do not necessarily bring out the best in people. Some of those arguments you heard have been going on since I was a child and I am sure will continue long into the future.

I'd like to make it up to you. Can I invite you to a civilized dinner with carefully selected friends? (As they say, you can pick your friends but not your family.)

Sincerely,
Paula

Asking parents to supervise dog

Dear Sue,

My son Dillon enjoys playing with your son Alex very much, and my husband and I think Alex is a really good kid.

However, the last couple of times Dillon has come home from your house he has had scratches and even a few small bite marks on his arm. Dillon tells me they are from your new puppy, Buster.

We love dogs, and we want Dillon to be comfortable with them. But at this time we have to ask that there be adult supervision when Dillon is in your home to prevent this sort of injury; we also want to make sure that the puppy is not harmed.

Please let me know your plans. I'd be glad to speak with you about this matter before the next time Alex and Dillon (and Buster) get together.

Sincerely,
Claire Thomas

Complaint about neighbor's dog

Peter and Susan Whitman
Rolling Meadow

Dear Peter and Susan,

We enjoy your dog Tucker almost as much as you do, but I am afraid we have lately been having some problems with him.

For the past few weeks, Tucker has come on to our property and has broken into garbage bags left out on Sunday night for pickup on Monday morning. Before you ask, we know it was Tucker because we caught him in the act.

He's making a mess and causing us a lot of extra work. And we're also concerned he might be harmed by bones and other things in the garbage.

We do have a town ordinance that prohibits free-roaming dogs. I'd hate to have to call the police.

Could you please find a way to keep him out of our yard?

Thank you.
Brad Kelly

Asking for cleanup after dog

Laura and Paul Foy
Rolling Meadow

Dear Mr. and Mrs. Foy,

It has been fun to see your children walk their new puppy these past few weeks. The dog is very cute.

Unfortunately, he seems to particularly enjoy our front lawn as a place to do his business. Your children have made no attempt to clean up after him.

As you may know, our town has an ordinance that requires animal owners to dispose of solid waste in approved containers.

I don't want to take away your childrens' joy with their new dog, but I must insist that the messes not be left behind. One of the lessons of having a pet (and a child, I might add) is that with the joy comes the responsibility.

I hope this letter is sufficient to deal with this problem.

Sincerely,
Liz Friedman

Complaining about teasing of dog

Bill and Jessica Brown
Rolling Meadow

Dear Mr. and Mrs. Brown,

We live a block away from you, at 98 Somerset Lane. Our twelve-year-old Shetland sheepdog loves to roam our fenced-in yard; it's his territory to protect.

I'm sorry to say, though, that for the past few weeks your two sons have decided it is entertaining to stop at the fence and tease our dog. Shelties are very gentle, but they can be easily riled up, and your boys have figured out exactly how to do so.

I have tried to ask the boys to stop several times, but instead they just ran away.

I am asking that you explain to your children that this is inappropriate behavior. I hope we can deal with this quickly and politely.

Thank you.
Susan Burke

Second letter to parents about teasing dog

Bill and Jessica Brown
Rolling Meadow

Dear Mr. and Mrs. Brown,

It has been a week since I made you aware of the actions of your sons in regard to my dog.

They have not stopped teasing him. And when I confronted them yesterday and asked them to stop they were rude and used inappropriate language to me.

I have spoken with the community association and with the town animal control officer, and I have found there are some steps I can take to deal with the harassment of our dog.

I would like to ask you one more time to tell your children that they must act responsibly.

We are only asking that our dog be left alone. We would rather not file a complaint about your children, but if that is the only way to deal with this situation we will do so.

Susan Burke

Declining request to care for dog

Dale Tyler
Rolling Meadow

Dear Dale,

Your trip to South America sounds great. You're lucky to be able to go somewhere warm in the middle of our winter.

You asked if I would be available again to take care of Buster while you are away.

As much as I enjoyed his company last year, I'm afraid that I won't be able to do so at this time. I've taken a job working at the library and I am out of the house five days a week.

I don't think that would be fair to Buster.

I do know of a woman across town who boards dogs at her farm. If you'd like, I'll pass along her phone number. Some of my friends speak very highly of her.

Sincerely,
Karen

Declining request to house sit

Janet Stevens
Rolling Meadow

Dear Janet,

You asked if I would be available to housesit your apartment while you are away for a week in December. When you first asked, I told you I would be happy to do so.

In rereading your note, I realized that you were also expecting me to care for your two cats. I am terribly allergic and could not possibly spend time in a place where there were cats.

I'm afraid I'll have to decline; I wish I could help but I can't.

Sincerely,
Emily

Objecting to loud parties

Dear Jay and Suzanne,

We hope you are enjoying your time at your winter home in Florida; you are certainly missing some pretty awful weather up here.

I'm afraid, though, that I must pass along a complaint about some activities taking place in your house. Your son Jeff, who is living there while attending college, has been having parties several times a week.

The street fills up with cars, and there is loud noise and music late into the night; on Saturday the party began around 9 P.M. and kept us awake until after 3 A.M. We have found beer bottles on our property and in the street, and we also fear that some of the guests are driving after drinking.

As you know, the town by-laws say that no loud music or other disturbances are permitted after 10 P.M.

I have spoken to Jeff about this several times. He was very polite and said he would take care of the situation but nothing has changed.

Because of our longstanding friendship, I am asking that you intervene and put a stop to these incidents. Otherwise, I feel I have no choice but to call the police and ask them to make a visit.

Sincerely,
Don

Withdrawing offer to help move

Tim Vaughn
Rolling Meadow

Dear Tim,

I really hate to do this to you, but I have to withdraw my offer to help you move to your new apartment next Friday.

As much as I would have enjoyed the activity, I hurt my back the other day doing ordinary housework and I don't think it would be very smart for me to try and lift sofas and bookcases.

My truck is still available, though.

Please let me know if you want the truck; I'd be happy to let you fill it up, and I can drive it and act as the supervisor of the move.

Sincerely,
Dick

Asking for return of loaned item

Dear Karl,

I hope you and Janet had a wonderful time on your vacation; the itinerary sounded fantastic.

When you were planning your trip you asked if you could borrow my digital camera. There are not many people I would trust with my expensive toy; you're one of just a few.

Can I come by soon to retrieve my camera? I'd like to use it for a family gathering next week.

Sincerely,
Chris

Asking for return or purchase of loaned item

Dear Mr. Rogers,

I am writing on behalf of my father, John Abbott.

As you may know he recently suffered a stroke and is recovering at a rehabilitation facility. When he is able, he will be moving to an assisted-living facility.

We are in the process of preparing his home for sale and getting his affairs in order.

About a year ago, when my father found he was no longer able to take care of his lawn, he loaned his riding mower to you and hired a landscaping service.

At this time, we would like to know if you would like to purchase the mower; the funds will help pay for his expenses at his new home. If you are not interested in buying the machine, please contact me to arrange its return.

Sincerely,
Clair Gordon

Reporting damage to loaned item

Dear Chris,

I am so appreciative of the loan of your camera. We used it through most of our trip.

But I'm afraid I have some bad news; despite my best efforts it was damaged in a fall in Switzerland. A careless waiter knocked it off the table in a restaurant.

But before you get worried, please know that I will take full responsibility.

I would like your permission to send the camera to the manufacturer for evaluation to see if it can be repaired to your satisfaction. If not, I guess I owe you a new camera.

I've already spoken to the manufacturer, and they say they will be able to give a quick report on the damage and tell us whether it can be fully fixed.

I appreciate your generosity in loaning me this valuable piece of equipment, and one way or another you'll have a great camera soon.

Sincerely,
Karl

Complaint about condition of returned item

Dear Linda,

Thanks for returning the dress you borrowed from me to wear at the cocktail party for the theater guild. I appreciate that you had it dry-cleaned.

However, when I examined the dress, I found that several rows of sequins were missing from the lower panel. I don't know if that damage occurred while you were wearing it or at the cleaner's.

Either way, I consider the dress damaged and in need of repair by a professional.

If you believe the damage occurred at the dry cleaner's facility, I would ask that you file a claim with them. Otherwise, please let me know and I will obtain an estimate from a seamstress here in town.

I was happy to be able to help you out with the loan of the dress. I'm sure you understand that I expect it to be returned in the same condition it was in when you picked it up.

Sincerely,
Jennifer

Asking replacement of damaged item

Dear Karl,

Thank you for sending me the report from the camera maker about the cost of repairs; they did quite a thorough diagnosis . . . and they're asking for a lot of money.

I am sorry to say that I don't feel comfortable with the proposed repairs. It doesn't take much to ruin a delicate piece of electronics and a lens, and I'm not convinced that these items can be repaired fully.

As you know, the camera was only a few months old when you borrowed it. Replacement cost is about $1,200. Please call me to discuss.

Sincerely,
Chris

Telling of breakage of loaned item

Dear Gina,

I hardly know where to begin, except to say I am so sorry. The punch bowl you loaned us for our anniversary party has been seriously damaged in a fall.

The morning after the party, as we were cleaning up, we put aside the bowl for special treatment. We were really trying to take care of it, but somehow it fell to the tile floor in our kitchen.

I know the bowl was an important family heirloom. We kept all the pieces, but I'm pretty sure it is beyond repair.

I hope you will forgive me, and I hope you will tell me what you want us to do. We can try to have it repaired or try to find a replacement to give to you.

I was so pleased that you loaned the beautiful bowl to us for our happy party. Again, I am so sorry about what happened.

Please call me.

Sincerely,
Judith

Apology for damage and offer to pay

Dear Veronica,

I am writing to again apologize for my unfortunate accident at your party. I can't believe that I spilled red wine on your beautiful white sofa.

You told me not to worry about it, but that's just about all I've been doing since Saturday, worrying. I am embarrassed and angry at myself for being so careless.

I have spoken with a local furniture restorer and he tells me he can clean the sofa or replace the cushion if necessary; I'd like to make this up to you.

Please give me a call to discuss.

Sincerely,
Lucy

Returned item not the right one

Dear Ralph,

Lisa told me that you brought back my scroll saw yesterday while I was at work.

I appreciate your effort in returning a borrowed tool, but I'm afraid you left with me a tool that is not mine.

The saw I loaned you was a Dewalt cordless circular saw; I'm looking at the box right here. The tool you left in my garage is a much lesser store-brand jig saw.

Perhaps you borrowed saws from two people. In any event, I am sure you can figure it out.

At your convenience, would you please pick this one up and return mine.

Sincerely,
Lou

Declining to lend vehicle

Stan Blanchard
Rolling Meadow

Dear Stan,

I have been rethinking your request to borrow our truck to move some furniture to your cottage on Eagle Mountain.

As much as I would love to be able to help out, I have come to the decision that my good old truck might not be up to the task. It's twelve years old and the only trips it makes these days is to and from the dump, and sometimes I'm a bit worried about whether it will make it back.

I think it would be much safer and comfortable for you to rent a newer vehicle from an agency. I'm sorry to disappoint you, but I am sure it would be a much bigger problem if the truck breaks down between here and the mountains.

Good luck!
Jim

Asking for more time with loaned item

Dear Tony,

I want to apologize for keeping your garden tiller longer than I had promised. I asked to borrow it for just two days and I still have it two weeks later.

First of all, all is well with the tiller.

But I ran into problems with the rainy weather and my own schedule, and I have not yet completed the work I wanted to do in the garden.

If it is okay with you, I'd like to ask your permission to hold on to the tiller for one more week. The weather for the next few days looks good for working in the garden.

I promise to return it by next Sunday, rain or shine. Please let me know if this presents any problems for you.

Sincerely,
Jeff

Declining more time with loaned item

Dear Jeff,

I'm sorry to hear you were not able to get your garden planted. I do, though, want to ask that you return my tiller as soon as possible.

I have been watching the weather forecast, and I need to get my own garden planted this week. Please arrange to return the tiller. I will probably be done with my work by Saturday, and if you want to call me then I expect I can lend it to you again at that time.

Sincerely,
Tony

Canceling trip because of financial difficulties

Ruth Andrews
Rolling Meadow

Dear Ruth,

When Jim and I signed up a year ago to accompany you on the trip to Norway we were really excited about the wonderful expedition through the fjords.

Unfortunately, a great deal has happened since then and it is with sadness we now find that we will not be able to go. We are faced with unanticipated health issues and expenses that we will not able to avoid.

According to the agreement, we are still within the time frame to receive a full refund of our deposit; I would appreciate your attention to getting the funds back to us.

We hope to be able to go with you on a future trip. Please keep us informed of plans you make for next year and beyond.

Sincerely,
Dolores Rector

Asking former roommate to remove items from apartment

Jonah Brennan
Rolling Meadow

Dear Jonah,

It has been six weeks since you moved out of the apartment. I hope your new job and rental unit are working out well for you.

When you left you said you would make arrangements to collect the remainder of your possessions, including your bed and treadmill. So far I have heard nothing from you, and your items are making it difficult for us.

A new roommate will be moving here at the beginning of the month. Would you please call me to arrange for me to let you in to remove your possessions? If I don't hear from you by the end of the month I will hire a mover to take some of the items to the landfill.

Thank you.

Ray

CHAPTER 7

Helping Friends

ESTRANGEMENT FROM FRIEND ❧ 48

TO AN ESTRANGED FRIEND ❧ 48

SEEKING TO RENEW ESTRANGED
FRIENDSHIP ❧ 48

THANKS FOR FRIEND'S CONCERN ❧ 48

THANKS FOR HELP IN CARING
FOR FAMILY ❧ 49

THANKS FOR HELP IN TIME OF CRISIS ❧ 49

OFFERING HELP TO FRIEND WITH
PERSONAL PROBLEM ❧ 49

TELLING OF LOSS OF JOB ❧ 50

SUPPORT FOR SOMEONE WHO LOST JOB ❧ 50

COUPLE TELL OF DIVORCE ❧ 50

TELLING OF DIVORCE ❧ 51

SUPPORTING A FRIEND GOING THROUGH
A DIVORCE ❧ 51

SUPPORT TO PARENT OF
DIVORCING COUPLE ❧ 51

DEALING WITH A DIVORCED COUPLE
AT EVENT ❧ 52

TELLING FRIENDS ABOUT
NEW RELATIONSHIP ❧ 52

TO FRIEND MARRYING AFTER THE DEATH OF
A SPOUSE ❧ 52

TELLING FRIEND OF HURT FEELINGS ❧ 53

APOLOGY FOR NOT HELPING ❧ 53

ASKING END TO POLITICAL DISPUTE
AMONG FRIENDS ❧ 54

ABOUT FRIEND'S ELDER PARENT
AS DRIVER ❧ 54

APOLOGY TO GROUP FOR BEING IN A
BAD MOOD ❧ 54

TO FRIEND ABOUT INAPPROPRIATE
WORDS ❧ 55

TELLING OF MOVE TO BE
WITH FAMILY ❧ 55

SEEKING INTERVENTION FOR FRIEND ❧ 55

Estrangement from friend

Dear Julie,

When we moved to Rolling Meadow five years ago, you were one of the first people to offer me your friendship. And I have been honored to have that friendship all the time since then.

But, after seeing you on the street yesterday, I am wondering if I have done anything to offend you. During our very short conversation I had the impression you were mad at me for some reason.

I can't think of anything I have done, but if something is bothering you, I would very much like to speak with you about it and set it right.

Sincerely,
Mary Lee

To an estranged friend

Pat Taylor
Rolling Meadow

Dear Pat,

I miss talking to you and getting together. The disagreement we had last month now seems so trivial and certainly not worth the end of our friendship.

Can we agree that there are certain subjects we will probably always feel differently about, and sweep them off to the side? A good friendship is worth so much more than winning an argument.

I'd like to get together soon for a cup of tea, my treat. Pick the time and place and I'll be there with a smile.

Fondly,
Kim

Seeking to renew estranged friendship

Dear Mona,

As I was sipping a cup of eggnog last night I was flooded with wonderful memories of years past when we were very serious in our search for the perfect holiday drink.

I don't recall the recipe, but I do remember two very close friends sharing laughs and having a wonderful time together.

In the years since, we have become estranged. To tell you the truth, I don't even remember the reason, and I don't really care. I miss the company of a good friend.

If you feel the same, please call me and let's get together. I'm hoping we can begin with a few spiked eggnogs.

Fondly,
Louise

Thanks for friend's concern

Katie Graham
Drinkwater Falls

Dear Katie,

Thank you for being such a good friend on Tuesday. You were there when I needed a shoulder to lean on.

We are really hopeful Jen and Ben can resolve the problems in their marriage. As her parents we are trying to be supportive but not intrusive. It is a very difficult line to walk.

Your support was great. You listened, offered some advice based on your own experience, and never asked for more than I was comfortable with talking about.

I really appreciate your friendship. And I hope when next we speak the news will be better.

Fondly,
Louise

Thanks for help in caring for family

Frances Connors
Rolling Meadow

Dear Fran,

I want to thank you for all you have done for me and my family during my mother's stay at Rolling Meadow Hospital.

We could not have asked for a better friend. You gave us emotional support, helped out with the children, and even prepared some great meals for the family.

We are happy that mom is recovering nicely now and are hopeful that all will be well.

If there is anything we can do to show our appreciation, please do not hesitate to ask.

Fondly,
Ellen Simpson

Thanks for help in time of crisis

Dear Fay,

I want to thank you for all you did during my mother's recent illness.

You were like one of the family in the way you supported all of us, my mother as well as my brothers and sisters.

The last couple of weeks of my mother's life were very difficult, but your assistance made it much less stressful for all of us.

You were a great friend to my mother, and a tremendous help to our family in our time of need.

Sincerely,
Janet Kent

Offering help to friend with personal problem

Mildred Nathan
Rolling Meadow

Dear Mildred,

We all miss you at our book club; it's just not the same without you there.

We understand that some personal matters require your full attention; we don't mean to pry, but we do want to know if any of us can be of help.

Please let us know if there is anything any of us can do.

And in any case, we hope that everything works out for the best and you will be able to join us again soon.

Sincerely,
Doris

Telling of loss of job

Dear Vince,

I wanted to let you know that my life has taken an unexpected turn recently.

A week ago I was laid off from my job at Lehrman & Lehrman. I'm trying to not take it personally; more than fifty of my coworkers got the same bad news on the same day. That doesn't make it easier on me and my family, but I only have to look around at the whole economy to see so many others in the same situation.

Although I certainly enjoyed my job and my situation, I also have come to understand that we should not be defined by what we do for a living but rather for who we are.

I wanted to let the people who knew me principally through my job know that I hope to continue our personal and professional relationships in the years to come.

I've already begun looking for a new job, and I have some prospects that are promising. I know there are many more jobseekers than jobs, but no one will be working harder at finding work than me.

In the meantime, I'm going to be pinching pennies. You may not see me out for dinner at places with real napkins and silverware for a while, but I'd be happy to meet you anytime for a cup of coffee.

And, of course, if you hear of any leads you think I might want to follow, please don't hesitate to pass them along. You won't hurt my feelings; in fact, that's the sort of news I'd most like to hear.

Thanks for your support over the years.

Sincerely,
Jeb

Support for someone who lost job

Dear Jeb,

I'm so sorry to hear about your job situation. I've enjoyed knowing you as a colleague and a friend, and I want you to know that I hope you'll continue to stay in touch.

In this economy everyone has to be a bit worried about their companies and their jobs.

I hope you'll join us in two weeks when we start up our softball league again. I'd be happy to sponsor you as a member.

And you can count on me to pass along any job leads I come across here at my company or elsewhere in town. I'd very much like to see you and your family continue to contribute to our community.

Sincerely,
Vince

Couple toll of divorce

To Our Friends,

Before the rumor mill spins too many times, Mark and I wanted to let you know directly from us about a major change in our lives.

After five years of marriage we have decided to go our separate ways.

It will probably not come as a complete surprise to most of you; we've had our ups and downs in recent years. We tried, but we've decided that we are better off going our own way. We expect our divorce will be final by the end of the year.

Once we came to a mutual decision, Mark and I found it was surprisingly easy for us to remain civil and cooperative about this; we hope to remain friends with each other outside of a marriage.

You are all dear to us and we hope we can keep you in our lives.

Fondly,
Linda and Mark

Telling of divorce

Dear Friends,

There is no easy way to say this, after twenty-six years of marriage, Bill and I are divorcing.

I expect this is not much of a surprise to many of you. Bill has not been at home for nearly a year, and we have not been acting as a couple for a while before then.

You may hear from Bill, but this letter is from me. I wanted you all to know that I'm ready to go on with my life, and that I hope I can still include you amongst my friends.

I will be calling each of you in coming weeks, but please don't hesitate to call me on your own. I'm fine, and I want to keep in touch.

Fondly,
Cynthia

Supporting a friend going through a divorce

Dear Jen,

I was very sorry to hear that you and Phil have decided to divorce.

We have been friends for many years, through the good and not-so-good times. I want you to know that I will be there for you and support you in any way I can.

Any time you want a strong shoulder to lean on, or want to get together, please give me a call. I am a really good listener and sometimes I even give a bit of advice, but only if asked.

Love,
Tina

Support to parent of divorcing couple

Patty Hill
Rolling Meadow

Dear Patty,

I just heard the sad news that your son Peter and his wife Susan will be divorcing.

I feel so sorry.

Knowing Peter and Susan as I do, I am sure helping their three beautiful children through this difficult time will be their first priority. And I'm sure you'll be there to help them as well.

Things seem so very different from when we were young. Today, it seems that there are so many diverse definitions for "family." One thing I do know is that with enough love from all sides, everyone should come through well.

I have always been a good listener; I hope you'll give me a call sometime soon.

Sincerely,
Pam Jacobs

Dealing with a divorced couple at event

Jan Hunter
Rolling Meadow

Dear Jan,

I am writing to invite you to a reception for congressional candidate Orlanda Houston at our house on Sunday from 3 to 5 P.M.

Orlanda, a longtime friend of ours, will be answering questions about her positions on the important issues we face. We are sure that when you meet her you will be as impressed as we have been for many years.

On a personal note, I will tell you that we have also invited Bob to this event. I don't know if he will be coming, but I thought you might want to know.

When you and Bob divorced you told us that even though you were not together as a couple, you hoped to maintain relationships with all of your friends. I hope you will consider our invitation in that context.

Sincerely,
Laura

Telling friends about new relationship

Dear Friends,

All of you, my dear friends, know that last year was one of the worst in my life. After forty-seven years of marriage to my wonderful Betty, I lost her to cancer.

Without the help and support of all of you I don't know how I could have dealt with this loss. I still miss her terribly.

I am slowly healing and coming to terms with the changes in my life. Although I will never forget Betty, I want all of you to know that there is now a lovely and remarkable woman in my life.

Angela, who I met through volunteer work at the community library, will be spending time with me this winter. I hope all of you will visit and meet her. I am sure you will see how extraordinary she is and how she has helped me get back to enjoying life.

Sincerely,
Rick

To friend marrying after the death of a spouse

Dear Joan,

I was so happy to receive your letter about your plans to remarry.

I have known for a while that there was someone special in your life, and from what you say Jim sounds like a wonderful man. If he makes you happy, I like him already.

I know how difficult this past year has been for you. We all loved Ray; he was an extraordinary man. You suffered a profound loss.

We will all never forget Ray, but we are excited to meet Jim and wish you all the best in your marriage.

Sincerely,
Jean

Telling friend of hurt feelings

Helen Rush
Rolling Meadow

Dear Helen,

We have been friends for a long time, and I hope you will forgive my gripe. But I have to tell you I was surprised and a bit hurt by your actions last week.

I have not often asked you for favors, but when I called on Tuesday and asked if you could give me a lift to and from an important doctor's appointment, I was very disappointed when you so quickly said no.

I was very concerned about the test the doctor was going to perform, and I had hoped to have the support of a good friend. Instead you said something about having to shop for shoes or something like that. To tell you the truth, I was so upset I couldn't even focus on your answer.

I would like to think that if the situation had been reversed I would have done anything I could to support you. As it turned out, I had to take a taxi to and from the doctor, something which just added to my discomfort and my disappointment.

I'm writing to explain what went on because I still value you as a friend and I hope we can continue.

Sincerely,
Edna

Apology for not helping

Edna Baker
Rolling Meadow

Dear Edna,

Thank you for caring enough about our friendship to tell me about how I hurt your feelings. I am very sorry I wasn't there for you.

The fault was entirely mine. To tell you the truth, I was distracted by other much less important issues in my life and I guess I didn't listen very well when you asked for a favor.

I am so sorry for how insensitive I must have seemed. Nothing should have been as important to me as helping you out when you needed me.

I promise to make it up to you.

Fondly,
Helen

Asking end to political dispute among friends

Rick Whalen

Dear Rick,

I think you would agree that our guys' night out at Gino's Restaurant last Thursday was not our most pleasant gathering. What started as a spirited discussion about the issues turned into a shouting match.

As a longtime friend, I'm writing to ask if we could come to an agreement to stay away from politics during this election season. Can we declare a moratorium, and stick to baseball, women, and the stock market? There's more than enough to jabber about in those areas.

Sincerely,
Dave

About friend's elder parent as driver

Barbara Grant
Rolling Meadow

Dear Barbara,

Please forgive me for what may seem to be an intrusion of your privacy, but I am concerned about the safety of your father and others on the road.

This morning while I was coming home from the grocery store, I saw your father behind the wheel of his car on Main Street. His driving was erratic and he seemed confused.

I followed him home because I was concerned that something was the matter. He attempted to turn the wrong way on a one-way street and did not stop at the stop sign on Water Avenue.

I know it is a difficult subject to bring up with an elderly parent, but for his safety and others on the road I think it may be time for him to give up driving.

With my best regards,
Ann Philips

Apology to group for being in a bad mood

To My Book Club Group,

Thank you all for putting up with me on Thursday. When I got home from our meeting I realized how unpleasant and out of sorts I must have seemed.

I really don't want to get into details—they've all been resolved anyhow—but I came to the club after several days of rather trying family issues.

I promise to be my otherwise cheerful and engaging self at the next meeting.

Regards,
Grace

To friend about inappropriate words

Judy Wood

Dear Judy,

As a friend, I wanted to let you know that you may have inadvertently caused Louise some distress the other day.

At our little post-tennis lunch on Tuesday you made an offhanded remark about the prices on the menu, and you said the economy was so bad we might have to sell our houses to pay the bill. I know you meant no harm, but you should know that Louise and her husband are facing severe economic problems, and she told me they were worried about losing their home in foreclosure.

Please don't tell her I told you about their circumstances. I don't think you have to do anything at all except be sensitive to the fact that she and Bob are going through hard times.

Sincerely,
Kay

Telling of move to be with family

Dear Friends,

I want to let all of you, my dearest friends, know that I will be moving away from Rolling Meadow soon.

The responsibility and expense of owning a home are becoming a bit much for me now. But most of all I miss seeing my daughter and her family.

I've decided to sell my home and move to Arizona. Betsey found a retirement community that is about five miles from her. That way I can still have my independence but see my loved ones often.

I will miss all of you. But I want you to know a little secret: I'll have a small guest room in my condominium. That means I'm taking reservations now for visits. I recommend the warm, dry winter; the golf courses are great.

I hope to see each of you before I leave, but I didn't want you to hear of my plans from someone else.

Regards,
Sam

Seeking intervention for friend

Dear Friends,

I'm writing to each of you as friends of Rick to ask if you will join me in trying to help him get out of the dangerous spiral he has entered.

I'm sure you all know that Rick has been drinking heavily, more so than some of us can ever recall. What started out as somewhat funny has turned into something that is quite serious.

I'd like to suggest that we get together and come up with a plan about how to help him. There are a number of agencies here in town where we can seek assistance.

Obviously we should all keep this amongst ourselves to protect Rick's privacy. I hope that he will agree to allow us to help him and that we then can be there for him as he gets assistance.

Please call me to discuss.

Tom

CHAPTER 8

About the Children

ASKING FOR RETURN OF
CHILD'S POSSESSION •◦ 57

OBJECTION TO TRANSPORTING
CHILD •◦ 57

TELLING NEIGHBOR OF CHILD'S
RECKLESS DRIVING •◦ 57

CONCERN ABOUT CHILD'S ALLERGIES
AT PARTY •◦ 58

ASKING PARENTS TO
CONTROL CHILDREN •◦ 58

SECOND REQUEST ABOUT
CHILDREN TRESPASSING •◦ 58

ABOUT INAPPROPRIATE
INTERNET USE •◦ 59

ABOUT CHILD'S EXCESSIVE VISITS •◦ 59

ASKING PARENTS TO PAY FOR DAMAGES
BY CHILD •◦ 60

ASKING NEIGHBOR TO SUPERVISE CHILDREN
AT POOL •◦ 60

COMPLAINT TO MOTHER ABOUT ACTIONS
OF BABYSITTER •◦ 61

ABOUT REQUEST TO TAKE CARE OF
FRIEND'S CHILDREN •◦ 61

Asking for return of child's possession

Audrey Martin
Rolling Meadow

Dear Audrey,

I am writing, mother to mother, asking to remind your son Ben to return the video game he borrowed from Tyler several weeks ago.

I'm sure you agree with me that it is best for youngsters to try to work things out by themselves, but Tyler tells me he has asked Ben for the return of the game several times. Tyler is quite upset about this.

Ben can drop the game off at our house any time after school or you can call if some other arrangement would be better.

Thank you,
Shelia Montgomery

Objection to transporting child

Diana Beck
Rolling Meadow

Dear Diana,

Two weeks ago you asked if I would be available to take your daughter Kara to her piano lesson after school and bring her home. I was happy to lend a hand.

I did not, however, think that you expected I would be available to do this on a regular basis. Kara showed up yesterday expecting me to drive her to her lesson and wait for her.

I am not always free to get away in the afternoon. Please find an alternate plan for Kara's needs.

Sincerely,
Cindy Cousins

Telling neighbor of child's reckless driving

Joe Smith

Dear Joe,

As your friend and neighbor on Hollingwood Drive, I find it necessary to inform you of a potentially serious matter.

I understand your son Josh just received his driver's license. We went through that experience with our two children and somehow survived, although I'm not sure I remember how.

I have seen Josh behind the wheel a number of times and must tell you that at this point I feel his driving is a danger not only to himself but to pedestrians and others on the road.

He drives much too fast on Hollingwood Drive. Yesterday when he was backing out of your driveway he was not looking in the rear-view mirror and almost hit some children.

In good conscience I have to say that Josh does not appear ready to be driving unsupervised.

I hope you do not feel I have overstepped my bounds, but I could not live with myself if something happened.

Sincerely,
Fred Beck

Concern about child's allergies at party

Dear Brenda,

Taylor was thrilled to receive an invitation to Morgan's birthday. She would love to be able to go, but I have one major concern.

As you may know, Taylor has a severe allergy to nuts, especially peanuts. She cannot eat whole nuts or any product that may contain small traces of nuts, and she can also have a reaction if others eat these kinds of foods anywhere near her. At school the nurse has control of an antidote, and as Taylor grows up she will have to learn how to deal with this problem on her own.

I hope we can speak soon to discuss this situation. I'd like to know that Taylor can participate in social situations with her friends; she very much likes Morgan.

I look forward to hearing from you soon.

Sincerely,
Tina Collins

Asking parents to control children

Doug and Arlene Porter

Dear Doug and Arlene,

We hope you and your family are beginning to enjoy your new home in Rolling Meadow; I know it takes weeks before everything is in its right place.

We live in the house directly in back of you on Spruce Street, and our back yards face each other. I hope we soon will have the pleasure of meeting you.

Before then, though, we do have one request that we would ask you to pass on to your children. Since the bus stop is on our street, your children have been using our yard to get to the bus stop and to meet their new friends.

In doing so they are intruding on our privacy and doing damage to our flower beds.

Morinda and I have raised four children of our own. We know most of the time young people don't realize they are being inconsiderate.

We have asked that they not do this, but I think it must come from you. We would appreciate your help.

Sincerely,
Bill and Morinda Gordon

Second request about children trespassing

Doug and Arlene Porter

Dear Doug and Arlene,

It has been two weeks since we wrote to you requesting you to ask your children and their friends to stop using our property as a shortcut to your back yard.

The situation has only gotten worse. We have been disturbed by noise early in the morning and late at night. We have also had to pick up candy wrappers, paper, and many cigarette butts.

I don't know how else to put this but to say that we consider this to be trespassing and an invasion of our privacy.

We have asked the children on several occasions to stay out of our back yard, but they have either ignored us or been rude in their response.

We would welcome the opportunity to meet you, and we certainly do not want to start out our relationship with a fight. We will ask one more time that you take control of your children.

If we don't hear from you we will consult with the neighborhood association and if necessary with the police. We hope there is no need to do this.

Sincerely,
Bill and Morinda Gordon

About inappropriate Internet use

Margaret Robbins

Dear Margaret,

Last week my son Ben invited your son Kevin to come to our home after school. They went upstairs to Ben's room to play on his computer in his bedroom.

Before we allowed either of our children access to the Internet, they agreed to rules we established that included not going to certain websites we consider inappropriate for their age.

While Kevin was with Ben, they violated those rules and visited a number of sites that we do not approve of. We know about this because Ben felt guilty and told us; we also have a piece of software on the machine that alerts us of visits to inappropriate sites.

We have already dealt with Ben.

I am asking that you tell Kevin that, while he is welcome to visit Ben, it is on the condition that he does not encourage our son to do anything counter to our family's rules.

Sincerely,
Sue Evans

About child's excessive visits

Dear Maryann,

I am very pleased that our Jill has become such good friends with your daughter Heather. She is a polite and bright girl, and I am sure you are proud of her.

We certainly welcome Heather to our house to be with Jill, but I find this is happening more often than we are comfortable with.

In the past two weeks Heather has come to our house every day after school. On three of those days my daughter was not even at home, but I let her stay because she said no one was at her house and she did not have a key to get in.

On several evenings, we invited Heather to dine with us.

I am concerned that Heather does not have a safe place other than our home to go to after school. Where would she go if we were not home? And my children are expected to begin their homework immediately after school, and that was difficult for Jill to do with a friend still at the house.

Please understand that we do not mind the girls getting together at our house from time to time. But I don't want the responsibility of caring for Heather every day, and as I said, I do worry about where she would go if we were away.

I hope you'll give me a call or come over to the house some time so that we can discuss the situation.

Sincerely,
Grace Ware

Asking parents to pay for damages by child

Dear Mrs. Strong,

Last week my daughter Alice invited a group of her classmates to our house to finish work on a science project.

We were happy to have the children in our house. However, I did want to tell you that your son Alex strayed from the family room into our living room several times. Despite our requests that he not touch any of our antiques, he handled and dropped a valuable clock that has been in our family for many generations.

He at first denied touching the clock, and then he abruptly left our house without so much as an apology.

The clock's crystal and part of its ornamentation were badly damaged. We took it to a repair shop in town, and we expect the final bill to be about $150.

We think it would be appropriate for Alex to take some responsibility for the damage he caused; that would certainly be what we would expect if an adult had broken a valuable possession.

I would appreciate hearing from you, and from Alex, after you have had a chance to discuss this with him.

Sincerely,
Amy Egan

Asking neighbor to supervise children at pool

Ben and Sylvia Miller

Dear Ben and Sylvia,

As you know, we recently had an in-ground pool installed in our backyard.

We put a great deal of thought into making the pool as safe as possible, including erecting a high fence with a locked gate. Our children have been instructed not to even go into the pool area without an adult present.

Your children have on several occasions attempted to pressure our son to let them use the pool when neither my husband nor I were there to supervise. As far as we are aware, he did not let them in to swim.

But yesterday our family returned home late in the day to find that your son and daughter had climbed the fence and were swimming in the pool.

At the advice of our attorney, we called the police and filed a report about the incident. I hope you understand that we have the fence and the rules to protect any youngster from the risk of drowning, and also to protect us from liability in case of an accident.

Please discuss this with your children. As your neighbors, we want to be on good terms with you, and we want our son to enjoy the pool with his friends. But we will be forced to ask the police to become more directly involved if any further trespassing or unauthorized use of the pool occurs again.

Sincerely,
Al and Laura Swain

Complaint to mother about actions of babysitter

Dear Martha,

My son Jason was happy to be invited to the sleepover at your house; he likes Kyle very much. But I want to bring something to your attention about what went on that night.

As I understand it, you hired a babysitter to watch the five boys, and she allowed them to use your library of DVDs without any supervision.

When we picked up Jason the next morning he was unusually quiet; he later told us he had been very frightened by some of the movies that were shown that night. From what we've been able to gather, many of the films were very violent, and some included sexually explicit scenes.

We feel that you, and the babysitter, should have more closely supervised the sleepover. I hope we can get past this unfortunate incident and remain friends, but I will want to know more about arrangements you may make before we allow Jason to spend time at your house.

Sincerely,
Christine Nolan

About request to take care of friend's children

Kim Urban
Rolling Meadow

Dear Kim,

I just got your note about your plans to spend the entire month of August in the south of France. C'est magnifique! I promise to envy you every day you are gone.

A few months ago when you asked whether Bill and I would be available to take care of Kathy and Sam while you were away, we didn't expect it would be for a full month—we were thinking more of a week or ten days.

We still want to be available to help, but we'd like to find a way to have it make a little less of an impact on our own summer. Do you think you could find another friend or family member to split childcare duties for the month? We could even switch on and off for a week at a time, which might be the best solution of all.

I hope this doesn't put a crimp in your plans. Please get back to me soon with your thoughts.

Sincerely,
Beth

CHAPTER 9

Social Engagements

APOLOGY FOR MISSING PARTY ❧ 63

APOLOGY FOR MISSING
ANNIVERSARY ❧ 63

APOLOGY FOR MISSING
SOCIAL EVENT ❧ 63

APOLOGY FOR SERVING
ALLERGENIC FOOD ❧ 64

DECLINING DINNER INVITATION BECAUSE
OF DISPUTE ❧ 64

ASKING FOR CHANGE IN DINNER
CLUB POLICY ❧ 64

WITHDRAWING FROM WEEKLY
DINNER GROUP ❧ 65

OPTING OUT OF ANNIVERSARY GIFT ❧ 65

UNABLE TO ATTEND REUNION BECAUSE
OF COSTS ❧ 65

UNABLE TO ATTEND REUNION BECAUSE
OF ILLNESS ❧ 65

RESPONSE TO REQUEST ABOUT VISIT ❧ 66

INFORMING FRIENDS ABOUT UNAVAILABILITY
OF SUMMER COTTAGE ❧ 66

ASKING FRIEND TO MAKE OTHER
ARRANGEMENTS FOR VISIT ❧ 66

DECLINING REQUEST FOR
LONG-TERM VISITOR ❧ 67

DECLINING REQUEST FOR FRIEND'S CHILD
TO STAY ❧ 67

ASKING VISITORS TO NOT
BRING PETS ❧ 68

LIMITING NUMBER OF
DINNER GUESTS ❧ 68

APOLOGIZING FOR
OVERBEARING GUEST ❧ 68

ASKING FOR VEGETARIAN MEAL
AT RECEPTION ❧ 69

Apology for missing party

Lois Brennen
Rolling Meadow

Dear Lois,

I just realized I made a terrible mistake. When we got the invitation to Stan's birthday I very efficiently put it on my calendar. This was one event that Tom and I definitely did not want to miss.

Unfortunately, although I put it on my calendar, I put it down for the wrong day.

We had hired a babysitter, picked out the perfect present, and were ready to show up at your door a week late when I looked again at your invitation today. I am embarrassed and annoyed.

So, first of all, a belated Happy Birthday to Stan. And secondly, please allow us to make this up to both of you. I'll call with some ideas.

Fondly,
Sharon

Apology for missing anniversary

Nancy Green
Woodlake Village

Dear Nancy,

I just came to the terrible realization that I forgot your anniversary a week ago.

Please accept my congratulations and my sincere apologies.

I hope you and Jim celebrated that important date in style; Chuck and I would like to take you out for dinner any coming weekend you're available.

Fondly,
Janice

Apology for missing social event

Jane Evans
Rolling Meadow

Dear Jane,

I want to apologize to you and Don for missing your wonderful dinner party on Saturday. Jim and I were very much looking forward to spending the evening with you and your guests.

As we were preparing to leave for your house I received a call from a friend that my mother had fallen. We ended up spending the evening with her in the emergency room.

The good news is that nothing was broken and she will be fine.

I apologize for not being able to immediately call you. As we rushed out the door we asked one of our neighbors to call you, and I understand that message was delivered rather late in the evening.

I trust you will forgive us, and we hope to join you and your friends on another occasion.

Sincerely,
Ruth

Apology for serving allergenic food

Sarah Milton
Rolling Meadow

Dear Sarah,

Please accept my sincere apologies for the blunder I made with dinner yesterday.

I was not aware you were allergic to shellfish. If I had known I would have chosen a main course that would have been appropriate for all of my guests and not caused you any embarrassment at the table.

That said, you were a most gracious guest. I hope you really did enjoy the leftovers we scrambled to prepare for you.

I hope you will join us again at our next dinner party; please call and discuss your concerns beforehand so that I can make sure you dine as well as all of our guests.

Sincerely,
Claudia O'Connor

Declining dinner invitation because of dispute

Dear Jessica,

Thank you for inviting me to the going-away party you have planned for Sam Bush. I'm certain it will be a very fine recognition of his service to the company.

As you may know, though, Sam and I have agreed on very little over the past couple of years except that we found a means to stay out of each other's way.

I wish him well in his new job, and I will tell him so if I see him at work.

Under the circumstances, though, I do not feel it would appropriate or comfortable for me to attend the dinner in his honor.

Sincerely,
Ben

Asking for change in dinner club policy

Dear Patrick,

Thank you again for including Wendy and me in your monthly dining group. As newcomers to the area this is a fine way to make new friends.

I do, though, have a question about the arrangements for paying the bill at the various restaurants we visit. At the first two dinners we attended the total bill was divided amongst all those at the table. We think this practice works quite well for food but not for wine and other alcoholic drinks that some members may order.

Wendy and I do not drink alcohol; we don't mind if others do, but it seems unfair to expect us to pay for drinks of others. (Some of the members of the group seem to be very serious connoisseurs of wine, and some of the bottles cost much more than entrees.)

Can I suggest we ask restaurants to produce one bill for the meals and another for alcohol? I hope this is acceptable to you and all of the others in the group.

Sincerely,
Alex Nagle

Withdrawing from weekly dinner group

Dear Bill,

I want to again thank you for including Anne and me in your informal weekly dinner group. As newcomers to the area we appreciated the introduction to new friends (and new places to eat).

Although it embarrasses me a bit to have to admit this, we have made the decision that we cannot continue. With two children in college and a third reading course catalogs, we need to reduce our expenditures.

Thank you again for asking us. Please pass along our regards to the others in the group.

Sincerely,
Jim

Opting out of anniversary gift

Dear Gretta,

We are looking forward to attending Marvin and Tina's 50th wedding anniversary.
It sounds like quite the party for such a special couple.
In your note you asked if Ron and I wanted to contribute toward the flat-screen TV you want to give them. I think it is a fine choice, and they certainly will enjoy it.

However, the amount you asked for is a little more than we feel comfortable giving. We would happy to make a smaller donation of $50, or we can give a gift of our own.

Please let me know.

Sincerely,
Fran

Unable to attend reunion because of costs

Gloria Ryan
Rolling Meadow

Dear Gloria,

I'm sorry to tell you that our family will not be able to come to the reunion in Rolling Meadow this year.
The past few months have been quite difficult for us. Ron has been laid off from his job, and my hours at the museum have been drastically cut. We simply can't justify the expense.
We will be thinking of all of you this summer and hoping for better times next year.

Fondly,
Kim

Unable to attend reunion because of illness

Katerina Sarne
Upper Valley

Dear Katerina,

I wish I had better news, but I don't. We're not going to be able to come home for the neighborhood reunion this year.

As I told you a few weeks ago, Lisa has been dealing with the nasty effects of Lyme disease. Lately she has been doing much better and our doctor is hopeful of full recovery, but she is unable to travel for extended periods.

Please pass along our best regards to everyone. We hope and expect to be there next year.

Fondly,
Kim

Response to request about visit

Dick and Dottie Becker
Upper Falls

Dear Dick and Dottie,

I am so glad that you will be able to join us at our home over the Memorial Day weekend. It will be great to see the both of you again and to catch up on old times.

In your note you asked if it would be possible to extend your stay for four more days beyond the weekend.

I wish we could accommodate that request, but we already have some family members who will be arriving the day after you leave.

If you would like, I can look around for rental properties or motels in the area. Please let me know.

Best regards,
Sue

Informing friends about unavailability of summer cottage

Dear Dave and Gretchen,

We hope all is well with you and your family. At long last spring is in the air, and that means summer can't be far behind.

For the past several years we have taken much pleasure in sharing our cottage on Mirror Pond with you and some of our other close friends. This year, though, I'm afraid we must do things a bit differently.

The expense of maintaining the house has gone up quite a bit, and for at least the coming summer we have decided to put the cottage on the market as a rental property. We already have several leads from people who are considering taking the cottage for most or all of the summer.

We hope you understand. And if we end up with some unbooked time in the fall, we'll let you know.

Sincerely,
Sandy Webb

Asking friend to make other arrangements for visit

Michael and Laura Jennison

Dear Mike and Laura,

We're very happy to hear about your new life with your baby boy. We remember well our own experiences with our children, so many years ago.

You asked about staying with us again this summer when you visit Rolling Meadow. We would, of course, very much like to see you and your son.

However, you said in your note that you plan on coming with the baby, a nanny, and your mother. I am afraid our small guest room is just not big enough for that many people, and it would also put a strain on the common rooms, including the kitchen and living room.

There is a lovely three-bedroom house just down the street that is available for rent, and I'm sure there are other possibilities. If you would like me to, I would be glad to find out rates and other information.

Please let me know your thoughts.

Sincerely,
Sara

Declining request for long-term visitor

Dear Jen,

I am thrilled to hear that you will be coming to Rolling Meadow to take a graduate course at RMU this spring.

You are and will always be one of my best friends. I'd be happy to squeeze you in for a few days when you arrive, but I'm sorry to say that I simply do not have enough room for you to stay the entire semester.

My apartment is little more than a closet. It's so small that I have to store much of my possessions at my parents' house in their basement.

When you come, I'd be happy to show you around and help you find a more permanent place to stay. In the meantime, I will be on the lookout for any sublets or short-term rentals.

Please give me a call soon to discuss details.

Love,
Beth

Declining request for friend's child to stay

Dear Catherine,

I am delighted to hear that your granddaughter Emily will be attending a seminar this summer at Rolling Meadow University.

It's hard to believe she is now a college student. Time flies so quickly!

In your note you asked if she could stay with Alan and me at our house. Unfortunately, I must say no.

We travel quite a bit in the summer and would be away. And in any case, our house is on the far side of town from the university. I think it would be much too lonely and isolated for a young woman.

I have heard, though, that the dorms are quite nice. I would be happy to meet Emily and introduce her to Rolling Meadow.

Please have her get in touch with us when she arrives.

Sincerely,
Brenda Noonan

Asking visitors to not bring pets

Phil and Mary Singer
Coverdale

Dear Phil and Mary,

We are thrilled you are going to be able to stay with us in Rolling Meadow over the Fourth of July. We'll be able to enjoy the fireworks show from our front lawn and have a lot of time to catch up on the last year's comings and goings.

In your note you asked if you could bring your two Shetland sheepdogs, Jackson and Friskie. While we are looking forward to meeting them, I'm sorry to say that we don't feel comfortable allowing them to come into our house. Our floors and our collection of antiques are not the best mix with dogs (or young children).

There is a very fine kennel about a mile from our house where you could board the dogs each night and still be able to visit them and take them for walks during the day. Please let me know if you want me to make reservations for your guys.

Sincerely,
Sue

Limiting number of dinner guests

Angela Price
Rolling Meadow

Dear Angela,

I received your note asking if your sister and brother-in-law can come with you to our house on Sunday. I am truly sorry, but I'm afraid that's not possible.

As you know, the dinner is a welcome home for our neighbors Marcia and Harry who just returned from Russia. I am working with a caterer on some special dishes, and all of the arrangements have been in place for more than a week. We simply can't add two more guests now.

I would love to see Mary and Johnny, but we have a very limited space and a special arrangement for the dinner. I hope there will be another opportunity to get together with them.

Sincerely,
Sue

Apologizing for overbearing guest

Monica and Harold Smith
Rolling Meadow

Dear Monica and Harold,

I want to offer my apology for some of the actions of one our guests at dinner last night.

As we told our friends, Phil is a colleague of Sam's at the university. He is very intelligent and has a fascinating background and many interests. Unfortunately, all of that was pretty much lost at dinner when he chose to lecture us all on his political views.

I know that Sam and I disagreed with many of Phil's positions, and I suspect most of our guests were also unhappy with his views and the fact that he pretty much monopolized the conversation around the table.

Please accept our apologies; you were most gracious and we all survived the evening. I hope you will come to dinner the next time we invite you. I guarantee you the guest list will be different in at least one name.

Sincerely,
Gail

Asking for vegetarian meal at reception

Lisa Ames

Dear Lisa,

Mitch and I would be honored to attend the wedding of your daughter Karen to her fiancé Paul.
Thank you for inviting us; we are honored.

We were asked to select an entree from the three dinner choices. Mitch and I are vegetarians. Do you think you could ask the caterer to arrange for two dishes without meat or dairy products for us?

The meal aside, we're sure you are so excited and happy at the prospect of the marriage. We look forward to seeing you at the ceremony and the reception.

Fondly,
Lori

Part 4

Personal Business

CHAPTER 10

Money, Contracts, and Credit Cards

CANCELING AN INSURANCE POLICY ❧ 73

ASKING RENEGOTIATION OF
LOAN TERMS ❧ 73

ASKING PAYMENT PLAN
FOR UTILITIES ❧ 73

ASKING HOSPITAL TO SET
PAYMENT PLAN ❧ 74

ASKING PAYMENT ASSISTANCE
FROM HOSPITAL ❧ 74

ASKING SPECIAL SHORT-TERM
CONTRACT ❧ 74

CANCELING MEMBERSHIP BECAUSE
OF EXPENSE ❧ 75

CANCELING SERVICE AND ASKING FOR
REFUND OF PREPAY ❧ 75

ASKING FOR REDUCTION IN COST OF
CARETAKING SERVICES ❧ 76

ASKING FOR REDUCED SERVICES
FROM LANDSCAPER ❧ 76

ASKING NEW BID FROM CATERER ❧ 76

ASKING CABLE COMPANY TO
REVIEW BILL ❧ 77

ASKING REDUCTION IN SIZE
OF PROJECT ❧ 77

DECLINING DOWNSIZED PROJECT ❧ 78

POSTPONING PLANS FOR
RENOVATION PROJECT ❧ 78

ASKING PAYMENT FOR
CONSULTATION SERVICES ❧ 78

DECLINING REQUEST FOR
FREE CONSULTING ❧ 79

SETTING RATE FOR MAKING REPAIR ❧ 79

JUSTIFYING BILL SENT TO FRIEND ❧ 80

DECLINING TO EXTEND LOAN ❧ 80

DECLINING TO INVEST IN COMPANY ❧ 80

CREDIT CARD RETURN PROTECTION
GUARANTEE ❧ 81

CREDIT CARD EXTENDED WARRANTY ❧ 81

CREDIT CARD PURCHASE PROTECTION ❧ 81

CREDIT CARD AUTO RENTAL LOSS AND
DAMAGE COVERAGE ❧ 82

CREDIT CARD BAGGAGE INSURANCE ❧ 82

CREDIT CARD EVENT TICKET PROTECTION ❧ 83

COMPLAINING ABOUT SUBSTITUTION
OF PRODUCT ❧ 83

ASKING FOR REFUND BECAUSE OF
REDUCED PRICE ❧ 83

Canceling an insurance policy

Harry Payton, account manager
Green Shield Health Insurance
Rolling Meadow

In regards to account 6767640

Please cancel our health insurance coverage for the above account effective July 1. Please refund any unearned premiums in the account.

Although we have been generally pleased with the coverage and customer care we have received on both personal and business policies, we find the most recent round of price increases unacceptable.

We have decided to enroll with another health carrier.

Thank you.
Neil Stevens

Asking renegotiation of loan terms

John Rogers, Loan Officer
Fastcash Loan Company
Rolling Meadow

Loan No. xxxxxx

Gentlemen,

I am writing in regard to the above-referenced loan.

According to the terms of my agreement with your company, I am to make monthly payments in the amount of $1,500 for the next twenty-six months until the full amount of the debt is paid in full.

I have kept current on payments for the past three years. However, my financial situation has changed and I am writing at this time to ask renegotiation of the conditions of the loan.

I want to meet my obligation; at this time I would like to explore extending the term of the loan to reduce monthly payments. I would like to set up an appointment with you as soon as possible to explore options.

Sincerely,
Carole McGinnis

Asking payment plan for utilities

Rolling Meadow Heating Oil Company
Billing Department
Rolling Meadow

Gentlemen,

I have been a customer of Rolling Meadow Home Heating Oil Company for the past ten years.

I have been impressed with your delivery and repair service and have no desire to change to another company.

However, in these difficult economic times and rising costs for fuel oil, it is becoming difficult for me to make my payments in a timely manner.

I am writing to seek advice on enrolling in an annual budget plan, and I would also like to know about available low-income assistance programs for home heating.

Sincerely,
Jim Carver

Asking hospital to set payment plan

Billing Department
Rolling Meadow Community Hospital

Re, Invoice xxxx

Gentlemen,

I am writing in reference to an invoice I received for physical therapy services at Rolling Meadow Community Hospital that are over and above the amount paid by my insurance carrier.

According to the statement the entire amount of $5,642 is to be paid within thirty days. I fully intend to pay this bill in full, but it is impossible for me to do so in one month.

I am therefore requesting the establishment of an extended payment plan. I look forward to hearing from the hospital to discuss this arrangement.

Sincerely,
Susan Phillips

Asking payment assistance from hospital

Billing Department
Rolling Meadow Hospital

To Whom It May Concern,

I am scheduled to have hip replacement surgery on March 16.

In checking with my medical insurance company, I have learned that the estimated cost of this procedure will be about $18,000. I will be responsible for a deductible of $2,000 plus 20 percent copay for a total of about $5,000.

I certainly need the surgery, but because of my limited income I am going to have difficulty paying my share of the cost.

I would appreciate a call to schedule an appointment to discuss options.

Sincerely,
Benjamin Butler

Asking special short-term contract

John Silver
Silver's Health Club
Rolling Meadow

Dear Mr. Silver,

We have been members of your health club for the past five years. We appreciate the quality and cleanliness of your facility.

Since we are now in retirement, we have decided to spend six months in Rolling Meadow and the remaining winter months at a home we have in Florida. For that reason, it no longer makes sense for us to purchase a full-year membership.

We would like to request a six-month membership, or a month-by-month rate, for the period from April 15 to October 15.

We very much want to continue our association with Silver's Health Club. We look forward to hearing from you.

Sincerely,
Paul Baker

Canceling membership because of expense

Clara Logan, Director
Rolling Meadow Theater Guild

Dear Clara,

It has been our pleasure to have held a sustaining membership in the Rolling Meadow Theater Guild for the past ten years. We have enjoyed attending all of the shows, concerts, and other special events during that time, and it was very nice to have a seat we could call our own.

I wish it was otherwise, but I am afraid that we will not be renewing our membership for next year. We are living on a fixed income and our expenses keep rising. Please understand that the Theater Guild was one of the last things we wanted to cut from our budget.

I expect we will continue to attend selected events at the theater, and I hope we will eventually be able to once again become a sustaining member.

Regards,
Liza Proctor

Canceling service and asking for refund of prepay

Janice Sullivan
Jan's Pet Grooming Services
Rolling Meadow

Dear Jan,

For the past year we have depended on you for the grooming of Jackson, our Shetland sheepdog. We were very pleased with your work, and we think Jackson felt very handsome after each visit to your shop.

Unfortunately, we find it necessary to reduce our spending, and Jackson's hair styling is something we have decided we cannot afford for the moment.

Earlier this month we signed up for your special deal that gave reduced prices for prepaid accounts. At this time, we are asking for a refund of the excess funds you hold; we understand that the previous two sessions for Jackson will be charged at full price. By my accounting that should leave $82 to be refunded.

Thank you again for your work.

Sincerely,
Shelia Thayer

Asking for reduction in cost of caretaking services

Jim Steadman
Jim's Caretaking Services
Rolling Meadow

Dear Jim,

As winter approaches we would like to consider hiring you once again to look after our vacation home on Mirror Pond. It makes us very comfortable to know we have a responsible caretaker watching our house through the cold months.

However, we find that we need to cut back on all of our expenses. We would welcome suggestions from you that would reduce our monthly bill by about half.

We have been contacted by another individual in the area who has offered to do the caretaking at a greatly reduced rate. He proposes draining the plumbing and turning off all utilities for the winter. He would check on the house in major storms and look in a few times a month otherwise.

Can you offer us a similar deal? We would be perfectly happy to work with you on that basis.

Sincerely,
Paul Baxter

Asking for reduced services from landscaper

John Dunn
Better Lawn Care Services
Rolling Meadow

Dear John,

I received your letter regarding your annual spring lawn care services and the proposed schedule for maintenance for the coming summer.

We have been customers for the past seven years and have appreciated the work you and your crew have done on our property.

Unfortunately, this year we find ourselves with much less money in our budget for landscaping. I would like to see a revised proposal from you that reduces the cost.

We would like to continue to use the services of your company. I hope you can work with us on this matter.

I look forward to hearing from you.

Sincerely,
Dan Barlow

Asking new bid from caterer

Erma's Catering
Rolling Meadow

Dear Erma,

Thank you for responding so promptly with your proposal for catering services for our daughter's wedding in June.

As we told you at the time, we were seeking bids from three other caterers. Your presentation—and the samples you provided for lunch—were the most impressive.

Unfortunately, the overall budget for the wedding has gone up just as the economy has gone down. We have decided we would like to engage you to cater the affair, but we need to reduce the cost by about 25 percent.

I would welcome a new bid from you with a total price that reflects the lower cost; we are open to any suggestions for ways to spend less. I recall that you mentioned a buffet rather than plate service as one way to sharply reduce the cost.

We look forward to hearing from you soon.

Sincerely,
Cheryl Robbins

Asking cable company to review bill

Rolling Meadow Cable Television Company
Rolling Meadow
Re, Account 6SJ7-Satler

Dear Customer Service,

I am presently a subscriber to Rolling Meadow Cable Company for cable television and Internet service. My television package includes a confusing group of special packages and services.

I would like to continue as a subscriber, but I have been offered packages from the telephone company and from a satellite service that each would save me about $300 per year.

I am writing to ask that someone at your company review my bill and call me with specific suggestions on changes to my account that would lower my monthly bill. My current monthly bill is about $100, and I would like to reduce that charge by at least $25.

I look forward to hearing from you soon.

Sincerely,
William Satler

Asking reduction in size of project

Allison Tuttle
Tuttle Architectural Services
Rolling Meadow

Dear Allison,

Jim and I want to thank you for the many hours you spent with us discussing the new addition to our home on Jefferson Lane. The proposal you submitted was stunning; you are truly talented.

Unfortunately, Jim's hours at the assembly plant have been sharply cut back. We hope this is just a temporary situation, but for the moment we're not ready to commit to the full project as you laid it out.

There were two parts to the job: redoing our kitchen and adding a new wing to the family room. We would like to go forward with the kitchen remodeling and ask you to hold off on the plans for the addition for the moment. We hope to put that back on the schedule in years to come.

If you are still interested in working with us on this scaled down version, please give me a call.

Again, thanks for your help.

Sincerely,
Eleanor White

Declining downsized project

Eleanor White
Rolling Meadow

Dear Eleanor,

There is certainly no need to apologize to me for taking up my time with drawing plans for your house. This is my job and I try to work with any prospective client to the best of my ability.

I'm glad you were happy with my design. And I fully understand your reluctance to spend too much money in these difficult times. I wish it was otherwise, but you are not the only one in your situation.

As far as your desire to split the job into two parts, I think if you are just looking to make some changes to the existing kitchen, a good contractor would be all you will need.

When you are ready to have full plans drawn for the addition, please call me and we'll get that part of the project underway.

Sincerely,
Allison Tuttle

Postponing plans for renovation project

Pat Connors
Connors Construction

Dear Pat,

Thank you for your proposal for the addition to our home on Southbury Road. We really appreciate the time you spent working with us; you are an extremely creative designer.

Unfortunately, some unexpected events have forced us to postpone our plans for the project. Although we were quite serious about going forward with the work just a few weeks ago when we met with you, at this time we cannot justify the expenditure on the addition.

I want you to know that once our family situation is back on an even keel we hope to be in touch with you to try to get the project back on the schedule.

Thanks again for your time and effort.

Sincerely,
Jack Spriggs

Asking payment for consultation services

John Ryder, Executive Director
Rolling Meadow Science Museum

Dear John,

It has been my honor to have served as a consultant to the Science Museum for the past three years.

When I retired from my position at the university I was pleased that the museum would value my expertise and experience, and I was happy to help. I still feel that way.

However, this difficult economy has forced me to take a hard look at my finances. I have launched my own consulting firm to assist schools, museums, and businesses in their educational and training programs.

I would be thrilled to continue assisting the museum. I would welcome the opportunity to meet with you and discuss a contract for my services for the coming year.

Sincerely,
Michael Freel

Declining request for free consulting

Kate Toole
Rolling Meadow

Dear Kate,

I am glad to hear that your computer is running faster now. It took some time, but I was happy to help clean up the corrupted files that were slowing it down.

I am also glad the work I performed rewiring your phone line has improved your wireless system in the house.

You asked about teaching you Photoshop, and that is something I can do. I would ask, though, that you do so as a client through my consulting company.

Although I'm always willing to pitch in and help a friend or neighbor when I can, I also need to pay my bills.

I've enclosed a brochure about my services, along with the price schedule for individual and group instruction.

Sincerely,
Jeff

Setting rate for making repair

Liz Vaughn

Dear Liz,

As a follow-up to our conversation at work yesterday, I was happy to look at your home computer and make repairs. Based on what you told me, it sounds like your machine may have been infected with a computer virus. I would recommend testing for that, installing an antivirus software program, and making necessary repairs to the operating system.

We did not discuss payment, but my standard fee for this type of service is $30 per hour plus the cost of software. I would estimate this job will require about four hours of my time.

If you do want to engage me, please give me a call and we can arrange a convenient time. I am free on the weekends and most evenings.

Sincerely,
Ron Macy

Justifying bill sent to friend

Wes Murray

Dear Wes,

I received your letter in which you express surprise that I sent you a bill for fixing your water heater.

I know we have been friends and neighbors for a number of years, and that relationship is important to me also. But I do operate a plumbing business, and I do have to earn a living. When you called me last Sunday, I came right over and spent more than four hours making repairs to the heater.

The bill I sent you was actually substantially less than I would have charged a regular client who called for emergency service on the weekend; I billed at my standard hourly rate.

I hope you understand the situation now. I would like to remain a friend, but I do expect to be paid when I am called upon as a plumber.

Sincerely,
Ed Long

Declining to extend loan

Dear Chuck,

I have received your letter asking for an extension on the due date of the personal loan I gave you six months ago.

I'm sorry, but I must insist that the loan be repaid as agreed. You asked for the money to help you get through a difficult personal time, and I was glad to be of assistance.

However, I am not a bank. To tell you the truth, in looking back I don't think it was the right thing for me to make the loan in the first place; this is the sort of thing that can ruin friendships.

The loan is due in full at the end of the month. I truly hope you can keep to the terms of our agreement and allow us to get out of an uncomfortable situation like this.

Sincerely,
Joe

Declining to invest in company

Dear Dick,

I have reviewed all of the information you sent me about the restaurant you plan to open in town. You certainly seem to have put a great deal of thought into this new venture.

I am flattered that you thought of me when you sought financial partners for this project. However, although I am impressed with your enthusiasm for such an ambitious undertaking, I have decided that I do not want to invest in the restaurant.

Restaurants are a risky business even in the best of financial times, but in the current economy I think we are going to see many fine establishments unable to succeed. From what I have read, dining at anything above fast-food level is one of the first things people cut back.

I do wish you well. If you do open your restaurant I promise to be one of your first customers.

Sincerely,
Kent

Credit card return protection guarantee

Universal Credit
Insurance Claims

In regards to account xxx-xxxx-6089

As instructed by customer service, I am writing to file a claim under the return protection guarantee offered to cardholders.

I purchased a suede jacket at a local clothing store just over a month ago; the jacket has not been used. Recently I decided I did not want to keep it. When I brought it back to the shop the manager refused to refund my money or offer a store credit, stating that the store policy only allowed returns within thirty days of purchase.

Your return protection guarantee allows me to obtain a refund within 90 days of purchase.

I am enclosing copies of the sales slip and the form from the website I was instructed to prepare. I await instructions as to what I am to do with the jacket and when my refund will be processed.

I greatly appreciate this guarantee program; although I have never used it before, it is one of the reasons I carry your card.

Thank you.

Joyce Nathan

Credit card extended warranty

Universal Credit
Insurance Claims

In regards to account xxx-xxxx-6089

I am filing a claim under the extended warranty plan included with my credit card coverage.

I purchased a 50-inch Samasonic high-definition plasma television a year ago last January; it came with a twelve-month manufacturer's warranty. I don't know how this sort of thing happens, but the TV worked flawlessly for a year and then failed suddenly exactly one week after it was out of warranty.

The manufacturer was very quick to point out that the screen was no longer under warranty and offered to arrange for a repair. The representative said a failure of the screen electronics would typically cost about $900, which is about half of what I paid for the television.

I was very pleased, though, to learn the details of your extended warranty program, which doubles the manufacturer's warranty. Enclosed is a copy of the sales slip for the television and the warranty card. Please contact me as soon as possible with authorization to have the television repaired.

Sincerely,
Mary Fuller

Credit card purchase protection

Universal Credit
Insurance Claims

In regards to account xxx-xxxx-6089

I am filing a Notice of Claim under the purchase protection portion of my credit card coverage.

On a recent trip, my hotel room in Topeka was burglarized and my new digital camera was stolen. I had owned the camera for just two months; your purchase protection covers such losses for up to 90 days.

As requested by your customer service representative, I have enclosed a copy of the police report on the theft as well as copies of the sales slip for the camera.

Please advise if there is anything additional needed to process this claim.

Sincerely,
Robert Gordon

Credit card auto rental loss and damage coverage

Universal Credit
Insurance Claims

In regards to account xxx-xxxx-6089

As requested by your customer services department, enclosed please find details requested in support of a claim under the Auto Car Rental and Damage Insurance Plan offered to cardholders.

I am enclosing the completed claim form provided by your representative. Also enclosed is the police report with photographs of the damage to the car, proof of my auto insurance coverage, an itemized repair bill from the garage, and a copy of the auto rental contract from the rental company.

According to your representative, the insurance plan will reimburse me for the difference between the amount paid to the rental company by my personal auto insurance policy and the total bill, including the deductible on my policy.

If there is any further documentation needed from me, please let me know.

Sincerely,
Jennifer Adams

Credit card baggage insurance

Universal Credit
Insurance Claims

In regards to account xxx-xxxx-6089

Enclosed please find my claim for reimbursement under your credit card baggage insurance plan for the luggage lost on a recent flight from Los Angeles.

I have received payment from the airline in the amount of $1,250 for my clothing and personal effects, the maximum they would pay. My full claim was for $1,735. Under terms of your plan, I am asking for payment of $485, the amount in excess of what I have recovered.

I am enclosing a completed claim form as requested by your customer service representative, along with copies of paperwork from the airline and copies of receipts for certain of the high-value items that were in my luggage.

Please advise if there is anything else you require from me.

Thank you.

Sam Waters

Credit card event ticket protection

Universal Credit
Insurance Claims

In regards to account xxx-xxxx-6089

I am submitting a proof of loss and documentation required to be reimbursed for the cost of two concert tickets. I was unable to attend the show because of a medical emergency.

When it became apparent I would not be using this ticket, I contacted the credit card company by phone, which constituted the Notice of Claim. Enclosed is a proof of loss, a statement from my physician, and the claim form from your website as requested by your customer service representative.

With this paperwork I am also enclosing the unused ticket. Please advise if anything further is needed to recover the cost of the ticket.

Sincerely,
Barbara Vincent

Complaining about substitution of product

Customer Service
Big Bob's Furniture

Dear Customer Service,

I recently ordered two custom upholstered easy chairs from your company, working from swatches of fabric and colors supplied by you. I have attached copies of the invoice and shipping manifest.

The chairs arrived today, and they use a different quality of fabric in a substantially different color. There was either a error in taking the order, or I received someone else's chairs.

Please call me to make arrangements to have them picked up.

I expect to receive a full refund, including reimbursement for shipping and handling costs.

Sincerely,
Rose Butler

Asking for refund because of reduced price

Dave Patrick, Manager
Great Buys
Rolling Meadow

Dear Mr. Patrick,

Yesterday afternoon we purchased a Signature HD 36-inch flat screen from Great Buys.

In today's newspaper I see that this same model is on sale for $150 less than the price we paid.

I am enclosing copies of my receipt and my credit card information. Please credit my account immediately.

If we do not hear from you within the next few days, I will return the television to your store for a credit and buy an unopened box at the sale price. I don't see how that helps you or me, but I will do so for $150.

Sincerely,
Chuck Cosgrove

CHAPTER 11

Disputes and Complaints

INSUFFICIENT FUNDS FROM FRIEND ❧ 85

RESPONSE ABOUT
INSUFFICIENT FUNDS ❧ 85

INFORMING RELATIVE OF
DEFAULT NOTICE ❧ 85

ASKING REPAYMENT OF LOAN ❧ 85

ASKING DETAILED DESCRIPTIONS
IN BILL ❧ 86

ASKING CARETAKER FOR
ITEMIZED BILLS ❧ 86

DISPUTING LEGAL BILL ❧ 87

OBJECTING TO SERVICE
OVERCHARGE ❧ 87

ASKING REMOVAL OF LATE FEE FROM
CREDIT CARD BILL ❧ 87

OBJECTING TO BILL FOR
PHOTO PROOFS ❧ 88

ASKING REFUND FOR
CLASS CANCELLATION ❧ 88

ASKING FOR SCHOLARSHIP PAYMENT ❧ 89

COMPLAINT ABOUT TUTOR ❧ 89

COMPLAINT ABOUT DISCREPANCY IN
HOURLY WAGES PAID ❧ 89

ASKING REMOVAL OF NAME FROM
MAILING LIST ❧ 90

SEEKING REMOVAL FROM
MARKETING LIST ❧ 90

Insufficient funds from friend

Susan Hood

Dear Susan,

I'm sure this was an oversight, but the check you gave me to pay for your portion of our group lunch at the Water Café has been returned to me by the bank for insufficient funds in your account.

The check was in the amount of $24.50, and the bank added a service charge of $15.

I would appreciate it if you would write a new check or give me the cash to cover the total of $39.50.

Sincerely,
Laura Burns

Response about insufficient funds

Dear Laura,

I hope you will forgive me about the check; I am not in the habit of bouncing checks.

I forgot to record the check (and a few others) in my register when I got home, and we didn't make a deposit until a few days later.

Enclosed is a new check in the amount of $39.50 to cover the check plus the service fee.

Again, my apologies.

Sincerely,
Susan Hood

Informing relative of default notice

Ron Gibbons
Rolling Meadow

Dear Ron,

I have just been notified by the Bank of Rolling Meadow that you are in default on your personal loan. As cosigner on the loan, they are demanding I pay off the note in full within thirty days.

Six months ago, when you asked me to guarantee the loan I agreed to do so with great reluctance.

At the time I told you it would be a substantial burden to your aunt and me if you could not make the payments. You assured me that your employment situation was changing for the better and you had no doubts you would be able to make the payments for the duration of the loan.

I am hoping that you are in a position to honor your obligation to the bank and to your family.

Please contact the bank immediately and inform me of the outcome.

Sincerely,
Ralph

Asking repayment of loan

Dear Bob,

Four months ago when you asked for a short-term loan we were happy to help; the purpose of the loan was to help you pay expenses until you started your new job.

Even though it was not the best time for us to be dipping into our savings, we wanted to help you out.

The agreement called for repayment after three months. I am quite concerned that we have not received any money from you and that you have not responded to our phone calls.

I am asking that you honor the term of the loan. I very much want to keep this all on a friendly basis, but I am not prepared to write off that amount of money.

I would like to hear from you within the next week.

Sincerely,
Paul

Asking detailed descriptions in bill

Rolling Meadow Health Clinic
Rolling Meadow
Attn. Accounts Payable

In regards to account 234093-6SJ7

Dear accounts payable department,

I am writing on behalf of my father, Henry Walters. Under power of attorney I manage my father's finances and pay his bills.

Your most recent statement in the amount of $694.09 did not include enough detail about services provided.

Before I pay the bill, I want to make certain that all charges are appropriate. And I need to check with Medicare and with my father's supplemental health care insurance company to see if any reimbursement is available.

Please send me a detailed description of each charge on this and all future statements.

Sincerely,
Shirley Davis

Asking caretaker for itemized bills

Dear Sam,

First of all, I want you to know how grateful we are to have someone like you available to help my father in keeping his house in good repair. He needs the help, and he could not live there alone without having someone to call to take care of all of the routine and emergency situations that come up with an older home.

I do, though, have one request to make. I have been taking over the management of his finances, including paying all of his bills.

The statements you have sent my father show only an amount due; they do not indicate the particular service performed and make no distinction between repairs and capital improvements.

I am in no way doubting your honesty. But for legal and tax purposes, I am asking that all billing be as detailed as possible. If you have any questions, please don't hesitate to call me. And I expect that I will be calling you in coming months to go over some of the work you have done in recent years so that we can calculate a cost basis in the event we sell the house.

Sincerely,
Peter Lyons

Disputing legal bill

Stephen Giger, Esq
Giger, Giger & Giger

Dear Mr. Giger,

I recently retained your law firm to represent me in filing for state assistance for my father who now lives in a nursing home in Florida.

At our initial meeting, you told us that you offered a set fee for elder care services of this sort, $1,200 plus any required state or local court fees. That was the basis of our agreement, and it was also an element of the contract we signed with your law firm.

We were pleased with the work you and your associate Wendy Fuller did on behalf of my father. We accomplished all we had hoped for, and his finances are now set.

However, I was upset to receive a bill from your firm today totaling $3,200. Instead of the set fee of $1,200, we were billed for thirty-two hours of legal work at $100 per hour.

Without questioning whether the two filings actually required nearly a full week's work, I am asking that you redraw the invoice to represent the agreed-upon set fee.

Sincerely,
Barbara Moss

Objecting to service overcharge

James Steele, manager
ABC Towing Company
Rolling Meadow

Dear Mr. Steele,

We used your service Friday night to bring our vehicle from downtown to the Last Gas Garage after we found it would not start. When we called for the towing service we asked the dispatcher the cost and were told it would be $50 plus $1 per mile.

When we arrived at the garage, the driver presented a bill for $50 plus $6 in mileage and an additional $50 after-hours fee.

We were quite displeased at the extra charge, but the driver would not release the car without payment.

I have checked with the town attorney and he informs me that your franchise for towing does not include the right to add a late-night fee. Before I pursue this with the town, I would ask an immediate refund of the $50 surcharge.

Thank you.

Mark Kelsey

Asking removal of late fee from credit card bill

Transvisacard
Whiteshoe, WI

In regards to card 555-567-3929-2039

Dear Customer Service,

I have used a Transvisacard for more than a decade and have never been late with a payment.

I recently returned from a two-week trip to Europe to find a bill that had arrived while I was away. I immediately paid the outstanding balance. I now find that I have been assessed a late fee in the amount of $35 plus interest.

According to the terms of the card agreement, I am supposed to receive 15 days in which to make payment. Your bill arrived within the two-week period I was away, and therefore I must assume that it was delayed in the mail.

I am asking that you remove the late fee and all interest charges.

I would like to continue using my Transvisacard, but I expect this accommodation as a longtime customer.

Sincerely,
Tessa Stevens

Objecting to bill for photo proofs

Rolling Meadow Photographic Services
Rolling Meadow

Gentlemen,

I recently brought my two children to a photo session at the elementary school. The photographer, Glen, was very professional and took many pictures of both children.

Before I came to the sitting I checked with the school to make certain there was no charge for the session. In addition, the paperwork I signed at the school stated that we could choose any photo from the proofs and would only be billed for packages we would choose to order.

We decided not to order any pictures, notifying your studio through the school.

In today's mail I received a bill for $50 for the photo sitting and the proofs.

I would like to believe this was an error and not a deliberate attempt to bilk customers. I will not be paying the bill, and I have also notified the school and asked them to advise parents that they are not responsible for any charges other than for packages they order.

Sincerely,
Terry McGuire

Asking refund for class cancellation

Kathy Bradley, Director
Rolling Meadow Community School
Rolling Meadow

Dear Ms. Bradley,

In September I signed up for a six-week exercise class at Rolling Meadow Community School.

One class was canceled because of bad weather and two classes were not held because of the illness of the instructor.

I just received a notice that registration is beginning for the spring session, offering a prorated credit for the missed classes in the fall.

Unfortunately, I will not be able to attend classes in the spring because of other commitments. Therefore, I am asking for a refund of half the course fee I paid in September.

Sincerely,
Wendy Taylor

Asking for scholarship payment

Mark DeMarco
DeMarco's Fitness Center

Dear Mr. DeMarco,

I am writing to request once again that I be paid the college scholarship you awarded me through the Rolling Meadow Business Council this past June.

As I told you in my previous letter, I was very proud to be awarded $1,000 toward my college education; your company received a good amount of publicity in our community.

However, it has now been four months and I have not received payment.

I really don't want to cause trouble, but I have decided that if I do not receive the promised scholarship money within two weeks I will notify the business council and the local newspaper. I think that will result in the sort of publicity you do not want to see in town.

Sincerely,
Patrick Early

Complaint about tutor

Katherine Dean
Tutoring Express

Dear Ms. Dean,

As you know, we have asked your agency to provide a tutor to help my daughter Nancy in algebra.

We're sorry to say that though Greg Falcone is a very well-mannered young man, he does not seem to be adequately prepared to be a tutor. We provided him with copies of Nancy's course curriculum and encouraged him to get in touch with her teacher, but he has shown no indication that he understands Nancy's needs.

At this time we would like to ask that you contact us to discuss a replacement for Greg. If this is not possible, please let us know as soon as possible so that we can make arrangements with other tutors.

Thank you,
Kelly Ernst

Complaint about discrepancy in hourly wages paid

Douglas Worth
Rolling Meadow

Dear Mr. Worth,

Two weeks ago you engaged me to tutor your daughter Tara.

We agreed that I would meet her on Tuesdays at 2:30 P.M. in the middle school library to go over her homework assignments and assist her with prealgebra and other math concepts.

The arrangement called for a rate of $30 per hour for ninety minutes of instruction. I received a check from you today and it was for just $30; the proper amount should have been $45.

I have spent a considerable amount of my own time preparing for this job, including conferring with Tara's math teacher to understand the lesson plans.

I hope this is nothing more than an error in calculation. If there is any problem with the agreement, please let me know as soon as possible.

Sincerely,
Joan Parker

Asking removal of name from mailing list

Rainy Days Gutter Repair
Rolling Meadow

Please remove my name from your postal and e-mail lists. I do not want to receive any solicitations in any form from your company or from any other company with which you do business.

Mary Jones
18 Circle Road
Rolling Meadow

Thank you.

Seeking removal from marketing list

Rolling Meadow Travel Agency
Rolling Meadow

To Whom It May Concern,

I recently made an inquiry to your agency about a special offer on a cruise to Alaska. I specifically asked for information about that one trip.

Since then I have been inundated with phone calls, mailings, and other solicitations from your company about everything from travel insurance to trips to Egypt. Many of these calls come from unrelated companies that must have received our number from your agency.

Please immediately remove my name and telephone number from your records.

We will be making our decision within the next few weeks. I will choose a travel agency that understands our desire not to be badgered by salespeople.

Sincerely,
Amy Greenwood

CHAPTER 12

About the Service We Received

ASKING CREDIT FOR SERVICE NOT USED ❖ 92

ASKING FOR REDUCTION IN RESTAURANT BILL ❖ 92

COMPLAINT ABOUT RESTAURANT SERVICE ❖ 93

COMPLAINING ABOUT BEING RUSHED AT RESTAURANT ❖ 93

COMPLAINING ABOUT QUALITY OF LINEN RENTAL ❖ 94

QUESTIONING LANDSCAPING BILL ❖ 94

COMPLAINT ABOUT LAWN MOWING SERVICE ❖ 94

DISMISSING LAWN MOWING SERVICE ❖ 95

OBJECTING TO RUDE SERVICE PERSON ❖ 95

SECOND REFUSAL TO PAY LANDSCAPING BILL ❖ 96

FAULTY REPAIR ❖ 96

THREATENING LEGAL ACTION FOR SHODDY REPAIR ❖ 96

REFERRING ACTION TO A LAWYER ❖ 97

ASKING REFUND FROM REPAIR SHOP FOR IMPROPER WORK ❖ 97

COMPLAINT ABOUT FAILED AUTO REPAIR ❖ 98

ASKING FOR ACCOUNTING OF HOME CARE SERVICES ❖ 98

DISMISSING DOMESTIC CAREGIVER ❖ 99

ASKING DETAILS OF CHILDCARE NEEDS ❖ 99

COMPLAINT ABOUT TRASH PICKUP ❖ 100

PROBLEM WITH QUALITY OF HOME REPAIR ❖ 100

QUESTIONING AUTOMATIC CHARGES ON INTERNET BILL ❖ 101

SEEKING CREDIT FOR CABLE OUTAGE ❖ 101

ASKING REMOVAL OF MISSED APPOINTMENT FEE ❖ 101

RESTAURANT SPECIAL EVENT ROOM NOT AVAILABLE ❖ 102

Asking credit for service not used

Tom Casey
Casey's Car Service
Rolling Meadow

Dear Mr. Casey,

After many years as a satisfied client, I am writing to express my great disappointment with your service last week.

We had arranged a pickup at our home in Rolling Meadow for January 22 at 5 A.M. to take us to the airport for an early flight. After waiting twenty minutes and repeatedly trying to reach your answering service, we were forced to prevail upon one of our neighbors to help us out.

I am writing to ask that you credit the amount of $65 to my credit card immediately.

I have already disputed this charge with our credit card company, but you can speed the refund by reversing the charge now. Once our account has been fixed, I would be interested in hearing an explanation as to why we were not picked up as scheduled. I will decide whether to call upon you in the future based on your response.

Thank you,
Wayne Griffin

Asking for reduction in restaurant bill

Margaret Leeds, Manager
The Red Lantern Restaurant
Rolling Meadow

Dear Ms. Leeds,

I am writing to complain about our bill for a recent visit to your restaurant.

We come to dine at the Red Lantern regularly and often take advantage of your widely advertised Early Bird specials, which runs from 5 to 6:30 P.M.

We arrived last Friday about 6:15 P.M. and found we had a short wait before we were seated. In any case, we were at our table no more than ten minutes later.

Our next wait was for our waitress; she did not take our order for about fifteen minutes. We had the Early Bird menu in our hands and we ordered items from it.

When the check came, though, our items were charged at full price. We told her that we had arrived during the Early Bird period and ordered from that menu, but she chose to argue, which embarrassed us.

We paid the bill, but the more we think about the situation, the more upset we became. I am writing to you now—and enclosing a copy of our credit card receipt—to ask that you look into this matter.

We very much want to dine at your restaurant, but we have decided to wait for your response before making any plans.

Sincerely,
Claudia Stewart

Complaint about restaurant service

Geno Romano
Romano's Forum Italian Restaurant

Dear Geno,

As you know we have been steady customers of yours for the past four years, coming in nearly every Sunday night.

The food has always been excellent, and the service has almost always been superb.

That is why we are truly puzzled over our last two meals at Romano's.

Last week, our regular table in the corner was not held for us and we were given a spot very near the entrance, which we found quite uncomfortable. The waitress, a young woman named Mary who we had not seen before, made several mistakes with our order—in fact, I don't think she got anything right the first time. And perhaps worst of all, the eggplant lasagna was cold and tough; for the first time ever, we sent it back to the kitchen, but it did not improve with reheating.

And then last night was nearly a repeat. We had to ask for bread, the appetizers arrived at the same time as the entrees, and the food in general was well beneath your standards.

In thinking about it, my wife and I realized that we did not see you or your wife in the restaurant on either night. Has there been a change in ownership? Were you away?

We really want a reason to come back. Can you give us one?

Sincerely,
Jim and Kathleen Martin

Complaining about being rushed at restaurant

David Glaser
The Cellar Restaurant

Dear Mr. Glaser,

I am writing to let you know about our dissatisfaction with the service we received at your restaurant this past Saturday.

We brought a party of six, arriving just after 6 P.M. The restaurant was unusually crowded, and we had to wait about forty minutes before we were seated.

Our real problem began once we were finally seated. We were treated as if there was a race to get us out the door.

Menus showed up the minute we sat down, and our waiter, a young man named Chad, stood there and asked to take our order before we even had time to look at them. We asked him to come back in a few minutes; he made it clear he was not happy with that.

Our entrees arrived while we were still eating appetizers; Chad came by to attempt to clear the main course dishes before we had finished. And before we even decided about whether to order dessert he came by with the check.

In all, we spent more time waiting for a table than eating our dinner.

For us the bottom line is this: we have enjoyed your restaurant in the past and we may consider coming back again. But we would like to hear from you about our experience last Saturday. Was this an unusual experience or have you decided to push diners through as if this was a fast-food restaurant?

Sincerely,
Eva Goodsmith

Complaining about quality of linen rental

Marcia Elwell, President
Custom Event Rental
Rolling Meadow

Dear Ms. Elwell,

I recently rented some linen napkins and tablecloths for the rehearsal party before my daughter's wedding.

The dry goods were delivered one hour before the event and the caterers had to immediately set the tables.

When we examined the linens we were shocked to find that many of the pieces had stains on them; at least one tablecloth was unusable. I have never seen such shoddy quality at a formal event.

We had no choice but to use the linens, hiding the worst of them as best we could.

I have just received your bill, and before I make any payment I want to discuss this with you.

I entertain on a regular basis and have occasion to recommend rental companies to colleagues and friends. I will make further judgments based on your response to this letter.

Sincerely,
Alice Kraus

Questioning landscaping bill

Chester Davis
Chester's Landscaping

Dear Mr. Davis,

When we returned home yesterday from a week's vacation we found in our mail a bill from your company for application of weedkiller and fertilizer on our lawn.

If in fact this was done while we were away, it was not with our approval. Although we have used your company's services from time to time for planting some shrubs and flower beds, we did not request—and do not want—dangerous chemicals and unnecessary fertilizer applied to our lawn.

Please remove the charge from our account.

Thank you.
Ed Boyd

Complaint about lawn mowing service

Gary Kever
Gary's Lawn Care and Maintenance

Dear Gary,

We have used your company for twice-monthly lawn mowing services and flower bed maintenance at our home on Winter Street for the past few years.

Recently, though, we have found that the quality of work is much less than we have come to expect. There was no edging performed around the house, the flower beds have received only minimal attention, and the driveway has not been swept clean of clippings.

We are surprised at this sudden turn toward sloppiness; we had come to expect much more from your company. I am asking that you send the crew out for a touch-up visit as soon as possible—without additional charge—and that you instruct your crew on our expectations.

I look forward to hearing from you soon.

Sincerely,
Bill Collins

Dismissing lawn mowing service

Gary Kever
Gary's Lawn Care and Maintenance

Account 6SJ7

Dear Gary,

Effective immediately, please discontinue lawn care service at our home on Winter Street in Rolling Meadow.

Two weeks ago I brought to your attention our dissatisfaction with the quality of work. We were unhappy to find no improvement since.

Thank you.

Bill Collins

Objecting to rude service person

Dan Connor
Dan's Appliance Repair
Rolling Meadow

Dear Dan,

We recently used your company to repair our gas stove; the work was accomplished as scheduled, but I am afraid that we were quite dissatisfied with the personal manner of Michael, the technician sent to our home.

Because it was raining quite hard that day, I made sure to have extra floor mats in the hallway and the kitchen. Michael seemed to go out of his way to avoid them and instead tracked mud all over the floor.

He also took several breaks to smoke a cigarette in our driveway, which I found to be quite unprofessional and rather annoying since we were paying an hourly labor charge.

When he was finished he departed very quickly, leaving behind in the kitchen several boxes that held the repair parts.

The unit seems to be working properly, but we do not want the same sort of experience the next time one of our appliances needs repair. I would suggest that you speak to Michael about his performance on the job. We will consider our options carefully before we call your company again.

Sincerely,
Karen Mayer

Second refusal to pay landscaping bill

Chester Davis
Chester's Landscaping

Dear Mr. Davis,

We have received a second bill from your company, marked "overdue," for landscaping services that we did not authorize.

In my previous letter to you I explained that we had not requested that weedkiller and fertilizer be applied to our lawn. Although we have used your company in the past, this is a service we have never asked for. I am perfectly happy with a "country" lawn; we do not feel the need to pretend we live on a golf course.

We have not signed any contract with your company, and you have no right to bill us for work we did not request.

I expect that we will not receive further bills from your company for this service.

Ed Boyd

Faulty repair

Mark Stanton
Stanton's Paving Company

Dear Mr. Stanton,

We recently had our driveway blacktopped by your company.

When we received your bid for the job, I pointed out several places where there were holes to be filled. I also made sure that the workers doing the job were aware of the problematic areas.

I was assured this would be taken care of before the job was done. I had to go to work, and when I returned home I found that they had not fixed these spots.

I have since called your office several times to ask that the holes be filled, but I have not received a response.

I want you to know that I do not consider the work completed to my satisfaction. I will withhold payment of the bill until it is.

I look forward to hearing from you.

Sincerely,
Jim Duffy
Cc: Rolling Meadow Better Business Bureau

Threatening legal action for shoddy repair

Mark Stanton
Stanton's Paving Company

Dear Mr. Stanton,

It has been four weeks since I notified your company about my dissatisfaction I had with the quality of work done on our driveway.

The uneven areas in the blacktopped driveway are now cracking and breaking away from the surrounding surface.

In the meantime I have received two bills from your company, the second of which includes a late charge and interest fee.

This is totally unacceptable. I expect the job to be completed to my satisfaction immediately. I have no intention of paying for shoddy work, and I certainly will not accept a late charge for work not yet completed.

I intend to consult with my attorney about legal redress if this matter is not attended to within ten days.

Thank you.
Ken Jones

Referring action to a lawyer

Mark Stanton
Stanton's Paving Company

Dear Mr. Stanton,

I have received your demand for payment for the driveway repaving done by your company.

As you know, I have been asking that the job be fixed to our satisfaction for two months now. We consider the job incomplete because of gaps and cracks in the work that were immediately apparent.

At this time I have no intention of paying any bill from your company until the job is completed. I am considering asking my attorney to begin a lawsuit.

Ken Jones

Asking refund from repair shop for improper work

James Magliozzi
Jim's Auto Repair

Dear Jim,

As you know, I have been a loyal customer of your garage for the past ten years since we moved to Rolling Meadow.

During that time I have generally felt that I have been treated fairly and honestly. On the few occasions where I questioned some work or asked about the details of a bill, we have been able to discuss the matter and resolve it amicably.

About a month ago I brought my wife's vehicle in for routine maintenance. Your mechanic Fred told me that the oil pump was in danger of immediate failure and needed to be replaced. I approved the job, although I was shocked at the bill, which came to more than five hundred dollars for parts and labor.

A week ago, while my wife was on her way to work and driving on the highway, the car stalled. Luckily she was able to make it over to the side of the road; the car was towed to a garage in High Point.

The mechanic at that garage tells me the oil pump had been improperly sealed and had failed. I am enclosing a copy of the bill from the shop and the towing service, which together total $600.

I expect a call from you as soon as possible to discuss this matter. I hope we can come to an acceptable resolution without my having to take any further action.

Sincerely,
Kevin Morris

Complaint about failed auto repair

Don Beaton
Beaton's Auto Sales and Service
Rolling Meadow

Dear Mr. Beaton,

Ten days ago, on May 5, I brought my 2007 Sand Cruiser to your shop for an adjustment to the suspension.

I discussed the problem in detail with your service advisor; he said I would receive a call later in the day with a diagnosis and estimate.

Instead, later that day I received a call saying the problem had been fixed. Although I was not happy that there had been no consultation about the estimated cost for the repairs, I paid the $467 bill and picked up the car at the end of the day.

Within a few minutes drive toward home it was obvious that the problem was not fixed.

I returned the next morning and left the car again. When I returned that afternoon I was told a new problem had been found and repaired.

Two days later the same problem returned.

I want you to be aware of this situation before I come in again on Friday to have the car worked on for a third time.

I expect this is the last time I will have to spend money and time dealing with the same problem. If your shop is incapable of handling the issue, I expect a full refund and will take the car elsewhere.

Sincerely,
Joshua Smith

Asking for accounting of home care services

Susan Reilly, Director
Elder Care Home Services
Rolling Meadow

Dear Ms. Reilly,

As you know, I have taken over paying mother's bills and overseeing my mother's health care under power of attorney and a medical proxy.

In reviewing invoices from your company for services to my mother from February through August of this year, I have come across what appears to be several instances where she was billed twice for the same service and one occasion where she sent two checks for the same invoice.

I have included copies of the statements in question. Please review them and contact me to discuss them as soon as possible.

I am withholding payment of the October invoice while I wait to hear from you.

Sincerely,
Susan Phillips

Dismissing domestic caregiver

Louise Gold, President
Gold Health Care Services
Rolling Meadow

Dear Ms. Gold,

As you know, my mother Rose Katz has been receiving caregiver services from your company for the past six months.

I live several hours away and engaged your company to provide a caregiver to accompany my mother to her doctors' appointments.

We had arranged for a caregiver to take my mother to Rolling Meadow Hospital on Thursday, October 16, for some scheduled tests.

No one showed up. The hospital and her doctor called, and we were trying to find someone who could help us on short notice but were unable. My mother, who had prepared herself for the test, was very upset.

This is unacceptable to us. Although this was not an emergency, we expect the best of care at all times.

Please cancel all future bookings you have scheduled for my mother. We have decided to hire another company to provide special services for my mother.

Sincerely,
Jennifer Katz

Asking details of childcare needs

Mary Englund
Rolling Meadow

Dear Mrs. Englund,

You recently engaged my services to provide childcare at your daughter's wedding in November.

As we discussed, I was to be responsible for as many as six children in a small room adjacent to where the adults were being served dinner. I was to entertain the youngsters with games and crafts and supervise their dinner.

This morning I called the restaurant where the reception will be held to arrange to bring supplies. I was told they were expecting twenty-two children.

Our agreement called for payment of $50 per hour for as many as six children, and $10 for each additional child. This fee covers wages and expenses.

Please advise me of the actual number of children who will be in my care. If we have more than eight children, I will be hiring additional helpers; I ordinarily plan on one adult for each six children.

I look forward to hearing from you soon, and no later than one week before the wedding so that I can arrange for proper coverage.

Sincerely,
Lori Palmer

Complaint about trash pickup

Jeff Clarkson, Director
Department of Public Works
Rolling Meadow

Dear Mr. Clarkson,

I live on Grove Road in Rolling Meadow and my trash is picked up on Monday mornings at approximately 7 A.M.

For the past five years we have been generally satisfied with the quality of service we have received. However, in recent weeks there seems to be either a new crew or a new attitude, and it has become quite disturbing.

The crew has begun playing music from the cab of the truck, loud enough for us to hear it more than a block away. In addition, the men seem to be in a competition to see how loud they can be with tossing the trash cans into the bin of the truck. And then finally, where previously the cans and lids had been carefully placed back on the sidewalk, in recent weeks there have been a number of instances in which they have landed on the street side of the curb.

We would appreciate it if the crew was asked to be more courteous and attentive to detail.

Thank you,
Judy Kaplan

Problem with quality of home repair

Robert Lynch, President
Rolling Meadow Roofing & Tile Co.
Rolling Meadow

Dear Mr. Lynch,

I am writing with my final request that your company adequately complete the work performed on my home. I want to give you this last chance before I seek outside assistance in protecting my rights.

As you know, your company installed new shingles and rain gutters at my home on Eagle Lane in Rolling Meadow.

After the first rain we found two significant leaks in the upstairs bedroom and a problem with drainage from the gutters over the garage. I notified your company about the problem and was promised it would be fixed.

One month later, the roof and gutters have not been repaired and we continue to have problems each time it rains.

I expect your company to fix the roof immediately, and I also want a refund to cover the cost of repairing damage to the walls and ceiling in the bedroom.

Please contact me immediately to arrange a time for the work to be done.

If this is not resolved within ten days (June 15), I will refer this matter to our attorney and also seek the involvement of the Better Business Bureau and the town licensing board.

Thank you.
Dave Anderson

Questioning automatic charges on Internet bill

Compucase Internet
Rolling Meadow

In regards to account 6SJ7-2347809278-PATTEN

Dear Customer Service,

Three months ago I contacted your company on behalf of my father to cancel Internet service; my father has been in a nursing facility and has not been at home for some time.

In reviewing my father's credit card statements, I see that you have continued to charge him for Internet service for each of the past three months.

Please immediately credit him for the canceled service and do not reinstate any service until it is authorized.

I have also notified my credit card company that I am disputing these charges.

Sincerely,
Peter Patten

Seeking credit for cable outage

Customer Service
Bloomquist Cable Company

Dear Customer Service,

I am writing to request a credit for two weeks of lost cable television and Internet service for our home at 78 Winter Street in Rolling Meadow.

The entire northeastern section of town was without cable service from March 2 to March 15 after an ice storm; I would have thought a credit would have been automatically applied to all bills.

Please send me a revised bill reflecting the period of time we were without service.

Sincerely,
James Florence

Asking removal of missed appointment fee

Walter Fisher, DDS
Rolling Meadow

Dear Dr. Fisher,

I am writing to ask that the $50 fee for a missed appointment on March 25 be removed from my bill.

I showed up on time for my appointment that day but found that you were running more than an hour behind schedule because of an emergency surgery you had to perform. I understand that these things happen, but I was surprised that your front desk had not called patients to let them know.

In any case, I was unable to stay and I advised the receptionist and asked her to call me when there was another opening on the schedule.

Please remove this charge from my account.

Sincerely,
Ryan Foote

Restaurant special event room not available

Joseph Sebastian
Sebastian's Restaurant
Rolling Meadow

Dear Mr. Sebastian,

On June 3, we brought a group of twenty guests to your restaurant to celebrate my father's eighty-fifth birthday.

We chose Sebastian's because we are frequent patrons and thought this would be a special treat for my father. Unhappily, it did not work out that way.

We had spoken several times with Gloria, your manager, before coming to the restaurant. She had promised us the use of one of the small private rooms adjacent to the main dining room.

When our party arrived we were told by James, the host on duty that night, that the private rooms were not available. He said another, smaller group was using one of the rooms and that the two others had been used earlier in the day for a function and had not been fully cleared.

We were offered a makeshift table right in the middle of the main dining room, two long tables placed one after the other.

At that point we had two bad choices: stay and be subject to all the noise and commotion of a very busy restaurant or try to find another place on a Friday night that could seat twenty people on short notice.

We chose to stay, but it was unsatisfactory. None of us, including the guest of honor, could hear any conversations going on at the other end of the table. And we did not receive anything close to an adequate level of service from the two waitresses who were working our table as well as several others in the area.

We were all very disappointed in the way the evening turned out, and we are not at all certain we will come back to Sebastian's or recommend your restaurant to others.

Sincerely,
Ed Craig

CHAPTER 13

About the Product

COMPLAINT ABOUT FLAT SODA ➣ 104

COMPLAINT TO MANUFACTURER ABOUT
WORK BY AUTHORIZED DEALER ➣ 104

OBJECTING TO PRICE RISE ON
FLORIST BILL ➣ 105

RETURNING PRODUCT UNDER UNCONDITIONAL
SATISFACTION POLICY ➣ 105

COMPLAINING ABOUT
RESTOCKING FEE ➣ 105

COMPLAINT ABOUT SUBSTITUTION
OF INGREDIENT ➣ 106

RETURNING PHOTOGRAPH TO
BE REFRAMED ➣ 106

COMPLAINT ABOUT DECEPTIVE
PRODUCT PACKAGING ➣ 106

COMPLAINT ABOUT QUALITY OF
FOOD PRODUCT ➣ 107

ASKING REIMBURSEMENT FOR REPAIRS
UNDER WARRANTY ➣ 107

COMPLAINT ABOUT HANDLING CHARGE FOR
GIFT CARD ➣ 108

Complaint about flat soda

Customer Service
Olde-Style Soda Company

Dear Customer Service,

We are regular buyers of your unusual flavors of soda; I only wish it was easier to find all of your products including celery tonic and sarsaparilla.

Unfortunately, the most recent case of celery tonic we purchased turned out to be a disappointment. We bought the case of twenty-four cans at a convenience store in Rolling Meadow, more than an hour from where we live.

When we got back home and opened the first can we found that it was completely flat and had lost most of its flavor.

The soda can and case had the following lot number: 6SJ7-100-09.

We would like a refund for the cost of the case; I have enclosed a copy of the sales receipt. We hope this was an isolated problem.

Sincerely,
Fred Tracy

Complaint to manufacturer about work by authorized dealer

Customer Service
Mason Doors and Windows
Clinton Park

Dear Customer Service,

I recently purchased a garage door manufactured by your company (Model 6SJ7-1800R) and had it installed by one of your authorized dealers, Gleason Garage and Tractor Company in Rolling Meadow.

A week after the door was put in place, we found a major leak allowing rain to come into the garage. I called Gleason and they sent a repair crew that claimed to have fixed the problem.

This same thing happened after two subsequent storms. Gleason is now claiming that the problem is not with the door or their installation but with the structure of my garage.

I consider this a completely unreasonable position. There is nothing unusual about the design of our home; even if there was, this should have been dealt with by the installers when the door was first put in place.

I did extensive research and chose a door from your company because of its specifications and your excellent warranty. I am asking you now to stand behind that warranty and insist that either your authorized dealer complete the job properly or that you send a crew of your own for that purpose.

I look forward to hearing from you.

Sincerely,
Gordon Tate

Objecting to price rise on florist bill

Ray Hale
Hale's Florist

Dear Ray,

Thank you for your fine work in providing flowers for my daughter Cynthia's wedding. The church looked lovely, and the corsages for bride, groom, and attendants were beautiful.

As you recall, you called me on the day of the wedding to say that the shipment of white roses you had received were not up to your standards; you asked permission to substitute white lilies. We agreed, and the lilies were very attractive.

I am writing, though, to object to the extra charge for the lilies on the bill we have received.

We had a contract for the entire wedding. While we appreciate the fact that you did not want to provide inferior-quality white roses, we feel that we should not be asked to pay a higher price for the substitution you made.

We accepted your bid for the wedding, and the enclosed check covers the agreed-upon amount.

Sincerely,
Pat Fitzpatrick

Returning product under unconditional satisfaction policy

Customer Service Department
Walter's Tool Company

Gentlemen,

I am returning the Henderson Hedge Cutter Model 6988 I purchased from your store three months ago.

After using this piece of equipment twice I have found it to be too heavy and awkward for me to operate. Although the cutter functioned well, it put too much of a strain on my shoulder and neck.

I am returning the item under your complete satisfaction guaranteed policy and expect a full refund of the purchase price. I have enclosed copies of the sales receipt.

Thank you for your consideration. I hope to make other purchases from your company in the future.

Sincerely,
Rick Morris

Complaining about restocking fee

Customer Service
Big Bob's Furniture

Gentlemen,

I recently returned two custom upholstered easy chairs ordered from your company. These chairs were not the color I ordered and I found them unsatisfactory.

I just received my credit card statement and have been reimbursed for the original purchase price and all shipping and handling fees. However, I was charged a $125 restocking fee.

Please remove that $125 charge from my bill immediately. The chairs were returned because of an error made by your company.

I have already notified the credit card company that I dispute the charge.

Sincerely,
Rose Butler

Complaint about substitution of ingredient

Customer Service
Great Brand Cereals

Dear Customer Service,

I have been a loyal buyer of your Crunchy Bran cereal for many years.

I was unpleasantly surprised, though, to find that you have changed the formula to substitute palm oil for canola oil in the "new" recipe you are promoting.

This is a step in the completely wrong direction. When I shop I always look at the nutrition statement and pay close attention to the amount of saturated fat in products.

I will not buy Crunchy Bran again, until and unless you produce a more heart-healthy version of the product.

I look forward to hearing from you.

Sincerely,
Gladys Owens

Returning photograph to be reframed

Clark's Photo Services
Rolling Meadow

Dear Mr. Clark,

I am returning the enclosed framed photograph, which was sent to your company for restoration, matting, and framing.

I am very pleased with the restoration and framing, but I am afraid that the matting is the wrong color. We had specified A15 (Sky Blue) but instead received an inappropriate shade of ochre.

Please correct the mistake. I will hold your invoice and pay the bill when I receive the work properly done.

Thank you.
Brian Martin

Complaint about deceptive product packaging

Customer Service
Sal's Macaroni Company

I was very disappointed to find what I consider to be deceptive packaging in your company's line of dried pasta products.

On a recent visit to my local supermarket I picked up a box of macaroni and was about to place it in my cart when I noticed that it contained only 15 ounces of product instead of a full pound. It was in the same-sized box your company has used for years; the only change was the weight.

There is no excuse to put 15 ounces of pasta in a 16-ounce box, and there is no excuse to use an oversized box for an undersized quantity.

There is no other way I can look at this except to think that your company—a brand I have used for years—was trying to sneak a price increase past shoppers who are not careful enough to study the label.

I will be studying your packaging, and those of brands I had never purchased before, to make sure that I get the most for my money and that I am not tricked into making a bad decision. I would be interested in hearing from you about this matter.

Sincerely,
Georgia Taylor

Complaint about quality of food product

Customer Service
Aunt's Minnie's Cookies

Dear Customer Service,

I have been a loyal customer of your products since I was a child, which makes me about as old as your company. I have always considered your cookies to be the highest-quality packaged baked goods on the market.

For that reason, I am writing to express my dismay at the "new recipe" vanilla cream cookies now on the market. As best I can tell, the change in the recipe means that the cream filling is about half the size it used to be, and the cookie itself has lost its distinctive crunch.

Is that your intent? Was this merely a bad batch or is this "new" recipe the inferior replacement for your original product?

I am enclosing the UPC code from the package.

I look forward to hearing from you before I buy any more of your products.

Sincerely,
Rose Walker

Asking reimbursement for repairs under warranty

Customer Service
Lawnpro Lawn Mowers

Dear Customer Service,

I purchased a LawnJoy power mower from your website in May; I have attached a copy of the invoice.

It was immediately apparent when I began using the mower that there was a leak in the fuel hose that caused the engine to shut off every few minutes. When I spoke to one of your customer service representatives, I was told to bring the mower to a local authorized repair shop and send the receipt to your company for reimbursement.

The confirmation code for this conversation was 6SJ7-0508.

As it turned out, the mower required a new fuel hose and primer bulb.

I submitted all receipts two months ago, on June 2. As of today I have not received reimbursement. Please advise the status of this case.

Sincerely,
Phil Green

Complaint about handling charge for gift card

Charles Herbert, Vice President for Sales
Happy Kids Toys and Accessories

Dear Mr. Herbert,

I am writing to tell you of my unhappiness with your company's policies regarding gift cards.

As a present for my young nephew, we decided to purchase a gift card and allow him to go shopping at your store. We thought it would be fun and educational for him to act like a customer and make decisions based on the amount of money he had available to spend.

When we called one of your stores to make arrangements for the card, we were told that there was a $5 service charge plus a $3.95 fee for shipping and handling.

As far as I am concerned, this is an outrageous attempt to gouge customers. What possible justification is there for a service charge? And why do you ask $3.95 for mailing a card that will travel across the country for the price of a first-class stamp?

From my point of view, we are loaning your company the amount of the gift card from the time of purchase until it is used. And I would also expect that many people who receive cards end up spending more than the value on the card.

We ended up deciding not to buy the card and instead sent our nephew a check that his parents can cash. That wasn't our initial intent, but we did not want to waste money on your fees.

If you would like to retain our family as a customer in the future, I would be interested in hearing your response to my complaint.

Sincerely,
Amelia Mosley

CHAPTER 14

Dealing with a Store

ASKING STORE FOR DISCOUNT ❧ 110

ASKING STORE FOR QUANTITY
DISCOUNT ❧ 110

ASKING STORE TO STOCK BRAND ❧ 110

ASKING STORE TO RESTOCK
PRODUCT ❧ 111

COMPLAINING TO SUPERMARKET FOR LACK
OF SUFFICIENT HELP ❧ 111

RETURNING PRODUCT BECAUSE
OF PRICE ❧ 111

NOTICE OF AVAILABILITY OF STORE CREDIT
FOR RETURN ❧ 112

REFUSING STORE CREDIT AND DEMANDING
FULL REFUND ❧ 112

ITEM NOT RETURNABLE TO STORE ❧ 113

REFUSING RETURN OF ITEM ❧ 113

REDUCING HOURS AT BUSINESS ❧ 113

Asking store for discount

J.D. Office Products
Rolling Meadow

Gentlemen,

As you know, the Rolling Meadow Historical Society has been a longtime customer of your company. I know we are not your largest customer, but we have been loyal in our patronage. As much as possible we have made it our policy to patronize local businesses. We are dependent on the community for our support and feel it is our responsibility for us to do the same.

We have no complaints about your company's quality or service. However, in this very difficult economy we have been forced to reduce our budget and look for the best possible deals in all of our expenditures.

To be frank, we could save a great deal of money by purchasing office supplies from an online company or one of the warehouse stores in Littleton.

We are asking that you work with us to make it possible for us to continue to get our office supplies from you. We are asking for discounts, special offers, and incentives that will allow us to remain a loyal customer.

Please call me to discuss.

Sincerely,
Sandra Hudson, Office Manager
Rolling Meadow Historical Association

Asking store for quantity discount

George Robinson, manager
Rolling Meadow Variety Store

Dear Mr. Robinson,

I was in your store recently and saw a lovely silver-plated jewelry box. The retail price on this piece was $16.

I am chairperson for a woman's group in Rolling Meadow, and we will be having our appreciation banquet in September. I plan to purchase 80 gifts for our members. My budget is $1,000.

For an order of this size, I am hoping for a quantity discount; I can offer $12.50 per unit.

I'm hoping this is acceptable to you and we can place an immediate order. I look forward to hearing from you.

Sincerely,
Brenda Miller

Asking store to stock brand

Jeff Connors, manager
Rolling Meadow Supermarket

Dear Mr. Connors,

We are regular customers at your store and generally appreciate the range of products available. However, we have been unable to find a particular product that we very much enjoy: SoyFlava Wasabi Salad Dressing.

I am hoping you can add it to your shelf. In fact, we'll buy an entire case if that's the best way to get the product to Rolling Meadow. But I'll also encourage my friends to come to the store to buy this dressing.

Please let me know if this is possible and when I might expect to be able to purchase it.

Thank you.

Sonya Flanders

Asking store to restock product

Tommy's Toggery
Rolling Meadow

Dear Manager,

For many years we have been loyal customers of your shop. Among our favorite products are the rain hats manufactured by the Webster Clothing Company. We use them for ourselves, and I have bought them as gifts for many of our friends.

When I visited your store last week, I was told that you are now carrying a different line. I have to say I found the replacement item much inferior to the Webster hats.

I am hoping you will bring back the Webster hats; we promise to buy at least six when they're back on the shelves. I look forward to hearing from you.

Sincerely,
Elaine Harvey

Complaining to supermarket for lack of sufficient help

Go and Save Grocery
Rolling Meadow

Dear Manager,

For the past three Sundays I have been quite upset with the level of service at your store.

Each time I have found lengthy lines at the checkout counters; this past week I waited more than thirty minutes before I reached the cashier.

I do not understand why more cashiers are not employed during times when the store is consistently jammed with customers. At this time, I have decided to drive ten miles to your competitor in Hadley Village; that supermarket always has plenty of cashiers on duty.

I would welcome a call from you if you have any news about staffing plans that would convince me to bring my business back to your store.

Thank you.

Marion Otter

Returning product because of price

Customer Service
Morgan's Department Store

Enclosed please find a leather handbag purchased from your store on May 15.

I'm afraid I made a mistake in buying the item; I thought the price was $150, but I was shocked to receive my credit card statement with a charge for $1,500.

Although I admit the mistake was mine, I do want to point out that the price tag is not clearly marked. And at the time I bought the bag I remember saying to the sales clerk that I thought $150 was a great price for such a high-quality purse. I wish she had corrected me.

Sincerely,
Shelia Gordon

Notice of availability of store credit for return

John Jablonsky
Highland River

Dear Mr. Jablonsky,

We are in receipt of the electric drill you recently purchased from our store. In the accompanying letter you stated that the reason for the return is that you changed your mind and asked to be credited with the purchase price.

At this time, we are only able to offer a store credit on returns unless there is a defect in the item; this policy is clearly printed on your receipt. Enclosed please find a coupon, valued at the full price of the drill, which you can use for future purchases at our store.

Thank you.

Holly Lightly, Manager

Refusing store credit and demanding full refund

Suzanne Yates, Owner
Suzanne's Boutique
Rolling Meadow

Dear Ms. Yates,

I was in your store earlier this week and purchased a sweater as a gift; I have enclosed a copy of the sales receipt.

As I was shopping, the clerk told me it was 100 percent cashmere; it was included in your sale of cashmere items.

When I got home and looked at the small print on the label, I discovered that it was actually a 50/50 mix of cashmere and mohair.

I brought the item back and was told that because I purchased it as a sale item, I could only receive store credit. There was nothing else in the store I thought appropriate, and in any case I feel that I was misled by your clerk.

Perhaps it was an honest mistake on her part, but I want to reiterate that the sweater was being offered on sale as a cashmere item.

I do not want to have to escalate this matter, but I am certain that if I was to contact the state attorney general they would back me up because the item was advertised as something it was not.

Please advise how you intend to refund my money.

Sincerely,
Kay Becker

Item not returnable to store

Susan Carroll
Rolling Meadow

Dear Ms. Carroll,

We recently received in the mail a leather skirt that you asked to return for a refund or store credit. In your cover letter you said it was a gift and you had no accompanying paperwork.

Although we promise to stand behind all merchandise sold at our store or through our online website, we regret to inform you that this item was not purchased from us. We do not stock the item, and the identification tags on the skirt do not match our system.

We are returning the item. We hope you will find the original seller.

Sincerely,
Brian Adams
Customer Service

Refusing return of item

Sheila Gordon
Rolling Meadow

Dear Ms. Gordon,

We have received the leather bag you purchased recently at our store. In the cover letter you stated you wished to return the purse; we regret to inform you that we are unable to accept the item since it has clearly been used.

As stated on all receipts, we are happy to refund or issue store credit for all items returned in new and unused condition.

We apologize for any misunderstanding you may have had about your purchase.

As a gesture of goodwill to a valued customer, we are enclosing a coupon good for ten percent off your next purchase at Morgan's Department Store.

Sincerely,
Elizabeth Bell
Customer Service

Reducing hours at business

To Our Loyal Customers and Artisans,

We want to thank all our faithful supporters for your patronage this past year. We are proud to operate the largest crafts cooperative in the state, and we look forward to many years of serving the community.

As we prepare to open for the season, we want to notify you of a change in our hours of operation. In order to decrease costs in this difficult economy, we have decided to reduce our operating hours; effective May 1 we will be open five days a week, closing on Monday and Tuesdays.

We hope this does not inconvenience any of our customers. As a reminder, we do schedule openings of the store by appointment in the evening and on days when we are closed.

We look forward to seeing old friends and new faces this season.

Sincerely,
Jo Perry

CHAPTER 15

Traveling About

COMPLAINT ABOUT TRAVEL
ARRANGEMENTS ❖ 115

ASKING TRAVEL AGENCY TO
REDUCE PRICE ❖ 115

ASKING REFUND FROM
TRAVEL AGENCY ❖ 116

COMPLAINT TO TRAVEL AGENCY ABOUT
UNEXPECTED FEE ❖ 116

COMPLAINT ABOUT MISSING
HOTEL RESERVATION ❖ 116

COMPLAINING ABOUT CONDITION OF
HOTEL ROOM ❖ 117

OBJECTING TO NOISY ROOM
AT HOTEL ❖ 118

SEEKING PRICE ADJUSTMENT ON
HOTEL RATE ❖ 118

ASKING REFUND FOR HOTEL
OVERCHARGE ❖ 119

ASKING AIRLINE TO PAY FOR UNEXPECTED
HOTEL CHARGE ❖ 119

COMPLAINT ABOUT CLEANLINESS
OF AIRPLANE ❖ 120

Complaint about travel arrangements

Martin Shore
Go Away Travel Agency

Dear Mr. Shore,

We recently returned from a cruise package arranged by Shirley Glover of your agency.

Although the cruise was for the most part enjoyable, we feel that we received poor advice from Ms. Glover.

When we first spoke with Ms. Glover, we said we had never gone on a cruise before. We asked for advice in selecting a good cruise line with an itinerary and activities that would be appropriate for our entire family, which includes my wife and I plus our eight- and ten-year-old daughters.

The cruise ship from Miami to the Caribbean was filled almost entirely with senior citizens. The relatively few events included things like napkin folding and wine tastings. There were no activities for children at all, and our children were all but ignored by the staff.

We ended up paying dearly for our children to be miserable the entire time.

Since returning I have inquired among my friends and I have found there are a number of cruise lines that make a special effort to accommodate and entertain children. We are certain Ms. Glover could have done a much better job in choosing one of those cruises for us.

I am writing to bring this to your attention and to tell you that we feel we are entitled to a substantial refund or credit from your agency. We plan to cruise again, and we will make our choice of travel agency based on your response to this letter.

Sincerely,
Kay Maddow

Asking travel agency to reduce price

Laura Butler
Go-Away Travel Agency
Rolling Meadow

Dear Laura,

Three months ago my husband and I booked a cruise to Alaska in July with your agency. We paid our deposit, and the remaining money is due in two months.

The cost for this cruise was $2,600 per person for a suite with a balcony.

In recent days we have seen ads from the cruise line indicating significant discounts on upcoming Alaskan cruises, including the trip we have booked. The sale rate is $1,900 per person.

Please adjust our reservation to reflect the new price; if necessary, we are willing to cancel our first plan and rebook at the new rate. Even with a penalty the price would be lower, but we fully expect your agency will be able to renegotiate the price with the cruise line without a penalty being assessed.

Please call me as soon as possible to advise us of the new price.

Sincerely,
Karen Cart

Asking refund from travel agency

Laura Butler
Go-Away Travel Agency
Rolling Meadow

Dear Laura,

I received your letter in which you inform us that we are not entitled to the $400 per person savings you are now offering on cruises to Alaska in July.

We are not satisfied with your explanation. If you are not able to obtain a reduction in the price of our trip by dealing directly with the cruise line, there is one other way for you to keep our business: pay us from the commission you earn on the sale.

We have used your agency for many years and have been happy with the arrangements you have made. However, there are many other agencies we could use. To put it bluntly, we're sure we can find someone who wants our business enough to always be on our side in any disagreement with a travel provider.

At this time we expect either a reduction in the price of our cruise to reflect the new price or a full refund of our deposit so that we can make a booking with another agency.

I look forward to hearing from you within the next seven days.

Thank you.

Karen Cart

Complaint to travel agency about unexpected fee

Mildred Swain
Atlantic Travel Agency

Dear Ms. Swain,

As you know, my husband and I have booked a fourteen-day Mediterranean cruise on the MS Puddle of the Seas through your agency.

We have made all payments as required and are ready to leave in just two weeks. However, in today's mail we received a $300 invoice from the cruise line for a fuel surcharge.

This is unacceptable. We have a contract with your agency and the cruise line at an agreed-upon price. We do not intend to be forced to pay this additional amount.

As our travel agent, we feel it is your responsibility to be our representative in obtaining the best price and overall package for us. We want the surcharge removed from our bill and travel documents issued, or we want to cancel the cruise and receive a full refund—without any penalties—immediately.

Please call me to discuss.

Sincerely,
Catherine Allen

Complaint about missing hotel reservation

John Reynolds, Manager
The Lake View Hotel

Dear Mr. Reynolds,

I am writing to tell you of my extreme displeasure with your hotel's reservations and front desk.

My wife and I had a confirmed reservation at your hotel for the night of May 15. This room was booked six months in advance in anticipation of attending an event at Fredonia University. At the time of booking we were informed that no credit card deposit was necessary for check-ins before 4 P.M.

We have stayed at the Lake View a number of times in the past and have plans to make future visits to the college.

When we arrived at your hotel on May 15, at 3 P.M., we were told by front desk clerk Pat Stevens that there was no record of our reservation and that there were no rooms available for the weekend.

Ms. Stevens made no effort to investigate why our reservation was not recorded. And when we asked if she could find us a room somewhere else in the area, she told us, "It is not my job to make reservations for you at other hotels."

We feel that Ms. Stevens was very rude and dismissive of us.

We were forced to book a room at an inadequate motel thirty miles away, and we missed some of the events we had planned to attend.

I want you to be aware of the treatment we received at your hotel. We will be very interested in hearing from you before we consider making future reservations at your establishment.

Sincerely,
Harold Barker

Complaining about condition of hotel room

Janice Fletcher, Manager
The Overlook

Dear Ms. Fletcher,

My husband and I were guests at The Overlook on the weekend of July 11 to July 13.

This was not our first visit; we have stayed at your hotel at least four times in the past five years. On each of our previous visits the accommodations and service have been outstanding.

Unfortunately, that was far from the case on our most recent visit.

We always reserve a no-smoking room, and our reservation in July included that notation.

Although the room we were given was marked as such, it was clear that the previous guests had smoked. The odor was very apparent in the room, and there was even a full ashtray on the balcony.

This should have been obvious to your housekeeping staff. We also found it odd that there was an ashtray in a no-smoking room and unacceptable that it had not been removed.

We immediately returned to the front desk and explained the situation. We were told there were no other rooms available; I am not certain if that was true.

We found the condition of the room, and the unhelpful attitude of the front desk, to be well below the usual standard we have found at your hotel. Unless we can be reassured that this sort of situation will not occur again, we will be forced to look elsewhere for accommodations on our next visit to your area.

Sincerely,
Monica Peterson

Objecting to noisy room at hotel

Stan Lawton, Manager
Rolling Meadow Value Inn

Dear Mr. Lawton,

My wife and I have relatives in the Rolling Meadow area and travel there frequently. We are regular guests of your establishment and have generally had nothing but good experiences there.

Last weekend, however, our stay was totally unacceptable.

Our room was located on a floor where there were many guests attending a wedding party. On the two nights we were at the Rolling Meadow Value Inn there was partying and noise from the rooms and hallways for nearly the entire night.

We called the front desk several times between midnight and 4 A.M. There were only brief periods of quiet during that time. On our last call, the phone was not answered at all.

We asked to have a room change for the second night but were told none were available. We were assured that the guests had been asked to be quiet.

That was not the case. We were forced to endure a second sleepless night with no assistance from the manager on duty.

When we checked out the next morning we again brought our complaints to the attention of the person at the front desk. We received a barely adequate apology.

As I said earlier, we have in the past been very pleased with the Value Inn. We will now have to decide whether we will have to look elsewhere in the future.

I look forward to your response.

Sincerely,
Ben Fletcher

Seeking price adjustment on hotel rate

Michael Greene, President
Superior Inns and Suites

Dear Mr. Greene,

Recently my family spent a week at your Superior Inns and Suites location in Waterford, Florida.

We checked in on a Monday. On Thursday the marquee outside the motel advertised a special weekend rate that was fifty dollars a night lower than what we were paying.

I immediately went to the front desk and spoke with the manager, Carla. I asked that our three remaining nights be charged at the reduced rate. She assured me that that would be the case.

When we checked out on Monday, the manager on duty—Raymond—refused to adjust our rate. He said there was no notation on the file and that he could not make changes to our reservation once we were in the room. He said we would have to take this up with the corporate office.

I assure you if Carla had not agreed to give us the special rate we would have checked out and gone to one of the other nearby motels; they were all offering special weekend prices.

I am enclosing a copy of our receipt. I feel it would be proper for your company to credit me $150 for the three days for which we were overcharged.

When making travel plans in the future, I will be very influenced by how I am treated in this instance.

Sincerely,
Jon Anderson

Asking refund for hotel overcharge

Virginia Ray, Proprietor
Ray's Guest House
Rolling Meadow

Dear Ms. Ray,

My daughter Molly was recently married, with ceremonies and a reception held in Rolling Meadow.

Several months ago, I contacted you to ask if you could offer a special rate to guests coming from out of town. You offered a discount of $25 per night for a block of at least five rooms.

As it turned out, six wedding guests stayed at your guest house that weekend, with five spending two nights and one three nights. I have just found out that all of our guests were charged the regular rate, without a discount. That amounts to an overcharge of $325.

I am sure this was an error on your part. I would ask that you either make refunds to the guests individually or send a check for $325 to me and I will see that our invited guests receive the refund.

I hope we will be able to recommend your guest house to friends and family in the future.

Sincerely,
Nina Hobson

Asking airline to pay for unexpected hotel charge

Customer Service
One World Airways

Dear Customer Service,

I am writing to complain about a problem with baggage service on Flight 6932 from Los Angeles to Providence on May 22.

To make it short, we arrived on time at 10:05 P.M., but our bags were not available until the next morning. As a result, I incurred several hundred dollars in additional expenses.

When we arrived at the baggage claim area to pick up our luggage, we were at first told there would be a slight delay. About forty-five minutes later it was announced that there was a mechanical problem that prevented the ground crew from opening the compartment on the plane and technicians would not be able to make a repair until the next day.

We were asked to either come back the next morning or have our bags sent to another location.

I was on a business trip and needed the materials in my checked baggage as soon as possible. I had to book a room in the hotel at the airport so that I could get my bags the next morning. It was too late to cancel another hotel reservation I had made about twenty miles away from the airport, close to my client.

Because of the problem with your airplane, I paid for two hotel rooms and was late for my meeting. The cost of the airport hotel room was $175.

I feel that One World Airways should reimburse me for the cost of the extra hotel room.

I have enclosed copies of my airline ticket and my two hotel invoices. I look forward to hearing from you soon.

Sincerely,
Jane Green

Complaint about cleanliness of airplane

Customer Service
Northern Airlines

Dear Customer Service,

I travel often for business and am a regular customer of Northern Airlines.

I am writing to complain about an unusually unpleasant experience on a trip I just completed. On March 2, I flew from Boston to Austin on Flight 6932.

The plane arrived late, and your ground crew apparently rushed to get the plane ready to fly out again. The plane was full of garbage from the previous flight. There was food in the seatback pockets, and two of the plane's three bathrooms were out of service.

Leaving aside health concerns and common decency, I also worry that your airline is neglecting service and maintenance of its airplane.

I am anxious to hear from you before I decide whether to use your airline again or recommend it to others.

Sincerely,
Rick Wardon

CHAPTER 16

Landlords and Real Estate

ASKING RETURN OF SECURITY
DEPOSIT ❖ 122

ASKING REDUCTION IN
APARTMENT RENT ❖ 122

ASKING LANDLORD TO TRADE SERVICES
FOR RENT ❖ 122

ASKING LANDLORD FOR EARLY
SNOW REMOVAL ❖ 123

ASKING LANDLORD TO
COMPLETE REPAIRS ❖ 123

COMPLAINT TO LANDLORD
ABOUT SAFETY ❖ 124

FOLLOW-UP COMPLAINT
TO LANDLORD ❖ 124

NOTIFYING RENTER OF NONRENEWAL
OF LEASE ❖ 124

LANDLORD NOT RENEWING LEASE ❖ 125

LANDLORD THREATENING TO
TERMINATE LEASE ❖ 125

TO LANDLORD ABOUT
BARKING DOG ❖ 126

LANDLORD THREATENING EVICTION ❖ 126

RESPONSE TO LANDLORD WARNING
ABOUT TRASH ❖ 126

LANDLORD CLAIMS DAMAGE
BY RENTERS ❖ 127

INFORMING LANDLORD OF DEATH
OF TENANT ❖ 127

ASKING TO BREAK LEASE BECAUSE
OF ILLNESS ❖ 127

NOTIFYING RENTER OF TRANSFER
OF OWNERSHIP ❖ 128

OFFERING TO SELL HOME
TO TENANT ❖ 128

INFORMING FAMILY OF DECISION TO
SELL HOME ❖ 129

ADVISING WORK REQUIRED BEFORE REAL
ESTATE CLOSING ❖ 129

Asking return of security deposit

Peter Martin
Rolling Meadow

Dear Mr. Martin,

It has been sixty days since I vacated Apartment 8 at 39 Pine Street at the conclusion of my lease.

According to the terms of the contract, I was to receive a refund of the security deposit, plus interest, within thirty days after moving out of the apartment. I have also checked with the town housing department, and they inform me that state law also requires return of deposits in that same thirty-day period.

As you know, you accompanied me on an inspection of the property on the day we moved out of the apartment, and you told me then that there was no chargeable damage and that I would receive a full refund.

Please send the check to me at my new address, listed on the letterhead above.

Sincerely,
Janice Sullivan

Asking reduction in apartment rent

Rental Office
Rolling Meadow Garden Apartments

I have received the proposed renewal lease for my unit at Rolling Meadow Garden Apartments.

I have to say that I was shocked to see a 20 percent increase in the monthly rent. I find it hard to understand why such a substantial increase would be asked, especially when there are many empty apartments in the complex.

As you know, I have lived here for four years. I have never missed a rent payment, and I believe I have been a model tenant in all other ways. I would like to continue to live here.

I am asking that you redraw the lease so that the rate does not increase for the coming year. I am willing to commit to living here for another year but not to paying 20 percent more.

I don't want to move, but if I must I will. At the same time, I'm sure you don't want to see another empty and nonrevenue-generating apartment. I look forward to hearing from you soon with a revised lease.

Sincerely,
Kurt Myers

Asking landlord to trade services for rent

Lloyd Hagen
Rolling Meadow

Dear Mr. Hagen,

As you know, I have been a tenant in the house you own on Broad Street for the past two years. I have been quite happy with my apartment, and I believe I have been a good tenant.

Unfortunately, I have just been laid off from my job. I am looking for other employment in the area, and I expect I will find new work within the coming months.

Until I find a new job, I would like to see if there is a way I could reduce some or all of my monthly rent by performing services for you at the house. I am a capable landscaper and painter, and I would be happy to do whatever jobs around the house you would ask.

I would appreciate hearing from you soon.

Thank you.
Steven Abbott

Asking landlord for early snow removal

Lloyd Hagen
Rolling Meadow

Dear Mr. Hagen,

I am writing to request you make arrangements for early morning snowplowing at Lakeview Apartments.

As you know, we have had a series of storms this winter, and on at least three occasions the parking lot was not plowed until after 9 A.M. even though the streets had been cleared during the night.

Most of us living at your apartment complex have to be at work very early in the morning. The fact that the lots are not plowed makes it difficult and dangerous for us to get to work by car.

I would appreciate it if you would ask the contractor you use to clear the lots to come by the apartments by 7 A.M. on snow days.

Thank you.
Joseph O'Brien

Asking landlord to complete repairs

Mr. Russell Cosgrove
Lake View Apartments
Rolling Meadow

Dear Mr. Cosgrove,

I moved into Rolling Meadow Apartments three weeks ago. At that time I brought to the attention of your building superintendent, Sharon Ross, a list of items that needed attention.

I noted a torn patio door screen, a leaky faucet in the bathroom, and a significant stain on the living room carpet. Each of these were noted on the inspection form that Ms. Ross and I signed on the day I moved in.

I was assured that this work would be accomplished within the first week of my tenancy. That has not happened.

Ms. Ross has repeatedly promised me that the apartment will be tended to, but as of today the problems remain.

I intend to be a very good tenant, and I do not want to cause any problems. However, I must insist that these three jobs be completed immediately.

Sincerely,
Terry Foley

Complaint to landlord about safety

James Clemens
Rolling Meadow

Dear Mr. Clemens,

In regards to my apartment at 69 Spruce Street, I am writing to formally notify you of a serious safety issue that has to be dealt with immediately.

The banister on the stairs in the front of the building is dangerously loose, nearly detached from the porch. Our local postal carrier has already informed all of the tenants that he will no longer climb the stairs to deliver mail, and instead we must visit the post office each day.

This is not only an inconvenience and a danger but also a liability risk for you as the owner of the house.

I feel that I have been a model tenant, and I am otherwise generally satisfied with my apartment. However, I must insist that repairs be done immediately.

Thank you.

Will Simon

Follow-up complaint to landlord

James Clemens
Rolling Meadow

Dear Mr. Clemens,

It has been ten days since I notified you of the loose railing at the apartment building you own on Spruce Street. No repair work has been done.

I do not want to cause trouble, but I must insist that the apartment be made safe for tenants and visitors. I have contacted the housing authority, and they inform me that if your tenants file a formal complaint, the housing authority will take over the collection of rent and hold it under escrow. If the work is not done within forty-eight hours after that, the authority will hire a contractor to make the repair and any others their inspectors deem necessary.

As a courtesy, I will wait two days before filing paperwork with the housing authority to allow you to have the work done.

I hope you will give this matter your highest priority.

Sincerely,
Will Simon

Notifying renter of nonrenewal of lease

Cathy Kay Keating
Rolling Meadow

Dear Cathy,

On behalf of our family we want to thank you for your kind words about my mother. We also want to thank you for being a good tenant for all these years in the first-floor apartment of her house.

At this time, though, I am sorry to have to inform you that we will not be renewing your lease when it comes to an end on December 31. We have decided to use both floors of the house as apartments for family members who live in the area.

We wanted to let you know of our decision as quickly as possible to allow you ample time to find another place to live.

Please continue to make your rent payments as before. Feel free to call me at any time if I can be of help. In any case, we will be in touch on December 1 to confirm your moving date and to arrange an inspection of the premises.

Thank you.

Sincerely,
Julia Brennan

Landlord not renewing lease

Sandra Davis
Rolling Meadow

Dear Ms. Davis,

As the end of your current lease approaches, I am writing to notify you that I will not be offering you a new contract.

We have decided to convert the home from its present configuration of two one-floor rental units into a single-family home that will be occupied by a family member.

You have been a good tenant, and I will be happy to provide references if you require them. Under the terms of the current lease, I am giving you the required two-months notice and asking you vacate the apartment by October 31.

Sincerely,
George Lester

Landlord threatening to terminate lease

Cynthia Edwards
19 Spruce Street
Apartment 3
Rolling Meadow

Dear Ms. Edwards,

It has come to my attention that you are keeping a dog in your apartment. We have received several complaints from other tenants about barking.

Under terms of your rental agreement, dogs and cats are not permitted in any unit. We do this in order to protect the right to quiet enjoyment by other tenants of their apartments and to avoid damage caused by pets to the premises.

I am asking you immediately find another home for the animal. Under terms of the lease, I am notifying you that we will conduct an inspection of your apartment within the next five days and reserve the right to inspect again on short notice to assure there are no further violations of the lease.

Failure to comply with the terms will cause us to terminate the lease and seek a court's assistance in collecting the full outstanding balance for the five months remaining under the contract, as well as retaining funds from your security deposit to pay for repair of any damage to the apartment.

Thank you.

Vincent Monroe

To landlord about barking dog

Vincent Monroe
Rolling Meadow

Dear Mr. Monroe,

I want to apologize and explain the dog-barking incident some of my neighbors complained of last week.

My sister was visiting me for a few days, and when making plans for her stay she never mentioned she was bringing her dog.

As soon as she arrived, I asked her to make arrangements to put the dog in a kennel. However, because of the holiday it took three days before the dog could be moved out.

Again, please accept my apology. This will not happen again.

Sincerely,
Jessica Reynolds

Landlord threatening eviction

Dennis Manning
Apt. 3
Rolling Meadow Apartments

Dear Mr. Manning,

I am writing to formally notify you of a serious violation of your lease for the above-referenced apartment.

For the past several weeks I have found uncovered garbage in the front yard of the house you rent. This represents a violation of the city health code, which requires all refuse to be placed in closed containers.

I draw your attention to Section VI, Paragraph 4 of the lease in which you agree to take care that garbage is properly handled to avoid attracting pests.

If this situation continues, I will hire a garbage company to remove the material and perform such other tasks as are necessary to meet the health code; the cost of such services will be deducted from your security deposit. At the same time, I will move to immediately terminate your lease.

I trust this situation will not continue. If you have any questions about the lease or your obligations under the contract, please contact me immediately.

Victor Millar

Response to landlord warning about trash

Vincent Millar
Rolling Meadow

Dear Mr. Millar,

I received your warning about the trash left outside my apartment last week.

Please accept my apology; I assure you it will not happen again. I had to leave town for a family emergency and a friend of mine was watching my apartment while I was away. In my haste to leave, I neglected to fully inform him of the rules.

Sincerely,
Dennis Manning

Landlord claims damage by renters

Michael and Martha Randolph

Dear Michael and Martha,

We hope you had a spectacular time at our house on Mirror Pond.

As you know, we don't often rent the house; it is a very special place and is decorated with many antiques and family heirlooms. We discussed these items when we showed you the house and asked they not be used by renters.

When we checked the house after your departure we noticed chips in four of the Waterford Crystal wine goblets. We also cannot locate the stopper to the Grafton Street decanter that is kept in the same cabinet.

I have enclosed a statement from a reputable department store showing the replacement costs of these items.

We have deducted this amount from the security deposit you provided and are forwarding a check for the remainder to you.

Sincerely,
Andrea Quinn

Informing landlord of death of tenant

Simon Youkilis, manager
Rolling Meadow Realty
Rolling Meadow

Dear Mr. Youkilis,

I am writing to inform you that my mother, Mary Barker, passed away last week.

Under terms of the rental agreement she signed with you for apartment 68 at 101 Southbury Road, the contract is therefore automatically voided at the end of this month.

As executor of her estate and under power of attorney, I will be visiting the apartment on March 15 to remove her possessions. At that time I would like to meet with you to conduct an inspection of the property and to arrange for the return of her security deposit to her estate.

We appreciate the consideration you showed my mother over the years.

Sincerely,
Sandra Jennings

Asking to break lease because of illness

Susan Rider, Property Manager
Spruce Street Apartments
Rolling Meadow

Dear Ms. Rider,

My wife and I have lived at the Spruce Street Apartments for the past twelve years. As you know, we recently renewed our lease with plans to stay for another year.

In recent weeks my wife's health has taken a dramatic turn for the worse, and it is now apparent that we must move to an assisted-living facility where she can receive the help she needs.

As longtime residents, I am writing to ask that we be released from the new lease.

It would be a substantial hardship on us to pay for this apartment as well as an assisted-living facility. We would very much appreciate your consideration for us in this difficult time.

I look forward to hearing from you.

Henry Martin

Notifying renter of transfer of ownership

Mr. Charles Powell
Rolling Meadow

Dear Mr. Powell,

Since the death of my mother, I have not had the opportunity to thank you for your kind words at her funeral; I will miss her very much.

I also wanted to let you know the status of her house where you rent an apartment.

The home will stay in the family for the time being. As executor of her estate, please continue to make payments as before. Make the check payable to me, at the address on the letterhead.

We will be clearing my mother's possessions from the upper floor, and we expect to offer those rooms for rent soon.

I am giving notice now that effective May 1, sixty days from now, the rent for your apartment will be increased to $700 per month. The rate has not been increased for at least five years and we feel this is an appropriate price.

My mother enjoyed having you as a tenant and we hope that relationship will continue.

Sincerely,
Julia Brennan

Offering to sell home to tenant

Mr. Charles Powell
Rolling Meadow

Dear Mr. Powell,

I want to thank you again for your kind words about my mother. She always thought highly of you as a tenant, and we were happy to have you living downstairs from her in case of an emergency.

Now that we have begun the process of dealing with my mother's estate, I wanted to let you know the status of her house. We have decided as a family to put the property on the market; all of us live a considerable distance away and do not want the responsibilities of being landlords.

If we do sell the home to a new buyer, there is no guarantee you will be able to continue renting your apartment. But we will certainly let the new owner know that you have been an excellent tenant.

Before we list the house with a real estate agent, though, we wanted to find out if you had any interest in buying the property yourself. We would certainly be happy to consider an offer based on a reasonable discount from the market value because of savings two would realize in real estate agency commissions and other costs.

As you know, the house is a very desirable rental property, and the cost of a mortgage would be offset to a large extent by income received from a tenant.

Please me know by May 1 if you have any interest in buying the house.

Sincerely,
Julia Brennan

Informing family of decision to sell home

Dear Children,

We know you all understand that this past year has been a difficult one for your father and me. It's not easy getting old, but we're both feeling better now and hoping for the best.

We have come to realize that our house has become a huge burden. Although we love our home, we simply don't want to be spending all of our money and much of our time on its upkeep.

After much thought we have decided to simplify our lives and give ourselves the time to enjoy ourselves in retirement. We can do without the plumber and the landscaper and the snow plow.

We have found a lovely two-bedroom apartment in a new senior development right here in Rolling Meadow. It has a view of Mirror Pond and a recreation center, and they'll take care of all the maintenance, lawn mowing, and plowing.

The way we look at it, this is a great way for us make our lives easier. And we think this will ease the burden on all of you, our children, as well.

It is our plan to put the house on the market soon. If anyone in the family has an interest in the house, we'd be happy to hear about it.

Love,
Mom and Dad

Advising work required before real estate closing

Sheila Jordan
Rolling Meadow Real Estate Agency

Dear Ms. Jordan,

We are looking forward to completing the purchase of the property at 67 Pine Street in five days.

However, as you know, one of the conditions of the contract of sale is that the present owners remove all the debris and trash in the backyard. This includes a stove, a car engine, a broken swing set, and an aboveground pool.

On the advice of our attorney, I am bringing these matters to your attention now. If the property is not fully in compliance with the contract, we will not attend the closing and we will ask for the return of our deposit currently being held in escrow.

Please advise your clients and let us know their intentions.

Thank you.

Stan Lawrence

Part 5

Community Organizations

CHAPTER 17

Membership Matters
and Events

INVITING NEW MEMBERS FOR
CIVIC ORGANIZATION ❖ 133

ACCEPTING INVITATION TO
JOIN CLUB ❖ 133

ACCEPTING NOMINATION TO
EXECUTIVE BOARD ❖ 133

ASKING SUGGESTIONS
FOR PROJECTS ❖ 134

DECLINING OFFER
OF CHAIRMANSHIP ❖ 134

RESIGNATION FROM COMMUNITY GROUP
FOR POLITICAL POSITION ❖ 134

RESIGNING FROM
COMMUNITY BOARD ❖ 135

RESIGNING AS CLUB PRESIDENT BECAUSE OF
FAMILY OBLIGATIONS ❖ 135

APOLOGY FOR MISSING MEETING ❖ 135

RESIGNING AS ASSOCIATION OFFICER
BECAUSE OF ILLNESS ❖ 136

WITHDRAWING FROM COMMITTEE BECAUSE
OF WORKLOAD ❖ 136

RESIGNING FROM
VOLUNTEER POSITION ❖ 137

CANCELING ENGAGEMENT
OF SPEAKER ❖ 137

DECLINING INVITATION TO SPEAK
AT EVENT ❖ 137

ACCEPTING INVITATION TO SPEAK
IN OPPOSITION ❖ 138

CALLING ON COMMITTEE MEMBERS TO
SHOW MORE DEDICATION ❖ 138

OBJECTING TO POLITICAL ACTIONS
BY ORGANIZATION ❖ 138

COMPLAINING ABOUT TICKET PRICE ❖ 139

REQUESTING NEWSPAPER COVERAGE
OF SHOW ❖ 139

COMPLAINING ABOUT FACTUAL ERRORS IN
NEWSPAPER COVERAGE ❖ 140

Inviting new members for civic organization

Dear Neighbors,

We are all very privileged to live in a place like Rolling Meadow. But in the words of the great Massachusetts orator Wendell Phillips, "eternal vigilance is the price of liberty."

Citizens for Government Accountability is a nonpartisan civic organization that is dedicated to providing just that sort of vigilance here on the local level. Our focus is on encouraging and assisting the best candidates, of any political persuasion, to run for office. And then once they are elected, we do our best to hold them to their promises and the highest level of ethics.

We are writing to invite you to join our organization. Enclosed is an invitation to attend our next open house, scheduled for September 12.

Please read the information in the pamphlet with this letter, and if you agree that good government is ours for the asking . . . please join us.

We look forward to seeing you.

Harold Eckersley, President

Accepting invitation to join club

Bruce Chao, Membership Director
Rolling Meadow Citizens for Government Accountability

Dear Mr. Chao,

Thank you for your invitation to join RMCGA.

From everything I have heard about the organization and the information you provided, I am honored to be asked and happy to accept the invitation.

We chose Rolling Meadow as the place we wanted to live in retirement, and having lived here for just a few months we are quite convinced we made the right decision. I agree completely with your philosophy about the need for eternal vigilance of the actions of our elected officials, and I want to enlist.

I will be attending the meeting on August 1 and look forward to meeting you then.

Sincerely,
Ron Harris

Accepting nomination to executive board

Jerry Orsillo, Chairman of the Board
Rolling Meadow Citizens for Government Accountability

Dear Jerry,

Thank you so much for your asking me to join the executive board of Rolling Meadow Citizens for Government Accountability. I am pleased to accept.

My wife and I have lived many places and been involved in many organizations in our working careers. But from the time we moved to Rolling Meadow to retire, we knew we were in a very special place.

I look forward to working with you and the other distinguished members of the board to give back to the community and to insist on the highest level of responsibility by our government officials.

Sincerely,
Ron Harris

Asking suggestions for projects

To All Members,

As we are about to begin another school year, I'd like to call upon all members to look for worthy projects that our organization can support.

In the past, the Friends of Rolling Meadow Schools has funded special projects, purchased laboratory and supplies and athletic equipment, and even made our members available as volunteers for school events.

We are also always looking for new ways to raise money to support our activities.

I look forward to hearing your suggestions at our annual kickoff meeting, scheduled for Wednesday, August 29, at 7 p.m. in the elementary school library.

John Howard, President

Declining offer of chairmanship

Scott Ray, Chairman
Rolling Meadow Citizens Action Committee

Dear Scott,

I am truly honored that the Rolling Meadow Citizens Action Committee would consider asking me to succeed you as chairman.

You have done such a tremendous job for the past two years, and all of us who live here are in your debt. I would like nothing more than to work toward continuing your efforts to improve the quality of life in Rolling Meadow.

However, I regret that I must decline the offer.

The next year is going to be a difficult one for my wife, Priscilla. She has some health challenges we must deal with and that is our first priority.

I wish you and the committee the best; I will try to help in any way I can.

Sincerely,
J. R. Reed

Resignation from community group for political position

Dear Mr. Chairman,

I am writing to inform you that I have decided I must resign my membership in the Lumbertown Chamber of Business Executives.

I was unhappy to see the chamber vote to become involved in a highly partisan political issue related to the upcoming national presidential election. While I fully support the rights of individuals to express any reasonable political position, I do not feel that our local business group should do so on behalf of its members.

I want to pass along my personal regards to the members of the Chamber of Business Executives and reassure all of you that I intend to continue to seek the growth of the Rolling Meadow economy and the success of our local citizens and government.

Sincerely,
Elaine Martin

Resigning from community board

Diana Sayles, Executive Director
Rolling Meadow Youth Group
Rolling Meadow

Dear Diana,

I have been honored to serve on the board of directors of the Rolling Meadow Youth Group for the past three years.

During my time on the board I have been amazed at the dedication and commitment of everyone involved in the organization. You truly make a difference in the lives of Rolling Meadow youth.

It is with regret, though, that I must resign from the board. My duties at work have increased to the point where I do not have the time to adequately assist the board in its important tasks.

I do intend to give my full and enthusiastic support to the organization in years to come.

Sincerely,
Alastair Patten

Resigning as club president because of family obligations

Dear Joe,

I am sorry to say that I must resign immediately from my post as president of the Mirror Pond Homeowners Association. It has been my honor to serve in the position.

Unfortunately, I am going to have to be spending a great deal of time assisting my elderly parents in Florida. I will be leaving to be with them immediately and have no idea how long I will be gone.

I am certain that as vice president you will do a fine job in my place. I think that all of the association files are in good order, and you should be able to jump right in on all of our projects. The one big job, of course, is the fundraising for legal costs to fight the proposed bar and nightclub on Highway 61. That file is right on top of the desk at the office.

Please feel free to call me on my cell phone if there is anything I can do to help you get up to speed.

Sincerely,
Richard Thomas

Apology for missing meeting

Anne Gordon, Chairman
Rolling Meadow Historical Society

Dear Anne,

Please accept my apologies for missing the board of directors meeting yesterday.

I should have been there. My only excuse is that some of my coworkers did not recognize the importance of the meeting and I ended up with a conflict on my schedule.

When I was appointed to the board I pledged to be hands on and involved with the terrific work you do. I realize this was not an impressive start, but I will do better.

I will review the minutes and promise I will be present and up to speed for the next meeting.

Please extend my apologies to the other members.

Sincerely,
Jim Paterson

Resigning as association officer because of illness

Dear Phil,

I have been honored to serve as the president of the Rolling Meadow Action Committee for Fair Housing for the past two years.

I am sorry to say that I must resign my position immediately because of a medical condition I recently became aware of. My doctors are hopeful, and so am I, but fighting this will require my full attention for months to come.

I am proud of what we have been able to accomplish in the years I've been associated with RMACFH and know that this fine work will continue. And we are very lucky to have so many other qualified and dedicated individuals who are available to take over.

As always, I wish everyone in our community the very best.

Sincerely,
Brenda Temple

Withdrawing from committee because of workload

Frances Murphy, Superintendent
Rolling Meadow School Board
Rolling Meadow

Dear Ms. Murphy,

For the past eighteen months I have had the honor of serving on the parents' advisory committee to the Rolling Meadow School Board.

When I was asked to join the committee, I promised that I would bring a fair and reasoned approach to this very important position. There is nothing more essential to our success as a community and nation than the education of our young people.

I hope I have succeeded in making progress toward improving the educational system.

However, I must inform you that I have accepted a new job with a local company. As a result I will not have the necessary time to devote to the advisory committee.

Therefore, it is with regret that I must resign the parents' advisory committee. I wish the board and the community the best, and I do hope to be able to become involved with smaller projects from time to time.

Sincerely,
Elaine Martin

Resigning from volunteer position

Evan Corn, Director
Rolling Meadow Museum

Dear Evan,

I have greatly enjoyed my time as a full-time volunteer at the Rolling Meadow Historical Museum. It was truly a delight to be a part of such an intelligent and creative group of people.

I realize that funding and sustaining a community organization is a very difficult task. I only wish the museum had been more successful in generating income and that I could earn a living from my work there.

Unfortunately, though, a volunteer job does not pay the bills.

Effective January 1, I will no longer be able to volunteer my time. I have accepted a full-time paid position as an information technology manager at the high school.

I wish everyone at the museum the best.

Sincerely,
Francine Stevens

Canceling engagement of speaker

Erica Denton
Rolling Meadow

Dear Erica,

We spoke several weeks ago about the possibility of engaging you as a guest speaker for the annual dinner of the Rolling Meadow Camera Club.

Although we would love to have you come to the dinner, I am sorry to say that we now find we do not have the resources to cover your speaking fee.

We continue to be admirers of your work and hope that sometime in the future we will be able to pay you to share your expertise and artistic vision with our members.

My apologies for any inconvenience this may cause you.

Sincerely,
Herb Saul, President
Rolling Meadow Camera Club

Declining invitation to speak at event

Robert Gray, Events Chairperson

Dear Mr. Gray,

Thank you for the invitation to speak at an upcoming gathering of the Rolling Meadow Conservative League.

I regret that I must decline. Although I may personally be in agreement with some of your group's positions, company policy does not permit executives to become involved in partisan politics. It is one of our core values to respect the diversity of opinion amongst our employees, suppliers, and customers.

Tim Orelly
Big Meadow Pet Food Company

137

Accepting invitation to speak in opposition

Eric Payne, Executive Director
Rolling Meadow Historical Association

Thank you for your invitation to speak at your weekly luncheon discussions. You asked if I would address the town's proposal to put a bicycle path through the old cemetery of the congregational church.

I know the historical association is in favor of this idea and has made plans for restoration of the area after the path is installed.

I want you to be fully aware of my opposition to the bicycle path proposal. I intend to do whatever I can to defeat what I consider a desecration of sacred land.

If you truly are willing to allow me to speak at your luncheon and present my point of view, I would be happy to do so.

Sincerely,
Ted Galvin
Pastor, Congregational Church

Calling on committee members to show more dedication

To Members of the Committee,

Six months ago when I accepted the chair of the Rolling Meadow Parks Advisory Committee I did so with great hope for change. At the first meeting I was very impressed with the enthusiasm and commitment from all those in attendance.

I am disappointed to report that I have seen very little of that energy since. There are many projects we all agreed to support, but at the most recent meeting I can't say that any of our ideas have moved toward action.

At the top of the list when I first joined the committee was an effort to seek corporate sponsorship to provide funds for activities at our parks and the community pool this summer. With opening day just a month away, I am calling upon all interested members of the community to join us at our next committee meeting and work with us in contacting businesses and organizations to seek their participation.

As a reminder, our next meeting is Tuesday night at 7 P.M., in the library of the high school.

Wendy Fuller, Chairperson

Objecting to political actions by organization

Dear Veronica,

As a longtime member of the Rolling Meadow Civic Action Committee, I have been proud of our actions in support of our community. We have acted in a nonpartisan way on behalf of many important causes.

Recently, though, I believe that the committee has become too closely allied with state senator Richard Precedente. This is a politician with whom I have had a number of very serious disagreements over the years, and that is precisely why I am upset we should not do anything to compromise our impartial reputation.

I hope you will join with me in steering the committee back to its former nonpartisan role. I want to continue to work with you and the other members of the committee, but I can only do so if we steer away from political partisanship.

Sincerely,
Rita Hull

Complaining about ticket price

Kerry Johnson, Director
Rolling Meadow Community Theatre

Dear Mr. Johnson,

I am writing to register my displeasure with the increase in ticket prices for the upcoming season.

I am well aware that in this difficult economy organizations such as the Rolling Meadow Community Theatre are facing fiscal difficulties.

But in my opinion, a 50 percent increase to the price of individual tickets, and a corresponding boost to the cost of a season subscription, is unreasonable.

In my situation—and I suspect there are many others like me—all this will mean is that I will attend three performances this season instead of six.

I think your group should spend more effort seeking sustaining donations and grants from major corporations and civic groups instead of pricing tickets out of the range of local residents, something that will hurt the organization in years to come.

I have been a regular patron of the community theatre for many years, and I hope you are able to continue your valuable contribution to Rolling Meadow.

Sincerely,
Lorna Vogt

Requesting newspaper coverage of show

Maryanne Jaune, Editor
Rolling Meadow Times

Dear Ms. Jaune,

The Rolling Meadow Art Museum will be opening an exciting new exhibit in our main gallery on Thursday, July 6.

"Rolling Meadow, The Pioneers of Photography" will include some of the oldest known images of our town, taken by early residents and by itinerant photographs who headed west in the 1870s.

Many of the images come from the private collections of the original residents of Rolling Meadow and are shown here for the first time. Perhaps the treasure of the show is a photo of Chester A. Arthur on the courthouse steps making an appearance in his successful campaign for the presidency in 1880. He is the only president (or presidential candidate) ever to visit Rolling Meadow; the small park across from the courthouse, Arthur Park, is named in commemoration of his visit.

I am enclosing information about this exhibit and the membership reception scheduled for the evening before its official opening.

We would appreciate coverage of the event in the Times. Our curator, Joan Gordon, is available to meet with a reporter any time in the next two weeks to give a tour of the exhibit and explain the background of the photos on display.

Sincerely,
Samantha Gris, Curator

Complaining about factual errors in newspaper coverage

Maryanne Jaune, Editor
Rolling Meadow Times

Dear Ms. Jaune,

The article in this week's Times about our new photography exhibit contains at least four significant errors of fact.

As director of public relations for the Rolling Meadow Art Museum, I provided the newspaper with a press release including the opening date and other information about the exhibit. I also invited you to send a reporter to speak with our curator.

Unfortunately, the article that appeared was based entirely on the release—no one at the museum was called—and it included incorrect information.

Our official opening has come and gone, but I would greatly appreciate it if you would assign a reporter to do a story about the exhibit itself. We will cooperate in every way to provide information and images from the exhibition that you can use.

I look forward to hearing from you soon.

Sincerely,
Robert Vinton, Director of Public Relations

CHAPTER 18

Fundraising, Donations, and Volunteers

FUNDRAISING LETTER ➻ 142

SEEKING VOLUNTEERS FOR FUNDRAISING
PHONE BANK ➻ 142

OPEN LETTER SEEKING SPONSORS ➻ 142

ANNOUNCING SCHOLARSHIP
BEQUEST ➻ 143

SEEKING ADDITIONAL CONTRIBUTION TO
COMMUNITY ORGANIZATION ➻ 143

MAKING MEMORIAL DONATION
OF BOOKS ➻ 143

ACCEPTING DONATION WITH
THANKS ➻ 144

DECLINING DONATION BECAUSE
OF TERMS ➻ 144

CLARIFYING ITEMS LOANED
NOT DONATED ➻ 145

RETURNING DONATED ITEMS ➻ 145

RESPONSE ABOUT OWNERSHIP OF ITEMS
ON DISPLAY ➻ 145

OBJECTING TO FUNDRAISING PLANS ➻ 146

COMPLAINING ABOUT LISTING OF
DONOR AMOUNTS ➻ 146

COMPLAINING ABOUT AGGRESSIVE
FUNDRAISING ➻ 147

OBJECTING TO PROFESSIONAL
FUNDRAISER ➻ 147

DECLINING REQUEST FOR
CONTRIBUTION ➻ 148

DECLINING REQUEST FOR CONTRIBUTION
FOR CAUSE ➻ 148

DECLINING TO OFFER DONATION BECAUSE
OF DISAGREEMENT ➻ 148

WITHDRAWING CORPORATE SUPPORT ➻ 149

WITHDRAWING FUNDING FOR
CAUSE ➻ 149

COMPLAINING ABOUT USE OF
DONATION ➻ 150

ASKING PROPER ALLOCATION FOR
ENDOWMENT ➻ 150

SEEKING SPONSORS FOR HOCKEY
TEAM ➻ 150

SEEKING COACHES FOR HOCKEY TEAM ➻ 151

SEEKING TO ARRANGE CAR POOL FOR
HOCKEY TEAM ➻ 151

OFFERING TO VOLUNTEER AT
LIBRARY ➻ 152

COMPLAINING ABOUT SCHEDULING
FOR VOLUNTEERS ➻ 152

Fundraising letter

Dear Neighbor,

Can you imagine what life would be like without the many wonderful offerings of the Rolling Meadow Community Center?

It's a thought that very few of us want to even consider. We count on the center to provide music, theater, and civic events all through the year. Our children expect to be able to use the gym and the athletic fields.

The entire operating budget for the center is paid by very modest membership fees, ticket sales, and the generous contributions of companies, organizations, and individuals like you.

We are well aware that these are difficult times for everyone, but we believe that our town's culture is a necessity. I'm writing to ask you to join your neighbors and business associates in making a contribution to the Rolling Meadow Community Center. We will thank you for any amount you can give.

Sincerely,
Sue Stephens

Seeking volunteers for fundraising phone bank

To Our Employees,

This coming weekend, Rolling Meadow Lumber Company will be offering its support to our local National Public Radio station in its annual fundraising drive. We will be lending our telephone lines and other facilities to the station.

We hope supporters of the station amongst our family of employees will join us in working the phones. We will have twelve phone lines to answer for twelve hours on each day; volunteers can sign up for blocks of two to four hours on each day.

We will provide a buffet lunch and our deep thanks to all participants.

To register to participate, please contact the human resources department.

Sincerely,
Melissa Pearl

Open letter seeking sponsors

Rolling Meadow Gazette

To the Editor,

As president of the Rolling Meadow Arts Council, I am writing to appeal to all the residents and businesses of our city to help us maintain a valuable community event.

Our annual summer street fair, scheduled for August 12 and 13, is in danger of being canceled because of lack of funding and sponsors.

This event has been an important part of summer for the past twenty-three years. It combines a parade, games and special activities, and an opportunity for local stores and artisans to sell their products and food. Speaking for myself, I attended as a youngster and have been thrilled to share this with my own children.

It is also important to acknowledge the economic impact of the fair on the community. We draw thousands of visitors from all through the area.

The town council voted last week to discontinue funding for setup of the fair and other expenses.

We ask businesses and individuals interested in making contributions or sponsoring some or all of the cost of the fair contact the council as soon as possible; time is running out.

Jean Craig, President
Rolling Meadow Arts Council

Announcing scholarship bequest

To All Members,

We are very pleased to announce that we have received a substantial bequest from the estate of our much beloved former member Harry Painter.

Harry's daughter Lisa has informed us that in his will he has asked that a scholarship fund be established through our club to encourage talented young people to pursue a career in photography. We are working with the Painter family to establish a sustaining fund that will generate enough income for an annual gift to students.

At our next meeting I hope to have full details, and I hope to also announce a formal recognition by the club to Harry's family.

Charles Vantage, President

Seeking additional contribution to community organization

To Our Valued Donors,

Asking for money is one of our least favorite tasks here at the Rolling Meadow Historical Society. You have already been very generous in your support of our work.

But the fact is that our budget is strained past the breaking point. Ticket sales and corporate grants have dropped off dramatically in the past six months, and we are in danger of having to drastically curtail many of our ongoing projects.

And so we turn once again to those who have helped us out in the past. You are among the people who truly understand the importance to the community of an institution like ours.

Can we ask you to once again support our society? Every contribution will make a difference.

If ever there was a time to show just how much you value what we do, now is the time.

Sincerely,
Rebecca Thompson
Executive Director

Making memorial donation of books

Janet Turner, Acquisitions
Rolling Meadow Public Library

Dear Ms. Turner,

I am writing to offer to the Rolling Meadow Public Library a donation of my husband's extensive collection of books about local history. There are more than two hundred titles in his collection, and many of them are rare and valuable.

As you know, Ron was deeply devoted to our local library and museum. After his tragic death in an automobile accident two months ago, we decided as a family that the best place for the books would be here in Rolling Meadow.

We ask only that the collection be maintained and not sold individually or as a group. Along with the books, we are making a contribution of $5,000 to be used to create a place to hold the books and for the operating expenses of the library.

I hope this is acceptable to you. Please call me at your convenience to arrange moving the books from our home to the library.

Sincerely,
Susan Wheeler

Accepting donation with thanks

Susan Wheeler
Rolling Meadow

Dear Susan,

On behalf of the Rolling Meadow Public Library, I want to thank you for your generous donation of your husband's fine collection of books about local history. We are happy to accept.

I want you to know that the library board has decided to place the books in our Golden Age room. After we catalog the collection, we would like to have a small reception to honor Ron and his family. And we will be announcing the renaming of the Golden Age room as the Ron Wheeler Historical Collection.

We will be in touch soon to arrange for the relocation of the books from your home to the library.

In addition to your personal loss, Rolling Meadow is without one of its local heroes after Ron's death. We hope our recognition of him at the library brings you some comfort.

Sincerely,
Janet Turner, Acquisitions
Rolling Meadow Public Library

Declining donation because of terms

Susan Wheeler
Rolling Meadow

Dear Susan,

Thank you so much for your generous offer to donate your husband's fine collection of books about local history to the library.

Unfortunately, we are unable to accept the donation under the terms you laid out in your letter. In our charter, we are barred from accepting any gift or donation that limits the library in any way in its operations.

In your letter you said that the library could not sell the books individually or as a group once they were in our possession. Although we would certainly be honored to have the books added to our collection, we would have to be able to sell or otherwise dispose of titles without restriction. I'm not saying this would happen now or in the future, but we are unable to agree to a permanent restriction.

I hope we can come to an agreement that would allow the donation of Ron's books.

We would like to place the books in our Golden Age room, and the library board would consider renaming that area in your husband's name.

In addition to your personal loss, Rolling Meadow is without one of its local heroes after Ron's death. I hope we can come to an agreement that will honor his memory in this way.

Sincerely,
Janet Turner, Acquisitions
Rolling Meadow Public Library

Clarifying items loaned not donated

Stephen Regan, Curator
Rolling Meadow Historical Association

Dear Stephen,

I was very pleased with the work you and your staff did on the special exhibit "The Golden Years of Rolling Meadow."

As a family we were honored to have my grandfather's collection of paintings and sketches made a part of this show. He was a very talented and gifted artist.

On the wall above my grandfather's work there was a plaque indicating that the artwork was a gift to the museum from the Van Dyke family.

I want to clarify that these paintings and prints were loaned to the museum, and we expect their return when the exhibit is taken down. That is what you asked for in your letter, and that is what we agreed to in our response.

I would appreciate a prompt response to this letter indicating that ownership of the artwork remains with the family and that the pieces will be returned when the special exhibit ends.

Sincerely,
Victoria Van Dyke

Returning donated items

Lester Jones
Rolling Meadow

Dear Mr. Jones,

Thank you for your recent donation of family heirlooms to the Rolling Meadow History Museum. We are very grateful to all of our supporters in the community.

I am sorry, though, to have to inform you that the manuscripts and paintings you gave to us are not originals and not of significant historical interest to be held or displayed by the museum.

We hope you will continue to treasure them in the family.

I have asked our shipping department to get in touch with you to arrange return of the items.

Again, thank you for thinking of us. We hope you will continue to be involved in the programs of the museum.

Sincerely,
Jane Wise, Curator
Rolling Meadow History Museum

Response about ownership of items on display

Dear Victoria,

Please accept my apology for the erroneous wording on the plaque accompanying your grandfather's artwork on display at the museum.

The paintings and sketches are indeed on loan from the Van Dyke family to the museum, as we agreed. They will be returned in mid-November when we will be changing the special exhibit to our annual holiday show.

Again, we thank you and your family for loaning us your grandfather's artwork. They were an important part of the exhibit.

We appreciate your many contributions to the museum and look forward to working with you in the future.

Sincerely,
Stephen

Objecting to fundraising plans

Mary Taylor, Scoutmaster
Rolling Meadow Blue Birds

Dear Mary,

My three daughters—Stephanie, Linda, and Pam—are all members of your scout troop.

Yesterday they brought home the calendars that are to be sold as this year's fundraiser. Each of them was given ten to sell at $10 apiece.

First of all, I think that is a very difficult assignment in this economy. It is especially difficult when there is more than one child from a single family trying to sell items to the same friends, family, and neighbors.

I think the idea of a calendar as a fundraising item is not a good one. We already receive many free calendars from companies where we shop or do business, and in any case, most of us have long ago moved our calendars from the refrigerator door to our cell phones.

In years past we have had events where money was raised through the sale of services or goods, car washes, plantings for flower boxes, and that sort of thing. I would hope these kinds of events could be resumed.

I know my girls will try their best to sell the calendars this year, but I am not optimistic that—at least for our family—the goals will be reached.

Sincerely,
Sue Tager

Complaining about listing of donor amounts

Rolling Meadow Memorial Hospital
Fundraising and Grants Department

Dear Fundraising Department,

As a resident of Rolling Meadow and a frequent contributor to community organizations, I want to express my disappointment with the manner in which Memorial Hospital handled its most recent appeal for funds.

Included in the letter I received was a brochure listing all contributors and the amount they gave in the past year. Although this may have been intended as a way of giving thanks to your supporters, I find it to be an example of poor judgment. Many of us consider our charitable giving to be a private matter, and we do not seek to be compared against others.

I would hope that the hospital—and other community organizations—ask permission from donors before listing their names and also reconsider whether exact dollar amounts should be published. Speaking for myself, your future policy on this matter will influence my decision on whether I again donate.

Sincerely,
Arthur Cooper

Complaining about aggressive fundraising

Maryjo Conrad, Chairwoman
Rolling Meadow Community Chest

Dear Maryjo,

As I hope you know, I have been a regular contributor to the annual fund of the Rolling Meadow Community Chest for the past several years.

When I was contacted by someone on your fundraising committee several weeks ago, I told the caller that due to some personal issues I was not financially able to contribute this year.

Since then I have been solicited by phone three more times. With each call, I find the approach more insistent and upsetting.

Although I support the good works of your organization, I must ask that you remove my name, telephone number, and address from your fundraising list.

When I am again able to make contributions to community organizations I will consider giving to Rolling Meadow Community Chest once again, but only if I am not harassed again by one of your fundraisers.

Sincerely,
Franklin Cheney

Objecting to professional fundraiser

David Logan, Executive Director
Rolling Meadow Art Museum

Dear Mr. Logan,

I am a longtime contributor to the operations and building fund of the Rolling Meadow Art Museum.

I was recently contacted on the telephone by a man asking for a donation. I always object to solicitation on the phone, but I was particularly annoyed by this call. The person on the line was obviously reading from a script, and when I stopped him to ask a question he became flustered. It was then I determined that he was working for a professional fundraising company hundreds of miles away in another state.

I realize that times are hard and the museum is in great need of sustaining gifts. However, I find it very objectionable that any part of a gift I might give would be used to pay an outside company making calls. From what I understand, some of these outfits keep 50 percent or more of the money they raise.

At this time, I have decided to withhold any further donations to the museum.

I feel you owe an explanation to the community about the use of outside fundraisers, including full disclosure of the percentage of money that will be paid to the company.

Thank you.

Carla Robbins

Declining request for contribution

Donna Perkins, Chairman
Rolling Meadow Art Society

Dear Donna,

I just received your letter asking for our participation in the annual fundraising gala for the Rolling Meadow Art Society.

This is a wonderful event for an excellent cause; I am sure you will do a fine job as chairperson of the committee.

I am sorry to tell you, though, that we have decided to reduce our charitable contribution. We plan to alternate our giving among a number of worthy organizations each year; I expect that we will return as sustaining members at another time.

Sincerely,
Melissa Pearl

Declining request for contribution for cause

Dear Fundraising Committee,

I have received your letter asking me to participate in the Rolling Meadow Green Action Council fund-raising campaign.

Although I consider myself an environmentalist, I choose not to contribute to an organization that is campaigning for a complete ban against clear-cutting of domestic forests. Although I appreciate your concern, I want to point out that the American Lumber Institute has worked closely with environmental groups to develop new methods for sustainable renewable forestry products.

I hope you will reconsider your group's position on this issue. In the meantime, I will give my political and economic support to those organizations with which I find common cause.

Harold Dean

Declining to offer donation because of disagreement

Evan Corn, Director
Rolling Meadow Historical Museum

Dear Evan,

Every time I walk through the museum I realize how fortunate we are in Rolling Meadow to have such an outstanding institution in our community.

However, I have decided to decline to make my annual contribution this year because of my disagreement with some management decisions. I am sure it will come as no surprise to you that I strongly opposed the plan to divert operating income to pay for the rehabilitation of one of our lesser properties to serve as the home for the museum's director.

In addition to representing a diversion from the key mission of the museum to preserve and promote our local heritage, this major expenditure of money amounts to a substantial increase in salary for the director.

My previous contributions have all been aimed at supporting the mission of the museum. At this time, I do not want my money spent on unrelated and ill-conceived matters.

Sincerely,
Karen Connor

Withdrawing corporate support

Jean Craig, President
Rolling Meadow Arts Council

Dear Ms. Craig,

For the last four years Richardson Tire and Auto Supply Company has been proud to be a corporate supporter of the Rolling Meadow Summer Festival.

We are a family owned business and our roots will always be in Rolling Meadow. This summertime event is a tradition very dear to us, and we along with the whole community would be deeply saddened if it were not to continue.

However, as it has many other companies, the difficult economy has affected our business and we simply are not able to offer our support this summer.

I plan to make a small individual contribution. When sales pick up again, we hope to resume our corporate donation.

Sincerely,
Philip Hurley, President
Richardson Tire and Auto Supply Company

Withdrawing funding for cause

Jean Craig, President
Rolling Meadow Arts Council

Dear Ms. Craig,

The Crossroads Restaurant has been proud to be a corporate sponsor of the Rolling Meadow Contemporary Art Museum for many years.

However, it is with regret that we inform you we have decided to immediately end all support for the museum.

Although we fully believe in artistic freedom, we do not want to be associated in any way with the exhibition of work by the photographer Peter Sherry scheduled to open next month.

We find Mr. Sherry's work to be highly objectionable. We do not want our customers to mistake our general support for the arts for an endorsement of his photography.

We will reconsider our involvement with the museum after the end of the exhibit.

Sincerely,
Robert Johnson
Crossroads Restaurant

Complaining about use of donation

To the Editor,

I have been a regular donor to the general fund of the Rolling Meadow Animal Rescue Organization.

I think it is important that we humanely care for animals and control against overpopulation, and I have been proud to be associated with the Animal Rescue Organization.

I was shocked to see photos and a story in last week's newspaper about a twentieth anniversary gala held in Rolling Meadow at one of the most expensive restaurants in town.

When I checked with the organization, I was told the party was paid for from the general fund. I think this was entirely the wrong message to send to donors; my contribution was intended to help animals in need.

I hope other donors will join with me in insisting that any future fundraising efforts by the rescue group come with a promise about the purposes for which the money will be used.

Sincerely,
Francis Crocker

Asking proper allocation for endowment

Commissioner John Davis
Parks and Recreation
Rolling Meadow

Dear Commissioner Davis,

Four months ago my wife and I made a substantial donation to the Parks and Recreation Department of Rolling Meadow.

We made this gift in honor of our grandchild, Michelle, who is confined to a wheelchair. The money from this endowment was to be used to finance wheelchair ramps and make other handicapped-accessible improvements to the Rolling Meadow parks.

We have just received the year-end report and our name is included with those who have made donations for the construction of a new swimming pool in Venetian Park.

That was not our intent, and under the terms of our donation—a legally binding agreement approved by the town counsel—we have the authority to ask for the return of our donation if the ramps and other improvements are not made.

Please advise the status of the project or your plans to return the money.

Thank you.

Phillip and Helen Cuomo

Seeking sponsors for hockey team

Rolling Meadow Rink Rats
Rolling Meadow

I feel confident in my belief that you share with me a great pride in Rolling Meadow's newest civic center, the Rink by the River.

Our beautiful skating rink is due to open in two months. When it does, it will be a center of activity for our children in elementary, middle, and high schools as well as the general public. And we also plan to use the building for other events including concerts, dances, and lectures.

The biggest hurdle was raising funds to pay for the construction of the facility, and for those who helped in the capital campaign we are very grateful. The names of all contributors will be posted in various locations in the building.

I am writing to you, as a representative of one of Rolling Meadow's prominent organizations, asking for your support in operations through the year.

I would like to invite you to sponsor a team, an activity, or a section of the building. We would be happy to list your company's name on uniforms, scoreboards, signs, and even in logos embedded in the ice.

I am enclosing a breakdown of some opportunities for involvement and would be happy to discuss this or any other ideas you might have. I hope to hear from you soon.

Thank you.

Mark Lacy, Chairperson
Rolling Meadow Rink Rats

Seeking coaches for hockey team

To Parents,

We are very excited at the upcoming grand opening of the skating rink here in Rolling Meadow. As members of the school district's athletics department, we look forward to the involvement of all of our students and the rest of the community in free skating as well as organized hockey leagues and figure skating classes.

Many of you have already committed your valuable time to fundraising for the construction of the rink; we thank you again for your involvement.

Now we are asking for your talents and skills in running activities at the rink.

We need coaches and assistants as well as general volunteers to help sell tickets, work at the skate rental shop, and perform other duties. You don't have to have won a gold medal at the Olympics (although we would be thrilled to have you on the team), but if you've played hockey or are an accomplished figure skater we're certain you have some skills you can share.

I look forward to hearing from anyone in the community who wants to join us in our new community gem.

Thank you.

David Simyoni, Athletic Director
Rolling Meadow High School

Seeking to arrange car pool for hockey team

To Hockey Moms and Dads,

With the number of practice sessions and games our children attend as members of the Rolling Meadow Hockey Club, I think it would be a great help to us all if we could organize a car pool. This will allow us to reduce the number of cars and parents in motion each day.

I would be happy to help organize the car pool. If you're interested, please send me a note telling me the number of days per week and the times you are available. It would also be helpful to know the size and type of vehicle you drive.

One possibility suggested by the coach is to try to get one or two vans or small trucks to carry all of the hockey equipment, and then we can transport the kids in ordinary cars.

I look forward to hearing from you.

Jean Baldelli

Offering to volunteer at library

Charlotte House, Director
Rolling Meadow Atheneum

Dear Ms. House,

My wife June and I recently moved to Rolling Meadow after retiring from careers in education in Minneapolis.

I would like to offer our services as volunteers in the library; we have done this sort of work in the past and have enjoyed it very much and met some great people. We have worked at the front desk, as research assistants, and as floaters to assist visitors.

I look forward to hearing from you soon. We're ready to be put to work.

Sincerely,
Harry Harmon

Complaining about scheduling for volunteers

Steven Monroe, Executive Director
Rolling Meadow Science Museum

Dear Dr. Monroe,

For the past four years I have been proud to volunteer my time at the Rolling Meadow Science Museum. It is one of my favorite activities since I retired as a professor from the university.

However, I am afraid that some recent changes in management are making it increasingly difficult for me (and many others) to continue to give our time.

For years, volunteers were asked to sign up for available slots on the schedule. This works very well for all of us because it allows the flexibility to fit our volunteer time in with doctor's appointments, travel plans, and other demands on our time.

In the past six weeks, though, the new manager of volunteer services has been assigning us to work schedules without consulting with us. I know for a fact that this has caused a great deal of upset among the volunteers and also resulted in a number of cancellations of shifts.

We are not paid for our time, and we should not be thought of us salaried employees whose working hours can be assigned by a manager. I hope you can address this problem before it becomes too great to solve. All of us would very much like to continue our association with the museum.

Thank you.

Julia Duffy

CHAPTER 19

School Days

WITHDRAWING CHILD FROM PRESCHOOL FOR CAUSE ➤ 154

SICK CHILDREN IN DAYCARE ➤ 154

COMPLAINT ABOUT SUPERVISION ON CLASS TRIP ➤ 154

SEEKING VOTES IN ELECTION FOR PTA PRESIDENT ➤ 155

RESIGNING PRESIDENCY OF PARENT TEACHERS ASSOCIATION ➤ 155

COMPLAINT ABOUT TEACHER ➤ 156

FOLLOW-UP ABOUT COMPLAINT ABOUT TEACHER ➤ 156

COMPLAINT ABOUT DISRUPTION BY OTHER STUDENT ➤ 156

ASKING TEACHER TO SEPARATE FRIENDS ➤ 157

ASKING TEACHER TO SEPARATE SQUABBLING FRIENDS ➤ 157

ASKING ATTENTION TO HEALTHY DIET AT SCHOOL ➤ 158

DECLINING TO COACH TEAM ➤ 158

ASKING SCHOOL TO SCALE BACK HOLIDAY TRIP ➤ 159

OBJECTING TO SPENDING STUDENT FUNDS ON SPEAKER ➤ 159

ASKING RECOGNITION OF STUDENTS WITH SINGLE PARENT ➤ 159

DIVORCED PARENT ASKS TO BE ON MAILING LIST ➤ 160

COMPLAINT TO PRINCIPAL ABOUT CONTINUED TEASING ➤ 160

COMPLAINING OF CHANGE TO ADVANCED PLACEMENT COURSE ➤ 161

COMPLAINING OF POOR JUDGMENT IN HOLDING EVENT ➤ 161

ASKING FOR CHANGE IN BUS STOP ➤ 162

OBJECTING TO THE INITIATION OF USER FEES ➤ 162

SUPPORTING USER FEE FOR SPORTS IN SCHOOLS ➤ 163

OBJECTING TO INCREASE IN STUDENT FEE ➤ 163

COMPLAINT ABOUT COURSE FEES ➤ 164

REQUESTING MORE COLLEGE AID ➤ 164

Withdrawing child from preschool for cause

Francine Willows, Director
Rolling Meadow Preschool

Dear Ms. Willows,

I am writing to inform you that we will be withdrawing our daughter Jessica from Rolling Meadow Preschool, effective at the end of this week. We have enrolled Jessica at another preschool in the area.

We have spoken several times in the past about our concerns that there was not enough structured play and educational activities at your facility; it seems to us that you are essentially providing a baby-sitting service, and we wanted more for our child.

We do appreciate the work of your staff. They are well-meaning people, and Jessica never complained about her treatment.

Thank you.

Sandra Michaels

Sick children in daycare

Barbara Lewis, Director
Rolling Meadow Daycare Facility

Dear Ms. Lewis,

I am very concerned about some health practices I have observed at Rolling Meadow Daycare Facility.

When I picked up my daughter Laura last Friday I noticed at least two children who were noticeably ill.

I know sniffles and other illnesses are inevitable, but the two youngsters I observed were clearly contagious. They were sneezing and coughing and touching toys and other objects; they should not have been allowed to attend daycare.

I reread the rules distributed to all parents by SDF, and I also consulted the health regulations published by the state and listed on the bulletin board at the entrance to the daycare building.

Both sets of rules clearly state that a child who is suffering from a contagious disease cannot be allowed to attend daycare. I realize this is an inconvenience to working parents—I am one myself—but the rule is there to protect all of the other children and their families.

I look forward to hearing from you about how this will be dealt with in the future.

Sincerely,
Sandra Mason

Complaint about supervision on class trip

James Miller, Principal
Rolling Meadow Elementary School

Dear Mr. Miller,

My son Andrew was one of the third-grade students who went on a field trip to the Natural History Museum last Wednesday.

When we first heard about this trip we were excited that Andrew would be having an adventure with his classmates and without his parents; that is an important part of growing up. However, when I learned about several incidents that occurred during the trip—including the fact that at least six of the children became separated from the group and had to be located by museum personnel—I became quite upset.

It is obvious that there was insufficient adult supervision for this trip. There were more than fifty students taken into the city and a very large unfamiliar building with only four chaperones.

That meant that each adult was responsible for about twelve children. I don't understand why parents were not asked to volunteer to go along. I have done just this sort of thing with my older child.

I am grateful that nothing seriously marred the adventure. However, I will be very hesitant to approve my son's involvement in future trips—and I will make my feelings known to the school board—if a better plan is not put into effect.

Sincerely,
Isabelle Raymond

Seeking votes in election for PTA president

Dear Parents,

I have been a member of the Rolling Meadow Parent Teachers Association for the past fifteen years, since my first child started school here.

I have always been impressed with the level of cooperation between parents and teachers in Rolling Meadow; we are indeed fortunate to have such a fine public school system.

After all this time as a member, I have decided that I would like to try to offer my experience to young parents just entering the system. I will be a candidate for president of the association this coming March, and I would appreciate your vote.

Sincerely,
Annabelle Lolavitch

Resigning presidency of parent teachers association

Rolling Meadow High School PTA

Dear Members,

I was honored to have been elected president of the Rolling Meadow Parent Teachers Association last October.

As the parent of two children in the school system I share with all of you a commitment to excellence for our students and our support for the teaching professionals on the staff.

Unfortunately, due to unexpected family issues, I no longer have the time available for the important work that needs to be done. The last thing I would want to do is shortchange the students, teachers, and parents of Rolling Meadow.

I am therefore resigning the presidency, effective at our next meeting on March 15. I hope I can still be of service to the association in another capacity.

Sincerely,
Kimberly Reed

Complaint about teacher

James Miller, Principal
Rolling Meadow Elementary School

Dear Mr. Miller,

My son Matthew is a student in the fifth-grade class taught by Anne Rose.

I am writing to express some concerns about Ms. Rose's ability to satisfactorily manage her students and classroom.

According to my son—and the parents of several of his classmates to whom I have spoken—much of the day is taken up with dealing with behavioral problems that seem to be beyond Ms. Rose's ability to handle.

Perhaps as a result, my son has been coming home with what seems to me to be an unusually heavy amount of homework. Some days the time he spends—even with guidance from my husband or me—can reach three hours. I think this is excessive and perhaps an indication that not much actual learning is taking place in the classroom.

As principal I think you may need to become involved before this school term progresses much further. I would be happy to meet with you to discuss these concerns.

Sincerely,
Julia Adams

Follow-up about complaint about teacher

James Miller, Principal
Rolling Meadow Elementary School

Dear Mr. Miller,

It has been two weeks since I wrote to you with my concerns about what was happening in Ms. Rose's fifth-grade classroom.

At your request, I met with her to discuss the situation. Although I am certain she means well, I am more convinced now that she is unable to control her students and classroom.

She told me she is often overwhelmed by chaos among the students, but she said that she felt she could handle it. She basically asked me to leave her alone so that she could do her job.

At this time I must ask for the opportunity to meet with you to discuss this. If you are not able to offer a solution to the problem, I may ask that you move my son to another teacher and classroom.

Sincerely,
Julia Adams

Complaint about disruption by other student

James Miller, Principal
Rolling Meadow Elementary School

Dear Mr. Miller,

My son Dennis, currently a student in the fourth-grade classroom of Fern Arnold, has done well academically in elementary school thus far. We think Ms. Arnold is a fine teacher.

However, Dennis has been having significant difficulties with one of the other students in the class. Billy Hudson seems to have singled out my son to tease and humiliate nearly constantly. According to Dennis, this happens every day at recess, on the bus, in the cafeteria, and within the classroom.

The situation has begun to affect Dennis's feelings about school and his own self-esteem. We believe that on at least one occasion he missed a day of school because he was afraid to come to class. In thinking back about the day, we're not sure he actually was as sick as he told us.

I am asking you to look into this situation and work with Ms. Arnold and other teachers to stop this abuse of my child. Obviously this has to be done in a way that will not cause further problems for Dennis.

I look forward to hearing from you as soon as possible.

Sincerely,
Carole Simmons

Asking teacher to separate friends

Christine Mason
Rolling Meadow Elementary School

Dear Ms. Mason,

My son Christopher is a student in your third-grade class. He thinks very highly of you, and by all indications he is developing very nicely in math and reading.

As you may know, we are new to Rolling Meadow; we moved here over the summer. Our son has developed a close friendship with one of the children of our next door neighbor, Mark Patton, who we think is a very nice boy.

This friendship has extended into your classroom, where Chris and Mark have been assigned as reading partners.

I don't want in any way to interfere with your job as a teacher or to meddle with our son's choice of friends, but I was hoping you could find a way to help Chris expand his circle of friends beyond Mark.

I would appreciate it if you would find a way for him to work with some other children on various projects in the coming school year.

Again, thank you for your fine efforts. We look forward to meeting you at parent-teacher night later this year.

Sincerely,
Judith Schultz

Asking teacher to separate squabbling friends

Dear Ms. Darcy,

My daughter Kasey is a student in your class; she speaks very highly of you, and we are quite happy with her academic progress.

There is, though, a problem that has come into the classroom from outside the school.

Kasey has had some sort of a serious disagreement with Sarah Martin, who once was one of her best friends. I do not know the nature of their disagreement and think it best as a parent not to get in the middle.

I am not asking that you get involved other than to separate them as much as possible. I am sure you are quite experienced in dealing with ten-year-old girls, and I would appreciate any assistance you can offer so that they can each concentrate on their schoolwork.

Sincerely,
Brenda Jones

Asking attention to healthy diet at school

James Beach, School Superintendent
Rolling Meadow School District

Dear Dr. Beach,

I was pleased to receive an invitation to join my son Brandon at "Take Your Parents to Lunch" day at Rolling Meadow Middle School. It's a good program and a great way for parents to learn about the learning environment in our school district.

I was, though, less than thrilled by the food choices available in the cafeteria.

The menu featured french fries, hamburgers, hot dogs, and macaroni and cheese. Beverages included a highly sugared fruit punch and whole milk.

The salad bar, to be charitable, looked very tired and little used. Even worse, the available dressings were highly processed and full of chemicals and fat.

Are we not teaching our children about the importance of a healthy, low-fat, and low-salt diet? Healthy eating is a message that should be addressed at school as well as at home.

I am afraid we are putting our children in danger of obesity, medical conditions, and wasteful spending, all things that could be rectified by more attention to the menu choices at the cafeteria.

I would be happy to work with a committee, if you want to establish one, to look into creating a more healthful set of lessons for our children.

Sincerely,
Kris Manchester

Declining to coach team

Janet Sullivan, Athletic Director
Rolling Meadow Boys and Girls Club

Dear Janet,

Thank you for inviting me to once again coach the girls' junior soccer team.

It has been a difficult decision for me, but I have finally come to the conclusion that I do not have the time to devote to the team this year.

I loved working with the girls and I hope to be able to volunteer again in the future when my work and personal schedule permits.

I would be happy to be available to consult with whomever you select to coach the team.

Sincerely,
Jane Nolan

Asking school to scale back holiday trip

Dear Principal Miller,

I fully realize the popularity of the annual winter break ski trip; it has become a tradition among fifth graders.

However, I think I am not alone amongst parents in feeling uncomfortable about the cost; the cost of transportation, lodging, food, ski passes, and incidentals is approaching one thousand dollars. It will be a problem for us, and I know from speaking with other parents that they also feel strained.

I am hoping that there is a way we can reduce the cost and make the trip more available to every student. Perhaps we could reduce the number of days from a full week. We could also contact several ski areas and see if there is one that is willing to offer a better package than the others.

I would be happy to serve on a committee to investigate ways to reduce the cost. Please feel free to contact me to discuss this.

Sincerely,
Jan Stewart

Objecting to spending student funds on speaker

Elizabeth Stanford, President
Rolling Meadow University

Dear President Stanford,

I am writing to express my strong objection to the use of student activity fund fees to pay for the upcoming appearance by writer and political "personality" Ann Cross.

Ms. Cross is a very controversial and polarizing figure. I find her positions to be highly offensive and almost always not based on the facts.

My objection, though, is not based on my opinion—or hers. I feel that it is wrong to spend so much money (according to newspaper accounts, about $20,000) on someone who is so polarizing in her positions. Are we going to spend the same amount of money to invite someone with opposing views?

Please understand that I fully support freedom of speech, especially at a university.

If Ms. Cross wants to come to our school and speak for free, or if a student group wants to raise money specifically to pay for her appearance, that is fine with me. I object to the use of the general student fund for someone—anyone—who is so far out of the mainstream.

Sincerely,
Madeline Turner

Asking recognition of students with single parent

Susan Evans, Assistant Principal
Rolling Meadow Elementary School

Dear Mrs. Evans,

My son Ben is a fourth-grade student at RMES. At dinner tonight he gave me a copy of a notice about an event you are hosting in the school next Tuesday: Fathers and Sons Day.

I am sure the school means well, but I think you should know that Ben was quite upset about the event.

By my estimate, of the twenty-eight children in his classroom, about one-third come from single-parent homes. Many of the children, including Ben, do not have a father in their life because of divorce. Others never knew their father, and a few have fathers who are serving in the military and are not at home.

Out of fairness to these children, and to expand the idea of diversity in the school, I would like to suggest that this event and others like it be reconsidered. How about having a "Mentors" day where students could invite any adult they know and respect to accompany them to class?

In Ben's case, I'm sure he would be thrilled to invite his uncle Ned, who is a very well-respected researcher at Rolling Meadow University. I know that Ben looks up to his uncle as a role model, and I think the other students would benefit greatly from meeting him.

I hope you will be able to make this sort of change and extending an invitation to this event and all like it to any adult whom a child considers an important part of his or her life.

Sincerely,
Jennifer Klein

Divorced parent asks to be on mailing list

James Miller, Principal
Rolling Meadow Elementary School

Dear Mr. Miller,

My children Stephen and Jennifer are students at the elementary school. As you may know, my wife and I recently divorced, and the children live with their mother during the week.

However, I do want to continue to be involved in their lives and their education. Please add my name and address for any mailings regarding school activities or concerns.

And while I am on the subject, I think this sort of consideration should be given to all parents. Whether we like it or not, there are more and more children who are being raised in single-parent homes or other nonstandard situations. Perhaps the school district should put out a general notice each year to tell all parents and caregivers that they are welcome and wanted.

Sincerely,
Kevin Barrington

Complaint to principal about continued teasing

Denise McAuley, Principal
Rolling Meadow Elementary School

Dear Ms. McAuley,

My son Brandon is a student in Ms. Holly's second-grade homeroom. I sent her a letter four weeks ago, and again two weeks ago, about the teasing and bullying that routinely takes place in her classroom. She has not responded, and according to Brandon the level of abuse has not changed.

I am enclosing copies of the letters with the details.

At this time I am asking that you investigate why this behavior by some is allowed to continue.

In any case, my husband and I feel that the situation has gotten out of control to the point where we would ask that Brandon be removed from Ms. Holly's classroom.

Please let me know your plans as quickly as possible.

Sincerely,
Betsy Hawkins

Complaining of change to advanced placement course

Joshua Cornyn, Principal
Rolling Meadow High School

Dear Principal Cornyn,

I am writing to express my extreme dissatisfaction with the school's decision to merge the two AP English classes into one for the coming term.

My daughter Emily has been in Mr. Peterson's course and has benefited greatly from it.

Combining the two sections into one class with sixty students is a very poor decision. These are some of our most capable students, and they deserve the chance to improve their chances for a scholarship and get a head start on their college classes.

While I understand that the school budget has been cut back severely and ways must be found to save money, I think there have to be other solutions. For example, I am aware that in other school districts parents are allowed to volunteer as aides in some of the elementary school classes.

I look forward to hearing from you about this matter.

Sincerely,
Clifford Arena

Complaining of poor judgment in holding event

James Miller, Principal
Rolling Meadow Elementary School

Dear Mr. Miller,

I am writing to register my disappointment in the judgment of school officials who decided to go ahead with the Spring Carnival at Rolling Meadow Elementary School last week.

As you know, the day was not at all Spring-like. It was windy, cold, and rainy, and I can't say that any of the children had a particularly good time.

I know we can't control the weather, but this storm had been forecast for a full week in advance. I don't understand why there was not a contingency plan to either postpone the event or move it indoors to the gymnasium.

My daughter Amy missed the next two days of school with a cold, and I was forced to reschedule my own work.

I hope that any future events have a plan A and plan B to deal with the weather. I would be happy to become involved in any committees dealing with events of this nature.

Sincerely,
Rose Patrick

Asking for change in bus stop

William Jenkins, Transportation Coordinator
Rolling Meadow School System

Dear Mr. Jenkins,

I am writing to ask that you make a change in the bus stop location for students who live in West Hagensboro.

The current stop is directly in front of my house at 68 West Street. I don't understand why this location was chosen—there is a park one block further up the road that would serve quite well as a gathering spot for students.

I am sorry to say that my objection is based on the rude and inappropriate behavior of many of your students.

They begin to gather at about 7:15 each weekday morning, and their noise wakes us up. A number of them smoke cigarettes and bring food, and they leave a big mess.

And in rainy or windy weather some of them have the temerity to come into our yard and wait on our porch, which only adds to the noise and garbage problems. I am also concerned about my exposure to liability claims if any of them are injured while on my property.

I would appreciate your prompt attention to this matter.

Sincerely,
Harry Owen

Objecting to the initiation of user fees

Timothy Orful, Chairperson
Rolling Meadow School Board

Dear Mr. Orful,

I am writing to express my strong objection to the decision by the school board to impose a fee on students who participate in sports activities.

I have two children attending Rolling Meadow High School. Both are good students and good athletes. My older son Kevin is a junior and will be applying to college this year.

He has excelled in lacrosse for the past three years, won several awards, and was a big part of the Rolling Meadow team that advanced to the state championships. We were hoping that this record would help him get a scholarship to Syracuse University, where he is applying for college in the fall.

Although we are fortunate enough to be able to pay the charge, the whole idea of a "pay to play" fee seems unfair to the student community. Sports activities are an important part of the educational experience, and it would be a shame if some young person was unable to participate because his or her family was unable to pay the fee.

I would be happy to serve on a committee or otherwise assist the school board in seeking other ways to fund the athletic program. I am aware of some school districts that solicit sponsorships from area businesses and organizations, and I think this is one of several possibilities that should be considered.

Thank you.

Ann Harper

Supporting user fee for sports in schools

Timothy Orful, Chairperson
Rolling Meadow School Board

Dear Mr. Orful,

I would like to express my support for the idea of imposing a user fee on those who participate in organized sports in the Rolling Meadow School District.

The purpose of schooling is to prepare our young people for jobs, not to entertain them (or the community) with expensive sports like football and baseball.

My wife and I are retired, and our children have long ago graduated and moved on to careers. We pay school taxes each year, and we do so willingly to support the youngsters.

But in these difficult economic times, I think there is no excuse for even considering raising taxes or cutting back on education in order to support sports activities. I strongly support the new "pay to play" policy.

Sincerely,
Stan Jeffers

Objecting to increase in student fee

Chancellor's Office
Rolling Meadow University

Dear Chancellor Tully,

I am writing to express my strong opposition to the increase in the student activities fee for the coming semester.

The purpose of the fee is to support student-organized and managed entertainment, special events, and guest speakers. While I appreciate the opportunity to take part in some of these events, I feel that I should have a choice as to whether I want to support these activities.

In the real world—outside the gates of the campus—the promoter of an event does not have the right to levy a tax on local residents to support a business.

It is hard enough for students and their families to deal with the high cost of a college education; we have had to contend with another increase in tuition and room and board this year. To require us to pay a substantial amount of money for extracurricular activities, whether we take part in them or not, is wrong.

In my opinion, funding for student activities should be on a pay-as-you go basis. I call upon you to act to change the process.

Sincerely,
Karen Baker

Complaint about course fees

Dr. Harry Grove, Superintendent
Rolling Meadow Community School
Rolling Meadow

Dear Dr. Grove,

I am currently enrolled in the French Cuisine cooking course at the Rolling Meadow Community School.

When I enrolled for this course, it was stated that the enrollment fee was $50 and that the instructor would collect an additional $25 for ingredients and supplies.

At the first class, the instructor said that the published cost of $25 was a mistake and that in fact the amount required was $45 plus an additional $35 for a cookbook. I had expected to pay $75 and was instead being asked to pay nearly twice as much, $130.

I did not want to embarrass myself in the class, but the morning after the first lesson I contacted the bursar's office to ask for my money back. I was told I could only receive 50 percent of my registration fee—only $25—and nothing more because the program had started.

As far as I am concerned, the details of this course were misrepresented. It may have been the fault of the instructor, but nevertheless the community school is made to look bad.

I am writing to ask that all funds I have paid, a total of $130, be refunded to me.

I look forward to hearing from you.

Sincerely,
Caroline Sawyer

Requesting more college aid

Marlon Waters, Director
Financial Aid Office
Rolling Meadow University

Dear Mr. Waters,

I am thrilled to have been accepted to Rolling Meadow University for the coming semester. RMU was my first choice.

However, I am concerned that the scholarship and loans offered in the financial aid package are not enough to permit me to attend. The package from RMU is considerably less than that offered by other schools where I have been accepted.

I would like to request an appointment with an aid counselor to see what can be done to make it possible for me to attend Rolling Meadow University.

I look forward to hearing from you. I am very excited about the prospect of attending RMU, and I hope you will help me make that happen.

Sincerely,
Greg Winters

CHAPTER 20

Church Business

ASKING HELP FOR FIRE VICTIMS ❖ 166

THANKING MEMBERS OF CHURCH FOR SUPPORT ❖ 166

CHANGING CHURCHES ❖ 166

CHURCH NOT MEETING FUNDRAISING GOAL ❖ 167

OPPOSING NEW CONSTRUCTION PLAN ❖ 167

OBJECTING TO POLITICAL CONTENT OF SERMON ❖ 167

OBJECTING TO USE OF CHURCH HALL FOR POLITICAL RALLY ❖ 168

Asking help for fire victims

Dear Members of the Church Community,

As most of you know, last week a sudden fire destroyed the home of the Cosgrove family. Matt and Pam and their four children have been members of our congregation for the past six years.

We are so happy that everyone was able to escape the fire safely. But they lost everything they owned, literally running out the door with just the clothes on their backs.

The Cosgroves are temporarily living at the Lakeside Motel, which is owned by Jim and Diane Fleming of our church; they have generously provided shelter for this family in their time of need.

I am writing to ask that you, too, come to their aid.

We are accepting donations of money as well as clothing, toys for the children, and other necessities. Please contact the church office to see how you can help.

Sincerely,
Tom Anderson, Pastor

Thanking members of church for support

To Members of the Church Community,

As most of your know, a month ago this week Tom and I lived through one of the most horrific events of our lives.

A fire started in our basement and quickly spread to the upper floors in our house.

Fortunately it happened in the afternoon while we were all up and around, and our family (and the cat and the dog and the parakeet) was able to get out safely.

And though the Rolling Meadow Fire Department was on the scene very quickly, there was nothing that could be done; we watched the fire destroy everything we owned.

We feel blessed that everyone was safe and unhurt, and we draw strength from all of you who have been so kind and supportive of us. The outpouring of support has been incredible.

As we rebuild our lives, I cannot imagine how we could have done it without the generosity and love of our friends and neighbors.

We will be forever grateful.

Sincerely,
Pam Cosgrove

Changing churches

William Swain, Pastor
Rolling Meadow Community Church

Dear Rev. Swain,

My husband Jim and I have been parishioners at your church since we moved to Rolling Meadow five years ago.

It is our opinion that in recent years you have sought to ally the church with a number of human rights positions that are in conflict with our own beliefs about individual freedom of choice.

We have spoken to you in the past about our concerns. At this point we have decided that we have no other choice but to leave the congregation.

We wish you and our friends at the church all the best and hope that someday in the future we can worship together in harmony.

Sincerely,
Leigh Vaughan

Church not meeting fundraising goal

Dear Parishioners,

One year ago we embarked on what we knew was going to be a difficult mission: raising funds to build an addition to our community center to accommodate the many children of working parents who needed daycare.

We had hoped to begin construction this coming April. Though we never doubted the support and generosity of our members, we could not have predicted the difficult economic times that would arrive.

Today, as things begin to look better for our individual and national bank accounts, we'd like to begin the final push toward raising funds to complete the job.

As of this date we have raised just over half of what we need to achieve our goal. We would like to invite those of you who have yet to give to make a contribution now. To our already generous members, we'd like to ask for just a bit more.

The daycare facility will benefit us all, allowing for more parents to keep working and helping to fulfill our church's mission in the community.

Thank you once more.

Harry Andrews, Building Committee Chair

Opposing new construction plan

Dear Fundraising Committee,

Eight months ago the congregation of Rolling Meadow Community Church approved plans for a major building project that would add a recreation hall and kitchen to our facilities.

Fundraising and pledge support is to begin in the next couple of weeks.

I'm sure all of you would agree that the economy we face today is very different from what it was just eight months ago.

At this time I think it would not be prudent to proceed with a project on the scale originally proposed. I believe we should make do with what we have—the building has served us well for eighty years—until financial times are better.

In my opinion, our church's funds and the energies of our members would be much better used to provide assistance to those in need in the days ahead.

Clara Tuttle

Objecting to political content of sermon

Dear Reverend Wells,

As a relatively new member of your congregation, I congratulate you on your fine work and the respect you enjoy in the community.

I have always looked forward to your sermons. I have found them to be very thoughtful and inspiring; you write well and you speak with great passion.

However, I am afraid that I feel that this past Sunday's address to the parishioners crossed the line from faith into politics.

I believe politics and religion are each noble causes and that neither should cross into the domain of the other. It would be my hope you would continue to motivate and provoke but stay clear of political matters.

Sincerely,
John Daly

Objecting to use of church hall for political rally

William Swain, Pastor
Rolling Meadow Community Church

Dear Rev. Swain,

I was very surprised, and more than a bit concerned, to learn about the rally and fundraiser held in the Community Church's hall for a local candidate for Congress.

My personal feelings about this particular candidate are not relevant; I strongly believe that the church should stay out of politics. We all believe in free choice, and that must extend into the voting booth as well.

I am also concerned that any partisan political activity associated with the church could endanger our tax status with the state and federal governments.

I am hoping this event was a one-time error and not the beginning in a change in the focus of our church, which I know we all value so deeply.

Sincerely,
Beverly Owens

Part 6

Politics and
Government

CHAPTER 21

Political Intrigue

REMAINING NEUTRAL IN ELECTION •❖ 171

DECLINING INVOLVEMENT
IN CAMPAIGN •❖ 171

DECLINING TO SUPPORT
CANDIDATE •❖ 171

CONCEDING ELECTION •❖ 172

DECLARING OPPOSITION TO
SCHOOL EXPANSION •❖ 172

CALLING ON POLITICIAN TO
STEP ASIDE •❖ 172

CALLING ON POLITICIAN TO RESIGN •❖ 173

CALLING FOR INVESTIGATION
OF POLITICIAN •❖ 173

OBJECTING TO PUBLIC FACILITIES USED FOR
POLITICAL PURPOSE •❖ 173

OBJECTING TO INVOLVEMENT OF SCHOOL
EMPLOYEES IN BALLOT ISSUE •❖ 174

ASKING POLITICAL MAIL TO STOP •❖ 174

COMPLAINT ABOUT CORPORATE
SPONSORSHIP OF POLITICAL
ORGANIZATION •❖ 174

Remaining neutral in election

Dear Harry,

In the upcoming election we are faced with the best of choices: two well-qualified and capable candidates for the same office.

Speaking for myself, I am faced with the difficult situation of having to choose between two good friends both seeking seats on the board of selectmen.

Therefore, I have decided to remain publicly uncommitted; I would be happy to see either of you win. In fact, I hope whichever of you does not prevail this time will run again next year for the open seat.

I hope you understand my position here. I would rather keep quiet than have to make a public choice between the two of you.

Sincerely,
Mary Ryan

Declining involvement in campaign

Dear Mike,

I received your campaign literature and request for volunteers in support of your upcoming bid for selectmen.

I was proud and honored to work on your successful effort to stop the expansion of the state highway through town and am glad to see that you continue to be interested in public service.

I want you to know that I will be voting for you in November and will do what I can to convince my friends to join me in supporting your candidacy.

At this time, though, family obligations prevent me from devoting time to what I hope is a successful campaign.

I wish you the best of luck.

Sincerely,
Alice Jones

Declining to support candidate

Dear Mike,

Thank you for writing to me about your plans to run for selectman in the upcoming election.

I am very pleased to see several experienced and well-meaning candidates putting themselves forward for this seat. I know you well and am sure you would be an able representative.

However, I have already given my support to Harry Stevens. He and I have worked together on many community boards and special projects in the past decade, and he asked me to endorse him some time ago.

I wish you luck in this election and in future involvement in the community. Although I will be voting for Harry, I would be happy to see either of you on the board of selectmen.

Sincerely,
Sam Miller

Conceding election

To All My Supporters,

The results of yesterday's election have now been certified, and we came up short by 986 votes, about 2 percent of the electorate.

I want to thank all of you for your help. Together we ran a fair, spirited, issue-oriented campaign. We never descended into personal attacks but kept the focus on matters that directly affected the voters of Rolling Meadow.

I am proud of what we did, and you should be, too.

I have personally congratulated Harry Stevens on his win. I also let him know that I would continue to speak out on behalf of what we stand for, and I intend to continue to be active in the community on those issues and more.

Sincerely,
Mike George

Declaring opposition to school expansion

Dear John,

I have received your letter asking for my support in the upcoming town election for the ballot initiative to borrow funds to pay for a major addition to the high school's gymnasium.

As you know, I have supported the school district on many projects over the past decade and hope to continue to do so. There is nothing more important than the education of our young people.

And as you also no doubt know, I feel that you are doing an outstanding job as principal.

This time, however, I will not support the borrowing plan for the expansion. The expansion of the gymnasium may be a worthy project but not in these difficult times.

I believe that all of our efforts should be directed toward increasing funding for teacher salaries rather than capital expenses. I would hate to see us with a new gym while teachers were being laid off for lack of funds.

Sincerely,
Mona Franklin

Calling on politician to step aside

Dear Mayor Blanko,

As a concerned citizen of Rolling Meadow, I call upon you to temporarily step aside as mayor until the charges brought against you by the Northfork County Attorney are decided in court.

The allegations of bid rigging are serious, but I agree with your statement to the press that you are entitled to the presumption of innocence and a fair trial.

In the meantime, though, I feel that nothing will be accomplished in town hall while these charges are pending. You can do the most for Rolling Meadow by allowing city council chairman Marvin Mora to temporarily take your office.

Sincerely,
Dan Martin

Calling on politician to resign

Dear Mayor Blanko,

As a voter and former supporter, I am calling upon you to immediately resign your position as mayor of Rolling Meadow.

The recent indictment of your personal secretary and the criminal investigation into the conduct of two town department heads demonstrate a pattern of lawbreaking and a lack of oversight by our chief elected official.

It is already clear that the town council has decided to block any off-budget expenditures and hold up any new contracts until the criminal cases are concluded. There is little chance that this situation will be resolved before the end of your elected term in ten months.

It is with sadness that I join those who have concluded that you have lost the confidence of the citizens of our town.

Janice Sterling

Calling for investigation of politician

Harry Macy, County Attorney

Dear Mr. Macy,

On behalf of Rolling Meadow Citizens for Accountability in Government, we ask the county attorney's office to begin an immediate investigation of the bidding practices of the office of Mayor Rodney Blanko of Rolling Meadow.

Our own inquiries, as reported by the Rolling Meadow Weekly Inquirer, found a sustained pattern of favoritism and questionable contracts awarded in the past three years. We are sending a copy of this letter to the newspaper as well.

It is our belief that Mayor Blanko has used his office for personal gain or to reward his campaign contributors and political allies with contracts that are not in keeping with prevailing rates. We also uncovered what we believe to be a pattern of appointing friends and relatives to no-show jobs in the parks and public works department.

We stand ready to provide copies of all of the information we have uncovered.

Sincerely,
Wilson Keith

Objecting to public facilities used for political purpose

To the Editor,

This past Tuesday evening the School Tax Override Committee held an organization meeting in the high school cafeteria. This group supports a ballot initiative that would raise taxes to increase funding for our schools.

Regardless of your position on the request for additional taxes to support the school system, I feel it was highly inappropriate—and possibly a violation of law—to allow the use of public facilities by a partisan political organization.

This event is indicative of the poor judgment shown by the school board in their oversight of the district. We should not be in a position where taxpayers are being asked to come up with more and more money each year, and we should not have to consider whether teachers, students, and administrators are using publicly funded facilities for improper purposes.

I call on the voters of Rolling Meadow to reject the tax override and to send a message to the school committee that we do not approve of their stewardship of the school system.

Rhonda Seymour

Objecting to involvement of school employees in ballot issue

Jerome Vickers, Principal
Rolling Meadow High School

Dear Principal Vickers,

I am writing to express my strong objection to the use of school facilities and supplies for the production of political literature in support of the tax override initiative that will appear on this November's ballot.

While I am a strong supporter of our school system, I do not support raising taxes in these difficult times. We all have had to pull in our belts this year, and the school district should be no exception.

It was wrong to allow school district employees and students to spend time preparing literature about the ballot initiative, and highly improper to use the school's printing equipment and paper to produce the flyer.

I will also be contacting the town attorney about this matter, asking that he open an investigation into this misuse of public funds.

Sincerely,
Stan Walsh

Asking political mail to stop

Jerry Reynolds

Dear Jerry,

It is very obvious to me that you are someone who feels very strongly about your politics. I do, too, but it seems we lean in very different directions.

You have me included on your list of people receiving political e-mails from you. Thank you for thinking of me, but I have to tell you that I find the messages offensive or uniformed—in my opinion.

I enjoy your company when we talk about things other than politics, and sometimes even when we debate the issues. But I would appreciate it if you would delete me from your list for mailings.

Sincerely,
Ron

Complaint about corporate sponsorship of political organization

Gina Giannopolis, President
Momma Gina's Pizza

Dear Ms. Giannopolis,

I have been a devoted customer at your pizza restaurants all through the northeast; when traveling with my family we would sometimes go far out of our way just to find one of your shops because we knew the product would be excellent.

I am dismayed, though, to find out that your company has made several major donations to national political parties and to one presidential candidate in particular.

As much as I enjoy your pizza, I find this candidate and his party distasteful.

While I certainly believe citizens have the right to express their views and make contributions to political parties or candidates of their choice, I think you are making a mistake by donating money as a corporation. I do not want to support the candidate you have chosen, and I do not want the money I pay for your products to end up in his campaign.

I have decided that our family will no longer patronize your restaurants, and I will be very active in informing as many people as I can about your corporate support of this politician.

If in the future you make a change to your policies in this regard, I would like to know about it, and I might reconsider my decision at that time.

Sincerely,
Brad Johnson

CHAPTER 22

Government Affairs

UNABLE TO ACCEPT GIFT BECAUSE OF
CONFLICT OF INTEREST ➻ 177

COMPLAINT ABOUT CLEANLINESS OF
COMMUNITY POOL ➻ 177

PROTESTING CLOSURE OF
TOWN FACILITIES ➻ 177

ENDING COMMUNITY SERVICE ➻ 178

PROTESTING CLOSURE OF
TOWN FACILITY ➻ 178

COMPLAINING ABOUT CUTBACKS TO
LIBRARY HOURS ➻ 179

OBJECTING TO CLOSURE OF LOCAL MOTOR
VEHICLE REGISTRY ➻ 179

UNHAPPY ABOUT END TO
SWIMMING LESSONS ➻ 180

COMPLAINING ABOUT BUS ROUTE ➻ 180

OBJECTING TO NEW
RECYCLING FEES ➻ 180

COMPLAINING OF
UNLICENSED DOGS ➻ 181

ASKING OVERSIGHT OF HANDICAPPED
PARKING SPOTS ➻ 181

OBJECTING TO PARTISANSHIP AT
TOWN OBSERVANCE ➻ 182

OBJECTING TO ACTIONS OF
ELECTED OFFICIAL ➻ 182

Unable to accept gift because of conflict of interest

Dear Mr. Simon,

I received your invitation offering an all-expenses paid, weeklong trip to the Bahamas for myself and my family.

Although I appreciate the offer, it would be inappropriate for me to accept a gift from a company that does business with the town. I note that your company has submitted a bid for sewer reconstruction in town, and that contract will come before the board in a few months.

The state board of ethics clearly states that to avoid a conflict of interest no elected or appointed official can accept a gift of any value from any supplier or bidder for government work.

Sincerely,
Don Roberts
Cc: copy to town counsel's files

Complaint about cleanliness of community pool

Jamie Gregg, Aquatic Director
Rolling Meadow Community Pool

Dear Mr. Gregg,

We are very fortunate to have a wonderful facility like the community pool in Rolling Meadow. Our entire family are regulars.

Over the past month, however, I have become very concerned about the cleanliness of the facilities. The showers have an accumulation of mold, the floors in the dressing room are dangerously slippery, and there have been times when the trash does not seem to have been picked up for days at a time.

As you can understand, these are significant health and safety concerns and also present the danger of liability lawsuits to the town.

I hope you will address this issue immediately. I look forward to hearing from you about this matter.

Sincerely,
Cheryl Golden

Protesting closure of town facilities

David Elder, Director
Rolling Meadow Visitor Service & Information Bureau

Dear Mr. Elder,

On behalf of the Rolling Meadow Retail Association, I am writing to ask that the town reconsider its plan to close the public restroom facilities in the visitor's bureau downtown.

Although we are certainly aware of the budgetary crisis faced by town government, it is also true that one of the main sources of tax income is the downtown business district. We want to do everything we can to encourage people to come downtown and visit our stores, galleries, and restaurants.

Although it may seem like a small matter, we feel that the lack of public facilities in downtown may add to the exodus of business to the suburban malls. Every dollar spent there hurts the downtown business district and our tax base.

As we did three years ago when our association helped pay for the landscaping of Venetian Park, we would be willing to work with the town to find additional ways to fund improvements that would benefit the downtown.

Sincerely,
Bruce Woods, Director
Rolling Meadow Retail Association

Ending community service

Tate Holdgate, Mayor
Rolling Meadow

Dear Mayor Holdgate,

It is with regret that I must inform you that the Flying Aspidistra Garden Club will not be able to provide plantings and landscaping services in public spaces throughout downtown Rolling Meadow this summer.

It has been an honor to do this for the town for the past five years; we were very pleased with the appreciation we received from residents and visitors.

Unfortunately, although we still have many willing volunteers, contributions to our club have dropped off severely in the past six months, and we are unable to purchase plants and flowers.

If the town has funds to pay for the greenery, we would be happy to donate our time to take care of them this summer and in years to come. I would welcome the opportunity to discuss this with you at your convenience.

Sincerely,
Kathryn McDougall, President
Rolling Meadow Garden Club

Protesting closure of town facility

Kenneth Olden, Mayor
Rolling Meadow

Dear Mayor Olden,

I am writing to protest the proposed closing of the Rolling Meadow Elder Daycare Facility. I know I am not alone in saying that this facility is one of the most valuable services offered by the town.

For the past three years this service has been a lifesaver for my family.

My mother is eighty-five years old and still lives in her own home here in town, just down the road from us. She is not able to drive and her walking is limited, but she still very much enjoys getting out and spending the day with others.

For the past four years I have brought her to the center every morning, and we're both very grateful for what it has offered her.

Without the center, my mother and many other older people will probably end up sitting in front of a television set all day long. And the town will lose some of its distinctive character.

Of all the things to choose to close in difficult financial times, I think this should be the very last. We owe so much to our elders, and the adult daycare center has been proof that our community cares.

I call upon you to reverse this decision. I would be happy to become involved in a committee to save the center.

Sincerely,
Elliot Newman

Complaining about cutbacks to library hours

Margaret Norman, Director
Rolling Meadow Library

Dear Ms. Norman,

I am very unhappy to see that the library board has decided to eliminate evening hours this summer. The chance to stroll downtown to the library and enjoy some time in the cool and quiet of the reading room is a treat many of us enjoy.

Everyone understands the difficult economy, but I have to believe there were alternatives to eliminating this much-appreciated pleasure; in my experience there were nights when every seat was taken.

I think closing the library early on Saturday or even closing it completely on a weekday would be a better solution. Perhaps we could get some of the downtown stores to sponsor night hours.

I would be happy to volunteer my time on a committee to explore these and other options.

Sincerely,
Randolph Perry

Objecting to closure of local motor vehicle registry

Mary Turner, Director
State Motor Vehicles Department

Dear Ms. Turner,

I am writing to object to the announced plan to the Rolling Meadow Motor Vehicles Department. In your announcement you said local residents would be able to use the bureau in Green Island, about ten miles away.

While I am in favor of saving tax dollars wherever possible, I also feel that the state should always remember who pays those taxes. I work Monday to Friday and don't have enough time during the day to drive to the next town to conduct business.

I think a much better idea would have been to split the hours between the two locations. Let the clerks from Rolling Meadow come to Green Island on Tuesday and Thursday, for example, and stay at the other facility the rest of the week. By doing this, two or three people have to commute instead of dozens or hundreds who need to conduct business with your agency.

Sincerely,
Lee Davies

Unhappy about end to swimming lessons

Peter Swift, Chairman
Parks and Recreation
Rolling Meadow

Dear Mr. Swift,

I was very unhappy to learn that the parks department has decided not to offer swimming lessons at Mirror Pond this summer.

I have been a resident of Rolling Meadow for the past fifty years, and all three of my children became good swimmers as a result of this instruction. Two of my grandchildren were looking forward to attending this summer.

I realize that this is being done in an attempt to save money, but I have to believe that there are other ways to fund this important offering to the community. We could seek sponsorships from local businesses, run fundraisers, and seek volunteer help.

I would be glad to work with others to find a way to keep this valuable community resource going.

Sincerely,
Sylvia Summers

Complaining about bus route

Jean Collier, Administrator
Rolling Meadow Regional Transit Authority

Dear Ms. Collier,

I was disappointed to see that the transit authority intends to make a change to the route of the number 9 bus for the upcoming winter season.

In its present route, that bus picks up and drops off passengers in front of the Rolling Meadow Senior Center. Many of the residents use the bus on their trips to and from downtown.

The new route would change the scheduled stop to three blocks away, on Orange Street.

I hope you will reconsider this alteration to the route. Senior citizens are among the most consistent users of mass transit. I feel that we should always look to find ways to make their lives easier, not harder.

Sincerely,
Paula Kinsley, Executive Director
Rolling Meadow Senior Center

Objecting to new recycling fees

Gerald Day, Administrator
Rolling Meadow Recycling Facility

Dear Mr. Day,

I have just read about the proposed revised fee schedule for the Rolling Meadow landfill.

I realize that expenses have gone up and that we need to avoid running a deficit at the facility. The 15 percent increase in charges for dumping household garbage will be painful but we can manage.

I do, though, think that the substantial increase in special fees for dumping things like tires, appliances, and other bulky items is going to be counterproductive. I fear that instead of encouraging people to properly dispose of unwanted articles you are going to end up with more and more of these items dumped in the woods or by the side of the road.

Please reconsider these fees. Most people want to do the right thing. Let's not encourage the wrong result.

Sincerely,
Jane Derr

Complaining of unlicensed dogs

Edward Lewis, Town Clerk
Town Clerk's Office
Rolling Meadow

Dear Mr. Lewis,

I am writing to formally request that the town take action against a neighbor who has three unlicensed and unchained dogs. These animals are left to roam the neighborhood and regularly cause problems with garbage cans and make a great deal of noise every time a truck drives by.

Several residents of the street have concerns the dogs might harm young children.

I have made several calls to your office in recent weeks, but I do not see that anything has been done.

The property is question is owned by Sam Zillo, at 63 South Road.

I want to make it clear that I do not blame this situation on the dogs. It is their owner who must take control.

I am sending a copy of this letter to the mayor's office and the chief of police. I would appreciate the courtesy of a response to let me know what will be done about this matter.

Sincerely,
Michael Snow

Asking oversight of handicapped parking spots

Richard Graham, Chief of Police
Rolling Meadow Police Department

Dear Chief Graham,

As the result of a recent fall, I have been forced to use a brace and crutches, and I received a temporary handicapped parking permit from the town.

I appreciate the availability of closed-in spaces for my car in downtown.

However, I am—for the first time—aware of how often this courtesy is abused by people who have no right to use the spaces.

I am writing to ask your department devote more attention to the policing of vehicles in the spaces.

Just this morning I had business at the town office building. Both of the handicapped parking spaces were occupied by vehicles that did not have permits; I was forced to park several blocks away.

I, of course, recognize that parking enforcement is not the highest priority for the town. However, that does not excuse the lack of attention to this matter.

The town receives a significant amount of revenue from parking tickets, and we already employ several meter attendants. I am asking that you direct officers on patrol to pay close attention to the use of the available spots in town and to send a message to those who do not belong there: respect the law and those of us who need a bit of help in going about our daily activities.

Sincerely,
Fred Poor

Objecting to partisanship at town observance

Rolling Meadow Gazette

To the Editor,

Our family has long made it a tradition to attend the Memorial Day observance at Venetian Park in Rolling Meadow.

I want to compliment the community organizations and service groups who participated in the event; as always, it was a moving moment.

However, I do want to register my displeasure at finding a number of state and local political candidates who took advantage of the gathering to seek to campaign for office and collect contributions from the attendees.

Although I recognize that elections are an essential part of our system and that campaign activities are protected as a constitutional expression of free speech, I also think we should hold our politicians to a high standard; this should always be a solemn and nonpartisan event.

I am not singling out a particular political party or candidate here; I was equally offended by representatives of both persuasions. I hope that others will join me in reminding candidates that they should be smart enough to realize that some events should be outside the realm of partisanship.

Thank you.

Matt Armstrong

Objecting to actions of elected official

Editor
Rolling Meadow Daily News

To the Editor,

Once again I want to compliment the county commissioners and everyone else involved in putting on the Tuckernuck County Fair.

We are a small county, but we know how to put on a great party.

I do, though, want to express my indignation at the actions of Bert Greider, county sheriff. At a booth just inside the entrance to the fair, the sheriff and several of his deputies were handing out free baseballs and other items with his name printed on them.

No matter how I look at this, it comes out wrong to me.

Either he was using taxpayer money to buy items that served no purpose but to promote his name, or he was appearing in uniform with deputies to give away campaign material. Perhaps he was doing both: giving away campaign material paid for by tax dollars.

Sheriff Greider owes the people of our county an explanation. And we should all keep this in mind at election time next fall.

Sincerely,
Ben O'Neil

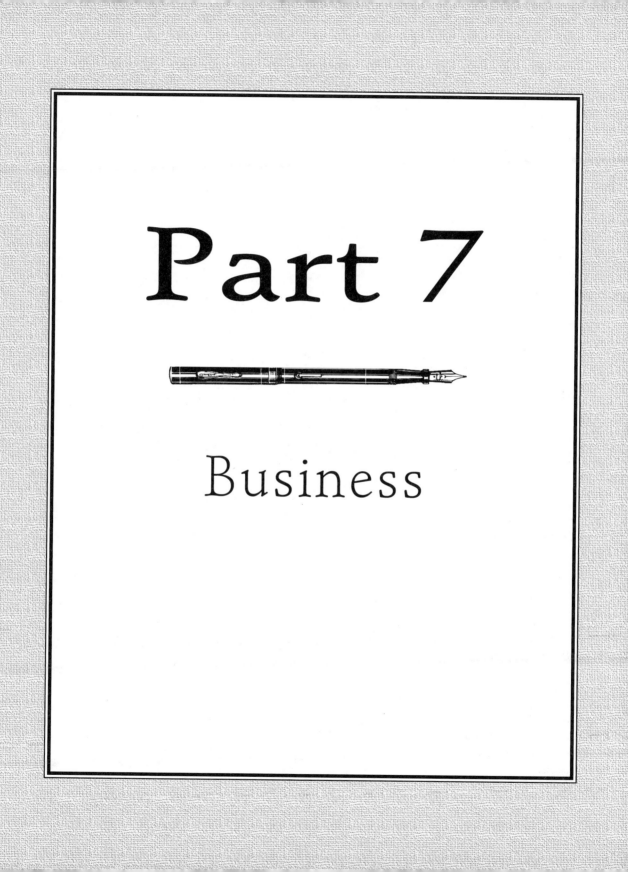

Part 7

Business

CHAPTER 23

Dear Boss

RESIGNATION WITHOUT
EXPLANATION ❖ 185

SIMPLE RESIGNATION FOR
ADVANCEMENT ❖ 185

LEAVING JOB FOR HIGHER-PAID
POSITION ❖ 185

RESIGNATION TO RETURN
TO SCHOOL ❖ 186

RESIGNATION BECAUSE OF
SPOUSE'S TRANSFER ❖ 186

RESIGNING JOB BECAUSE OF ILLNESS ❖ 186

RESIGNING JOB BECAUSE OF
FAMILY RESPONSIBILITIES ❖ 187

NOTIFICATION OF RETIREMENT ❖ 187

COURTESY LETTER TO EMPLOYER
ABOUT RETIREMENT ❖ 187

REQUESTING CHANGE TO PART-TIME
EMPLOYMENT ❖ 188

DECLINING INTERNSHIP ❖ 188

REQUEST FOR INFORMATION ABOUT
VACATION TIME ❖ 188

Resignation without explanation

Thomas Ellis, Personnel Director
Rolling Meadow Real Estate Agency

Dear Tom,

I am writing to tender my resignation as sales associate for the Rolling Meadow Real Estate Agency, effective immediately.

Thank you for the opportunity to work for the organization for the past six months.

Mary Ann Falcone

Simple resignation for advancement

Chase Davenport, Principal
Rolling Meadow High School

Dear Mr. Davenport,

It is with regret that I write to inform you that I will be resigning my position as a teacher's aide at Rolling Meadow High School, effective at the end of the spring semester.

I have been offered a full-time teaching position at Woodbury High School.

It has been an honor and a pleasure to have worked with you and the entire staff at Rolling Meadow High. I am well-prepared for my new job.

Thank you for giving me the opportunity to start my teaching career.

Sincerely,
Donna Curren

Leaving job for higher-paid position

Jill Hogan, Principal
Rolling Meadow Elementary School

Dear Jill,

It is with regret that I tender my resignation as a third-grade teacher at Rolling Meadow Elementary School.

I have been offered a similar position at Stepping Stones Charter School at a significantly higher salary. I am very excited at the prospects of my new job but also saddened that the Rolling Meadow School District is unable to obtain community support for a budget that would allow teachers a living wage.

Like many other teachers here, I greatly respect you and the entire team here. I am deeply indebted to you for the guidance and support you have extended. I came here fresh out of college, and your direction made me the teacher I am today.

I wish you, the staff, and the students of Rolling Meadow the very best.

Sincerely,
Judith Davis

Resignation to return to school

Peter Mann, Director
Rolling Meadow Historical Association

Dear Mr. Mann,

It has been a privilege and a pleasure to work with you and the rest of the staff at the Rolling Meadow Historical Association for the past two years. At this time, though, I am writing to tell you of my decision to resign my position in the technical services department to return to college and obtain a degree in museum studies.

You have been a most generous mentor, and I thank you for all you have done. I hope to stay in touch, and I hope someday to return to the historical association as a professional staffer.

Sincerely,
Tessa Sawyer

Resignation because of spouse's transfer

Jack Dwyer, Sales Director
Rolling Meadow Times

Dear Mr. Dwyer,

It is with regret that I submit my resignation as sales assistant for the Rolling Meadow Times. It has been a privilege to work for the company for the past six years.

On a personal level, I will also greatly miss the chance to work for you; you are a fine manager and I feel that I have learned very much here.

After putting my wife through several moves because of my career, this time it's her turn. Marylou has accepted a teaching position at a college in Ohio, and we will be moving next month.

I thank you for your offer to provide references and to refer me to sales jobs in Ohio.

Thank you again.

Sincerely,
Phillip Baxter

Resigning job because of illness

Maynard Fletcher, President
Rolling Meadow Savings Bank

Dear Mr. Fletcher,

It is with sadness that I submit my resignation as head cashier for the Rolling Meadow Savings Bank. My medical needs are such that I feel I cannot perform my job to the benefit of the bank.

I have been privileged to work here for the past fifteen years. When I was diagnosed with cancer six months ago, my colleagues at the bank sustained me and made it possible for me to continue to hope for the best.

Now I must devote my time to my treatment and struggle with this disease. I thank you again for the opportunities I have had and the support I received.

Sincerely,
Roger Wilson

Resigning job because of family responsibilities

Beverly Kale
Director of Human Services
Rolling Meadow Electric Company

Dear Ms. Kale,

Please accept my resignation as quality control auditor for the Rolling Meadow Electric Company, effective at the end of the month.

For the past five years I have had the honor of working with the talented and supportive colleagues of this company.

Because of family matters that require my full-time attention, I will not be able to perform my professional duties.

Thank you for the opportunity to work here and all you have done personally to make my time so pleasant and my tenure so successful.

I would be happy to work with the human resources department to help transition my duties to another staffer and to determine a final day of employment that least impacts operations.

Sincerely,
Tracy Nagle

Notification of retirement

Joseph Cunningham, Director of Operations
Rolling Meadow Printing

Dear Joe,

I am writing to inform you that I have decided to retire from the company, effective June 10.

Forty-five years ago, I know I never imagined a time like this would come. I was just a young kid, fresh out of school, with big dreams and empty pockets. I came here for a job and ended up with a career and an extended family of friends that I will always treasure.

As much as I still enjoy my work, I feel I owe it to my wife and family to enjoy the fruits of my labors after all of these years.

On a personal note, I want to thank you for your friendship and guidance. I would be happy to do whatever I can to assist you in training my successor.

Best regards,
Sam Curtis

Courtesy letter to employer about retirement

To Stan Borden, Sales Director
From Hank Murray

As you know, I plan to retire this June.

Before I set an exact date, I would like to know if there is any particular time that would be best for you and the company. I would be happy to help train my replacement or assist in some other way.

Please let me know your preferences.

Requesting change to part-time employment

Linda O'Connor, Personnel Director
Rolling Meadow Manufacturing Company

Dear Ms. O'Connor,

I would like to request consideration of changing my work status from full time to part time.

I currently work forty hours per week as receptionist in the executive offices. I enjoy my job very much, but I have found it impossible to balance the needs of work and taking care of my newborn child.

If you would be open to such an arrangement, I would suggest the possibility of a job-sharing agreement with another person with similar needs. I know of several other new mothers here in town who are looking for a part-time job of this type.

I look forward to meeting with you soon to discuss this; I truly hope there is a way to accomplish this.

Sincerely,
Tara Nolan

Declining internship

Jill Hensley
Hensley Galleries

Dear Ms. Hensley,

Thank you very much for your offer of an internship this summer. I am honored to have been offered a position at such a prestigious gallery.

Unfortunately, I must decline. I have accepted a paid summer job at another gallery in Rolling Meadow.

As much as I would have wanted to work for you, I also need to save money for college expenses in the fall. I will be majoring in art history with a minor in retail management; I hope someday to be considered for full-time employment at a gallery like yours.

Thank you again for considering me.

Sincerely,
Jessica Christopher

Request for information about vacation time

To Human Resources
From Ellen Smart

I am hoping to be able to take a vacation in September. Please let me know how much accumulated vacation time I have available.

I understand there is an option to add as many as four unpaid days. Can you please advise me on the process involved?

Thank you for your assistance.

CHAPTER 24

Employee to Employee

SEEKING ALTERNATIVE TO LAYOFF ◆ 190

ESTABLISHING GUIDELINES FOR
HOLIDAY GIFTS ◆ 190

DECLINING INVITATION TO RETIREMENT
PARTY FOR CAUSE ◆ 191

LAYING OUT THE RULES OF THE
COFFEE CLUB ◆ 191

OBJECTING TO DELAY IN
WORK SCHEDULE ◆ 191

WITHDRAWING OFFER TO TAKE FRIEND'S
WORK SHIFT ◆ 192

Seeking alternative to layoff

Patrick Eally, Director of Sales

Dear Patrick,

Since the beginning of the year, the sales department has been working under a general directive to reduce our expenditures by 15 percent. At this time I can report that we have met, or even slightly exceeded, that goal through cutbacks in new hiring and the elimination of many sales training and conference expenses.

I received today your memo in which you ask for a layoff of three staffers to further reduce our budget.

Before I do that, I would like to meet with you to see if there are not other ways to help our company succeed in this difficult economy without dismissing some of our best salespeople.

I think it would absolutely send the wrong message to our customers if we were to dismiss any of the men and women who sell our products. They are the face of our company, and their regular visits to clients are our best—and sometimes our only—way to put our products in front of buyers.

In my opinion, we have the best sales force in our industry. Our products are excellent, but we do have competitors. It is the expertise of our sales force that distinguishes us from the others.

We all are cautiously optimistic that the current economic downturn will soon reach bottom and that sales will begin to pick up in the next year. I would like to discuss ways that we might keep our company poised to take advantage of the rebound.

Among the possibilities are deferred bonuses, a carefully managed program of unpaid leave for some employees, and the use of web-based catalogs to reduce or eliminate the cost of printing and shipping sales collateral.

I'm available to meet with you at any time that is convenient.

Chuck Francona, Sales Manager

Establishing guidelines for holiday gifts

To All Employees,

As we prepare for our annual holiday party on Monday, December 22, at 6 P.M. at Rocco's Restaurant, I wanted to make a special request regarding gifts offered as part of the "Secret Santa" event.

First of all, in fairness to everyone, I want to remind everyone that the value of gifts is to be no more than $20.

Secondly, I want to ask that we all remember that our staff is wonderfully diverse and everyone's beliefs and culture is worthy of respect. We are asking that gifts as well as cards and wrapping not be of a religious nature.

Let's celebrate the holiday season in a way that does not make any of our employees feel uncomfortable.

If anyone has a question about this policy or seeks advice about the appropriateness of a particular gift, please call me or see me in my office well before the party.

Sincerely,

Mary Lou Shoote, Administrative Assistant

Declining invitation to retirement party for cause

Dear Mary,

I received your e-mail about the retirement party for Stan Bailey. Thank you for inviting me, but I will not be attending. I think it would be awkward for both of us if I were to attend; we have had many disagreements over the years.

Please make it clear to anyone who inquires about my absence that I wish Stan the best in retirement. I certainly will express that to him privately at an appropriate time.

Thanks,
Jim Brennan

Laying out the rules of the coffee club

Dear Debbie,

I hope you are enjoying your new job with Wilson Textiles. I've been here eleven years now, and I think it is a great place to work.

I wanted to let you know that the coffeemaker in the break room is not owned or provisioned by the company; it is maintained by a group of us in an informal club.

There is, as you know, a vending machine in the room, and you can always use it.

If you prefer better coffee (much better, actually) and would like to join us in our club, please see me sometime at lunch or on break and I will explain how we collect money for coffee and filters and the rules about responsibility for maintaining the equipment.

Regards,
Marsha

Objecting to delay in work schedule

Riccardo Mayor
Shipping department supervisor

Dear Riccardo,

I want you to know first of all how much I enjoy working here at the plant; we have a great group of people and a fine operation.

I am writing, though, to ask you help in a matter that is causing me difficulty. When I was hired as a "floater" in the department, I fully understood that my work hours and days would change from week to week; my role is to fill in any gaps that result from vacations, personal days, and other needs of the company.

That sort of arrangement was, and is, fine with me. However, I was told I would receive each monthly schedule at least two weeks before the end of the previous month. This is important to me so that I can arrange for child care and tend to personal appointments.

For the past several months, my assigned hours have not been made available to me until just a few days before the next month's schedule is to begin. It truly does not matter to me what days I work in a particular time period, but it is very difficult for me to handle my personal life when the schedule arrives so close to its starting date.

I would appreciate your assistance in helping me do my best for the company. Please let me know if there is anything I can do to help make the scheduling process go more smoothly.

Sincerely,
Barbara Dugan

Withdrawing offer to take friend's work shift

Jean,

I am very sorry to have to do this to you on such short notice.

I had agreed to take your shift this coming Friday, but I've just been asked by my mother to help her with an unexpected visit to the hospital for a medical test. I'm sure you understand that I have to help her.

I've checked with a few others in my department and I haven't found anyone who could help both of us for Friday. I'm hoping you can make some other arrangement.

Again, my apologies.

Jessica

CHAPTER 25

Money Matters

ASKING PAYMENT OF INVOICE ➥ 194

SECOND LETTER ASKING
FOR PAYMENT ➥ 194

THIRD REQUEST FOR PAYMENT ➥ 194

PLACING OVERDUE ACCOUNT
WITH ATTORNEY ➥ 195

DENYING DISCOUNT BECAUSE TERMS
NOT MET ➥ 195

QUESTIONING INVOICE
FROM SUPPLIER ➥ 196

QUESTIONING INVOICE FROM
SERVICE SUPPLIER ➥ 196

TELLING PROVIDER TO SUBMIT BIDS
FOR SERVICE ➥ 196

REJECTION OF BID FOR SERVICES ➥ 197

NOTIFYING COMPANY WHY THEY DID NOT
GET BUSINESS ➥ 197

ASKING CHANGE TO CONTRACT BEFORE
SERVICES DELIVERED ➥ 198

DISMISSING SERVICE COMPANY
FOR BUDGET ➥ 198

ASKING RENEGOTIATION OF FEE
FOR SERVICES ➥ 198

ENDING AGREEMENT WITH PROVIDER
BECAUSE OF ECONOMY ➥ 199

SADNESS AT CLOSING OF
LONGTIME BUSINESS ➥ 199

Asking payment of invoice

Mark McNamara, accounts payable
Rolling Meadow Paint and Supply

Account # 56780

Dear Mr. McNamara,

I am writing to bring to your attention the outstanding balance of $853.03 owed by Rolling Meadow Paint and Supply. This amount has been due and payable for the past two months.

We have always appreciated your business and look forward to serving you in the future. Perhaps this matter has been overlooked.

We will be expecting full payment of the above account as soon as possible. As stated in the bill of sale, invoices unpaid after 90 days will be subject to a 1.5 percent per month interest charge.

Sincerely,
Alice MacNeil, accounts receivable

Second letter asking for payment

Mark McNamara, accounts payable
Rolling Meadow Paint and Supply

Account # 56780

Dear Mr. McNamara,

On May 15 we brought to your attention the fact that Rolling Meadow Paint and Supply has an outstanding balance of $853.04. The invoice was 60 days old at that time.

To this date we have not received payment.

We value your business and want to do whatever we can to make it possible for us to continue our professional relationship. The invoice is now subject to a 1.5 percent per month interest charge, retroactive to the initial billing date.

Please contact me as soon as possible to discuss this matter. If we do not hear from you within ten days we will be forced to turn this invoice over to our collection agency.

Sincerely,
Alice MacNeil, accounts receivable

Third request for payment

Mark McNamara, accounts payable
Rolling Meadow Paint and Supply

Account # 56780

Dear Mr. McNamara,

Three months have passed and we have not received payment or other response from your company in regards the outstanding balance of $853.03 for the above-references account.

At this time we are unable to accept any further orders from your company until your invoice, plus interest charges, is paid in full.

Please immediately forward a check to us in the amount of $891.99 for products delivered plus interest on the outstanding balance. If we do not receive full payment by June 15, we will be forced to place this account in the hands of our attorney and collection agency.

You have been a valued customer in the past and we hope to continue a relationship with you in the future. If you have any questions, please feel free to contact me.

Thank you.

Alice MacNeil, accounts receivable

Placing overdue account with attorney

Mark McNamara, accounts payable
Rolling Meadow Paint and Supply

Account # 56780

Dear Mr. McNamara,

This is to inform you that the above-referenced account has been placed in the hands of our attorney for collection.

We value you as a customer and hope to deal with you in future, but we must insist on full payment of your outstanding balance.

If you wish to make arrangements for payment before legal action is begun, please contact their offices as soon as possible. All inquiries should be directed to:

Harris Sayle
Sayle, Sayle & Santos
98 Main Street
Rolling Meadow
(382) 555-1234

Sincerely,
Alice MacNeil, accounts receivable

Denying discount because terms not met

Accounts Payable
Big Box Homebuilders

In regards to invoice 88774-BBH

We have received your check for the above invoice.

The amount of the invoice was $2,100.50. The check we received was for $1995.48, with a notation that a 5 percent discount was applied.

Under terms of our bill of sale, and as clearly marked on the invoice, we offer a 5 percent discount to any customer who makes payment within 15 days of receipt of an invoice. Your check was dated and received more than 45 days after the invoice was sent. We apologize for any misunderstanding. We would appreciate prompt payment of the outstanding balance of $105.02.

And we would be happy to honor the early payment discount on any future purchases.

Eileen Ross, accounts receivable
State Lumber Yard

Questioning invoice from supplier

Buy the Foot Lumber
Rolling Meadow
Fred Black, Account Manager

Dear Mr. Black,

We have received your invoice number 254-100-231, dated July 1, in the amount of $18,394.34.

We note that the price per linear foot for Argentinean lignum vitae is listed at $8.75; the purchase order we issued, based on your bid of May 10, called for a price of $6.50.

The purchase order specifies that any discrepancies in quantities, quality, or price must be approved in advance and that variances from the bid may result in rejection of invoices.

Please provide an explanation for the discrepancy between the bid and invoice amounts.

Sincerely,
Barbara Grosbeak, accounts payable

Questioning invoice from service supplier

Thomas Mary, Manager
Better Than Nature Landscaping

Dear Tom,

We have received your invoice for landscaping services provided in May of this year; a copy is attached.

The invoice includes several items that appear incorrect. One line item includes a charge in the amount of $1,820 for installation of sod. We are not aware that such work was performed, and if it was it was not included in the bid for services accepted by our company in January.

We also note that the hourly rate for landscaping services is listed at $18.50 while the rate in the bid we accepted was $16.30 per hour.

We are assuming this was an error. Please correct the invoice and resubmit it for payment.

Sincerely,
Barbara Grosbeak, accounts payable

Telling provider to submit bids for service

Lori Reader
Lori's Hair and Beauty Salon
Rolling Meadow

Dear Lori,

For the past four years your salon has provided hair cutting services for the men and women who reside at our adult home. We think you do a fine job, and the residents look forward to this service on Saturdays.

Because of some funding we receive from the town, we have now been advised that we must put this service out for bids from any other qualified providers.

We hope that you will participate in this bidding process. In the Friday issue of the local newspaper there will be a formal notice and instructions on how to submit a bid.

Sincerely,
Lois Graham, Executive Director
Rolling Meadow Adult Home

Rejection of bid for services

Roland Maddow, Sales Manager
Rolling Meadow Tile and Paving
Rolling Meadow

Dear Mr. Maddow,

Thank you for your bid for the repaving of the employee parking lot at our company. We appreciate your interest and the attention to detail that you displayed in preparing the offer.

At this time, though, we have decided to accept a lower bid from another company already engaged in some construction work here on our grounds.

We will keep you informed if our future plans include a similar project and would look forward to receiving a bid from you at that time.

Sincerely,
Harold James

Notifying company why they did not get business

Judith Cranston
Judy's Wedding Services
Rolling Meadow

Dear Ms. Cranston,

I don't often feel it is necessary to let someone know why I did not choose to give them my business, but we were rather upset about the way one of your employees dealt with us.

We considered three wedding planning services in Rolling Meadow when we began to make plans for the wedding of my daughter Sharon next June.

When we spoke with you on the phone, you spent nearly an hour asking us in great detail about our expectations, personal preferences and styles, and the amount of money we had in our budget. We were quite impressed with the thoroughness of the interview, and we were looking forward to the proposal from your company.

On Monday, my daughter and I met with Courtney from your office. From the moment we sat down with her it was obvious that she either had never read the information you had collected or had chosen to completely ignore it.

This is a second marriage for my daughter and her fiancé; they are both well-established professionals. They were looking for a low-key, sophisticated dinner with tasteful music.

What Courtney presented might have been appropriate for a spring break party, but it was not in any way related to our expectations.

We feel that we wasted several hours of our time, and we have chosen to use a different company.

Sincerely,
Fay Mitchell

Asking change to contract before services delivered

Annie MacDonald
Annie's Catering
Rolling Meadow

Dear Annie,

We are looking forward to our daughter's wedding this coming September, and we are excited about the food you will be offering our guests.

However, I am writing to ask that we make changes to the agreement to reduce the cost by at least $3,000. I don't think I have to explain the difficulties all of us are facing since the assembly plant closed.

Under terms of the agreement, with six months to go before the wedding we are permitted to cancel the contract for a $250 fee. I hope you will waive that charge and allow us to negotiate a new deal. Otherwise we will reopen talks with other caterers in town.

We still very much want you to provide the catering. I hope you will agree to work with us on a somewhat more modest arrangement.

Sincerely,
Lorna Mayo

Dismissing service company for budget

David Campbell, President
Klean Windows
Rolling Meadow

Dear Mr. Campbell,

Thank you for your services over the year in providing window cleaning services at our plant on Industrial Road in Rolling Meadow.

Effective June 1, please discontinue your services at our facility. We have decided that we will be performing window cleaning with our own maintenance staff.

We are doing so strictly for budgetary reasons; we have been very satisfied with your company's work over the years.

Thank you.

Kent Jones, Controller
Rolling Meadow Textile Company

Asking renegotiation of fee for services

Benjamin Klein
Klein Financial Services
Rolling Meadow

Dear Ben,

For the past ten years we have been fortunate to be able to engage you to provide the parents of our high school seniors with a series of lectures on how to pay for college.

The feedback from those who attended has always been positive, and we hope this exposure has benefited your company as well.

Unfortunately, this year's school budget has been cut drastically, and we have had to cancel or sharply curtail almost every activity not directly related to the classroom. We realize the irony of this coming as parents are scrambling to find money for college as their investments and income decline.

I am writing to ask if you would consider donating your time for a shorter introductory course for parents. Although we cannot be directly involved in solicitations for business by commercial entities, I think you could expect to receive a reasonable number of private, paying clients as a result of involvement with the school.

Please call me to discuss.

Sincerely,
Louise Burden, Principal
Rolling Meadow High School

Ending agreement with provider because of economy

John Horton
Klean Sweep Lawn Care
Rolling Meadow

Dear Jack,

We have very much appreciated the work you have performed for the past five years keeping our lawn and flower garden in top shape.

Unfortunately, we need to cut back on our expenditures and have decided we will not be hiring your company for the coming spring and summer.

Please understand we are in no way dissatisfied with your work, and we certainly will recommend your services to anyone who asks. But for the moment, we're going to have to do it ourselves.

Sincerely,
Jeff Katz

Sadness at closing of longtime business

Peter Douglas
Douglas Variety Store

Dear Peter,

It was with great sadness that I learned that Rolling Meadow is going to lose one of its most treasured and unique establishments.

Your store has been a source of pleasure for most of us who grew up in Rolling Meadow and our children and grandchildren.

Where else will we be able to buy needles and thread, the daily newspaper, and cotton candy all in one place? Rolling Meadow is diminished by the absence of your store.

Good luck in whatever else you do.

Sincerely,
Moses Earle

CHAPTER 26

Customer Service

ANNOUNCING DELAY IN SHIPPING •• 201

OFFERING DISCOUNT PROGRAM
TO CUSTOMERS •• 201

ADDING CUSTOMER LOYALTY CARD •• 201

ENDING DISCOUNT PROGRAM •• 202

CANCELING FREE CRAFT CLASSES •• 202

LANDSCAPING BUSINESS
RAISING PRICES •• 202

REDUCING OFFERINGS
AT STORE •• 203

ADDING CHARGE FOR DELIVERY •• 203

ADDING FEE FOR SERVICE •• 204

DISCONTINUING DELIVERY •• 204

APOLOGY FOR UNAVAILABILITY
OF PRODUCT •• 204

Announcing delay in shipping

Phillip Avery, President
Avery Automotive Supply

Order 6SJ7-050909

Dear Mr. Avery,

In regards to the above order, we regret to inform you that due to problems at our overseas supplier there will be a delay of four to six weeks in delivery.

The rescheduled delivery date is August 19.

We sincerely apologize for any inconvenience this may cause you. As a gesture of good will, we will credit your account for 10 percent of the purchase price for future orders.

This particular part requires highly specialized manufacturing processes, and we have been unable to locate an acceptable alternative supplier who could deliver units of the quality we, and our customers, demand.

Please feel free to call me if you have any questions.

Sincerely,
Bruce Atwood
Customer Service

Offering discount program to customers

To Our Valued Customers,

We are very proud of our facilities and plan to upgrade much of the equipment in coming months. We will also expand our offerings of fitness classes and nutrition consultants.

As we enter the new year, we want to offer our valued members a pair of special offers.

All members who prepay for a one-year extension to their contract will be given two extra months for no additional charge.

In addition, any member who refers a friend or relative who joins the club will receive a two-month extension on his or her contract.

John Higgens

Adding customer loyalty card

To Our Valued Customers,

The staff and management of Caplan's Kosher Chinese Restaurant would like to take this opportunity to thank you for your business and support this past year.

We are very aware that in this economy every family has to carefully watch how they spend their money. We have always tried to keep our prices low while maintaining the highest possible quality.

To show our appreciation for your continued patronage we are introducing a Customer Loyalty Card. With every $25 spent at our restaurant (before tax) we will place a $2 credit on your card; our computer system will keep track of your purchases and do all the math. The loyalty card balance can be applied to any future purchases; for full details please see the enclosed description of the plan.

Please use the enclosed card the next time you dine with us. All you need to do is give it to the cashier when you pay your bill.

We hope to see you again soon.

Sincerely,
David Caplan

Ending discount program

To Our Patrons,

For the past several years we have been pleased to be able to offer members of the local automobile club a 10 percent discount on merchandise in our gift shop.

Unfortunately, our budget for the coming year does not permit us to participate in this program. Effective January 1, we will no longer offer this discount.

We do promise to do whatever we can to offer the best possible value to patrons at our gift shop.

Sincerely,
Susan Hunter, Executive Director
Rolling Meadow Contemporary Art Museum

Canceling free craft classes

To Our Patrons,

It is with considerable regret that we announce the end of our Saturday afternoon children's craft classes.

We have been happy to offer these free classes for the past five years. It has been a joy to get to know the young people of our community; we hope we have launched the career of a few great artists of the future.

In this economy, though, we could no longer afford the cost for an instructor and supplies. We considered charging a fee, but in calculating the actual cost of the classes we came to the realization that we would have to charge a fairly high rate for the class.

We are looking at ways to obtain sponsorship from some of our suppliers as well as from community organizations that would allow us to resume the classes; we want to be able to offer them for free to all children from all circumstances.

Again, our apologies. We would love to hear from any of our customers with ideas on how to resume these classes.

Beverly Higbee, President
Higbee's Toy Store

Landscaping business raising prices

To Our Customers,

We have been proud to serve the residents of Rolling Meadow for more than a decade. We want to thank all of our valued customers for their support, many have been with us all that time.

We take pride in providing the best and most comprehensive gardening and landscaping services in the Rolling Meadow area. Our customers are very important to us, and we think we represent the best value in the lawn care business.

We know that this is a very difficult time financially for everyone, and we have always worked very hard to keep our costs stable; there have been no price increases since 2005.

Unfortunately, the rising cost of fuel has impacted our business in many ways. The cost of operating our trucks and power equipment has gone up considerably, but so has the cost of fertilizer, pest and weed control, and other products that are also directly or indirectly affected by oil prices.

Enclosed is our price sheet for the upcoming season. Although the cost of most services will remain the same, we have been forced to raise some prices.

As a courtesy to our long-standing customers, we have a special offer: if you prepay for lawnmowing services for the season we will offer a $100 credit that can be applied to any special landscaping services.

Please call to discuss your upcoming schedule. We hope to once again serve you for all your landscaping needs.

Sincerely,
Ron Nash
The Complete Gardener Landscaping and Lawn Care Service

Reducing offerings at store

To Our Valued Customers,

As owner and proprietor of Rolling Meadow's only locally owned electronics and home entertainment store, I want to thank you for being a supportive customer of ours.

For the past twenty-two years we have dedicated ourselves to offering the best service as well as reasonable prices. We have managed to hold on even as our town has been surrounded by "big box" stores that seek to compete only on price.

I am writing to tell you that we have decided to make a change in our operations to concentrate on our strength: the ability to deliver custom service and support along with the highest-quality products. We intend to enhance the services we can deliver that the discount stores cannot: free consultation in your house, custom installation, and free lifetime support from our electronics specialists.

I hope you will visit our store soon so that we can show you our latest line of professional-grade high-definition televisions, home audio systems, and intercom systems. We intend to specialize on products that are not available at the discount stores because of the complexity required for training of technicians and installation.

And as a thank-you for your previous business, we have enclosed a coupon worth $100 off your next order.

We look forward to seeing you soon.

Angelo Caruso, Owner
Caruso's Home Entertainment Center

Adding charge for delivery

Dear Customers,

We want to thank all of our valued customers for their support during our first year of business.

We are proud to offer our special menu of organic vegetarian fare in Rolling Meadow. Our philosophy is to provide quality ingredients, good taste, and fair prices.

Effective June 1 we will be adding new menu items and a daily early bird special that offers a significant discount to our customers. Our existing regular menu will continue without any price increases.

At the same time, because of the rise in cost of fuel and insurance, we find it necessary to add a $5 fee to deliveries in the Rolling Meadow area. We apologize for any inconvenience this may cause.

We look forward to seeing you soon.

Robin Carr, Owner

Adding fee for service

To All Members,

We are always seeking ways to keep our costs down so that membership fees can be kept as low as possible.

Effective December 14, we will be changing the policy regarding personal training offered to our members. In the past we have offered this service free of charge to all members, but we will now ask only those who use the counseling to pay an additional $25 per month.

At this time we do not expect to increase monthly membership rates.

Thank you for your support and patronage.

Jim Stricker, Manager

Discontinuing delivery

To Our Customers,

At Roma Pizza we are committed to providing the best quality at the most affordable price.

Because of high fuel costs and liability insurance expenses we have decided to discontinue delivery service of our pizzas and other menu offerings.

We apologize for any inconvenience to our valued customers.

As a special offer, enclosed please find four 10 percent discount coupons that can be used on any orders between now and December 1.

We look forward to seeing you again soon.

Anthony Roma

Apology for unavailability of product

Dear Valued Customer,

We apologize again for the delay in shipping the Hot Mama fleece-lined parka you ordered on September 12.

Our supplier has just notified us that this product will not be available this season. We have therefore canceled your order and your credit card will not be charged.

We apologize for any inconvenience. As a token of our good will, we would like to offer you a 10 percent discount on any other parka in our current catalog; please use coupon code 6SJ7 in any online order or give that code to the customer service representative if you place a telephone order. The coupon will be honored on any one purchase between now and January 1.

Sincerely,
Bruce Caplan

CHAPTER 27

Hiring and References

APOLOGY FOR MISSING INTERVIEW → 206

APOLOGY FROM INTERVIEWER FOR
MISSING INTERVIEW → 206

ASKING FOR MORE INFORMATION
FROM APPLICANT → 206

ASKING ABOUT DISCREPANCY ON
JOB APPLICATION → 207

EXPLAINING GAP IN RESUME → 207

FOLLOW-UP AFTER JOB INTERVIEW → 208

SUGGESTING ADDITIONAL TRAINING FOR
JOB APPLICANT → 208

UNABLE TO OFFER JOB → 208

TO FORMER COLLEAGUE ABOUT
HIRING RELATIVE → 209

MAKING COUNTERPROPOSAL TO
JOB OFFER → 209

DECLINING TO OFFER JOB → 210

DECLINING TO REHIRE ASSOCIATE → 210

UNABLE TO OFFER A JOB TO FRIEND'S
FAMILY MEMBER → 210

DECLINING TO CALL ABOUT JOB
FOR FRIEND → 211

DECLINING TO RESPOND TO
REFERENCE CHECK → 211

ASKING FOR REFERENCE → 211

DECLINING TO ALLOW USE OF NAME AS
A REFERENCE → 212

ASKING END TO USE OF NAME AS
A REFERENCE → 212

Apology for missing interview

Kenneth Hull, Director of Marketing
Rolling Meadow Manufacturing Company
Rolling Meadow

Dear Mr. Hull,

I very much apologize for missing my job interview yesterday.

An emergency arose involving a family member; I wanted to contact you but there was no opportunity to do so.

I realize this is an inauspicious first impression for someone who very much wants to be considered for the job position we were to discuss.

I assure you that missing appointments for any reason is out of character for me.

If you will be so kind as to give me a second chance to meet with you, I hope to demonstrate to you how much I want to work at Rolling Meadow Manufacturing Company.

I hope to hear from you soon.

Sincerely,
Carol Hay

Apology from interviewer for missing interview

Dear Sharon,

I want to apologize for missing your job interview yesterday. An emergency came up in another area of the company and I was called away.

Unfortunately, I was unable to get in touch with you before the time of your appointment.

I hope this hasn't soured you on the company and you will give us another chance. I was very much looking forward to meeting you; you come very well recommended and your background looks very strong.

Please call my secretary to set up another interview. This time I promise to be there.

Sincerely,
Scott Chase, Sales Director

Asking for more information from applicant

John Smith
Rolling Meadow

Dear John,

Thank you for your letter of application for the administrative assistant position currently open in our marketing department.

I am impressed with your credentials and work experience.

In reviewing the resume you submitted, though, I note a six-month gap at the beginning of the year in 2009. To get a better picture of your background, we would ask that you explain what you were doing in that period.

After we receive this information we will continue to process your application.

Sincerely,
Eleanor Hudson, Marketing Director

Asking about discrepancy on job application

Henry Sheenan
Rolling Meadow

Dear Mr. Sheehan,

Thank you for your resume and letter of application for a position at Rolling Meadow Real Estate Company.

On your resume you list a master's degree in accounting from Rolling Meadow University. It is part of our ordinary process to fact-check academic degrees and employment records. The university reports they could find no record of your attendance or the granting of a degree.

Before we proceed further in evaluating your candidacy for a position with our company, I would ask that you please contact me to discuss this matter.

Sincerely,
Linda Baker, Human Resources Director

Explaining gap in resume

Eleanor Hudson, Marketing Director
Rolling Meadow Manufacturing Company

Dear Ms. Hudson,

Thank you for your letter and your review of my resume in application for a position in the marketing department at Rolling Meadow Manufacturing Company.

I am very excited about the possibility of working for your company, and I know I would do a good job.

You asked about the six-month gap in my resume at the start of 2009. I apologize for leaving that open, but I found it difficult to fit a long story into a short space on the resume.

After two years of employment as an installer for Rolling Meadow Tile and Design, I decided that I wanted to make better use of my college degree and pursue a job in marketing and eventually management. I also had the advantage of being young and single, and for the first (and I expect, the only) time in my life I decided to head out on a backpacking trip to see a bit of the world.

It was a great experience, and I've gotten it out of my system. I intend to make use of what I learned in Europe and Asia in my career in marketing.

Please let me know if you have any other questions. I look forward to hearing from you soon.

Sincerely,
John Higgins

Follow-up after job interview

Karen Lewis
Rolling Meadow Advertising Agency

Dear Karen,

It has been two weeks since I met with you and interviewed for the position of assistant advertising director. Please forgive me if I seem a bit impatient, but I really want you to know how excited I am about the prospect of working with you.

If I am offered the job, I promise to bring that enthusiasm with me to work every day.

Please let me know if there are any other questions you might have for me or if you would like to meet again.

Sincerely,
Dick Maloney

Suggesting additional training for job applicant

Dan Sullivan
Rolling Meadow

Dear Mr. Sullivan,

Thank you for your application for the position of education coordinator at the Rolling Meadow Children's Museum.

Your academic credentials are excellent, and I was very impressed with your presentation at the interview. However, we are unable to offer you the job at this time because you lack certification as a teacher or equivalent experience working in programs for children.

If this sort of job is indeed your goal, I would suggest you consider taking specific classes and obtaining certification from an accredited university or by working as a teacher's assistant. Please feel free to call me to discuss this; I may be able to point you in the right direction.

Sincerely
Bill Wilson, Executive Director

Unable to offer job

Jessica Cummings
Rolling Meadow

Dear Jessica,

It was nice to receive your letter telling us about your success in college and your interest in coming back to work again this summer at our shop.

We have been privileged to have you on staff for the past two years; you were an excellent employee and a lot of fun to have on the staff.

Unfortunately, we are not going to be able to add any staff for the summer this year. Sales have been very slow this year, and we are searching for ways to be able to keep our full-time staff on the payroll.

I wish I had better news. We wish you the best of luck in finding a summer job; please feel free to list me as a reference.

Sincerely,
Rick Jones, Owner
Rolling Meadow Camera Shop

To former colleague about hiring relative

Mark Harris

Dear Mark,

It was good to hear from you again. It seems like only yesterday when we were both newly minted lawyers about to begin our careers at Morgan, Chase, Reynolds, and Burns.

I am glad that private practice has agreed with you. Speaking for myself, I remain happy staying at the firm and letting other people worry about bringing in new clients.

I have reviewed your son's resume, and it is quite impressive. Any law firm would be lucky to have him.

Unfortunately, our company does not have any job openings at this time. I will, though, keep his resume on file, and I wish him the best of luck.

Regards,
Kent Burns

Making counterproposal to job offer

Cherry Smith, human resources
Rolling Meadow Lumber Company

Dear Ms. Smith,

Thank you for your offer of employment as senior financial analyst in the accounting department of Rolling Meadow Lumber Company.

I am very excited about the prospect of joining the team. As you stated in your offering letter of March 15, the initial salary will be $47,500 per year with an annual review. Benefits include a family health plan, participation in an employer-matched 401(k) pension plan, and vacation leave of one week in the first year of employment, two weeks in second through fifth year of employment, and an additional vacation day added in each subsequent year after that. You also offered $10,000 toward moving expenses.

My only concern is this: I have checked with two moving and storage companies and have obtained estimates of $22,000 and $25,000 for the cost of transporting our possessions from Littleton to Rolling Meadow.

I would like to ask for an increase in the moving and relocation allowance to match the lower of the two estimates, $22,000. We will pay for any unexpected costs over that amount.

I hope this is agreeable to you. I very much want to come to work at Rolling Meadow Lumber, and I look forward to hearing from you.

Sincerely,
Lyle Mayflower

Declining to offer job

Jill Maxwell
Waterford

Dear Ms. Maxwell,

On behalf of the partners of Moore, Miller and Olsen, we want to thank you for coming to Rolling Meadow to interview for the position of associate counsel at our firm.

All of us who met you found you to be a very impressive young women with excellent credentials. We are confident you have a bright legal career ahead of you.

At this time, though, we are unable to offer you a position with our firm. Your areas of specialization and experience do not match our needs; we expect you will be more successful applying to a larger law firm with a wider range of clients.

We wish you the best of luck in your future endeavors.

Sincerely,
Lawrence Horton, Senior Partner
Moore, Miller and Olsen

Declining to rehire associate

Jessica Fisher
Rolling Meadow

Dear Jessica,

I was very pleased to hear that you have returned to town after being away for the past year to attend to family matters. I'm sure it was a difficult time for you and your family, but I also know the satisfaction that comes from being able to help those you love.

You asked if it would be possible for you to come back to work here at the store. I wish I had better news to give, but we are currently at full staff and in this economy we cannot afford to overstretch our budget.

There is the possibility of some evening hours this summer. And you have my word that if we have another opening you will be at the top of the list of people I call.

Again, welcome back. Please stop by the store some time so that we can chat.

Sincerely,
Janice Fowler

Unable to offer a job to friend's family member

Beverly Norton
Rolling Meadow

Dear Beverly,

Thank you for the opportunity to meet your lovely and talented granddaughter, Tara. I have already called her to let her know the situation, but I wanted you to hear directly from me as well.

Last winter when you said she would be spending the summer with you I was very excited about the possibility of Tara filling the seasonal internship opening at my gallery.

I am afraid, though, that in drawing up our budget we have found that we cannot afford to add an intern this year. I wish it was otherwise, but this year has already resulted in a loss for our business, and I do not expect a recovery until next year at the earliest.

Tara is a great job candidate. I wish her well in finding a job in this difficult economy.

Sincerely,
Julia

Declining to call about job for friend

Jack Gallagher
Rolling Meadow

Dear Jack,

You asked if I could help your son in his job search by calling my former employer; I'm afraid that wouldn't be of much help.

I retired from Rolling Meadow Advertising ten years ago, and I don't know of a single contemporary of mine who is still with the company. That really drives home the passage of time, but that's the fact.

I will, though, be happy to act as a reference to his character when he does make contact with an employer.

Sincerely,
Jim Frank

Declining to respond to reference check

Eric Raymond, Sales Director
Rolling Meadow Insurance Agency

Dear Mr. Raymond,

I have received your request for a recommendation on behalf of a former employee of this company, Parker Reis.

I can confirm that he was employed here from May 2008 through September 2008. Unfortunately, I am unable to provide a recommendation.

Sincerely,
Nicholas Singer
Waterford Title and Insurance Company

Asking for reference

Dear Mr. Curtis,

I have greatly enjoyed the opportunity to intern with you this summer. I learned a great deal and deeply appreciate your guidance on my career goals.

You went out of your way to share your knowledge and experience. I am more convinced than ever that I want to pursue a career in retail management.

With your permission I would like to use your name as a reference. I feel I have the confidence now to apply to some of the upscale stores in my hometown.

I am sure a good reference from you would be a great help.

Sincerely,
Tessa Simmons

Declining to allow use of name as a reference

Dear Lacey,

I received your request to serve as a reference in your applications for a position in retail management.

Unfortunately, I do not feel that I can help you. As I explained in your exit interview at the end of your summer internship, I felt there were a number of areas where you needed a great deal of improvement.

You are very bright and personable, but your lack of organizational skills greatly interfered with your work as store manager. If I was asked about your background, I would have to address that issue.

I hope you can improve your skills, and I wish you luck in your future career.

Good luck.

Sincerely,
Patrick Curtis

Asking end to use of name as a reference

Dear Glen,

At the time you left Diamonds Music, I was happy to serve as one of your references.

I said at the time that as your immediate supervisor I was happy to tell potential employers that you had been a knowledgeable salesperson and that your work ethic was excellent.

Six years later, I am still getting queries from perspective employers. I now feel that too much time has passed for me to make any comments on your current skills and qualifications.

I wish you luck in your future career. I must ask, though, that in the future you do not use my name as a reference.

Sincerely,
Patrick Curtis

CHAPTER 28

Employee Affairs

POLICY ON ACCEPTING GIFTS ❧ 214

INFORMING EMPLOYEES OF POLICY
REGARDING GRATUITIES ❧ 214

NOTICE OF DRESS CODE ❧ 214

REMINDER TO DEPARTMENT HEADS ABOUT
SUMMER DRESS CODE ❧ 215

POLICY ON BEREAVEMENT LEAVE ❧ 215

POLICY ON HOLIDAY SCHEDULE ❧ 215

POLICY ON RELIGIOUS
OBSERVANCES ❧ 216

POLICY ON DISPLAY OF POLITICAL
MATERIAL ❧ 216

POLICY ON OFFICE RELATIONSHIPS ❧ 216

OBJECTING TO PARTY ON
COMPANY TIME ❧ 217

DIRECTIVE FROM EXECUTIVE TO CHANGE
PARTY TIME ❧ 217

ADVISORY TO EMPLOYEES ABOUT
FLU OUTBREAK ❧ 217

NOTIFICATION OF SMOKING BAN ❧ 218

TOTAL BAN ON TOBACCO USE
BY EMPLOYEES ❧ 218

ADVISORY ON UPDATES TO ALCOHOL AND
DRUG POSSESSION POLICY ❧ 219

POLICY ON CELL PHONE USAGE
IN WORKPLACE ❧ 219

BAN ON PERSONAL MUSIC PLAYERS ❧ 220

ASKING CLARIFICATION OF LIABILITY
COVERAGE ❧ 220

RESPONSE TO QUESTION
ABOUT LIABILITY ❧ 220

ENDING COMPANY SUPPORT FOR
HOLIDAY PARTY ❧ 220

CHANGE IN POLICY REGARDING SNACKS FOR
NIGHT STAFF ❧ 221

ASKING TIMELY DELIVERY OF
MEETING MINUTES ❧ 221

SUGGESTING TIGHTER AGENDA FOR
STAFF MEETINGS ❧ 221

> **NOTE TO READERS:** Although, in general, any business may make hiring, termination, or policy decisions on any reasonable and nondiscriminatory basis, be sure to check with your company attorney or an employment law specialist if you have any doubts about the legality or propriety of a policy or action in the workplace.

Policy on accepting gifts

To: Employees of Rolling Meadow Lumber Company
From: Kirsten Thomas, human resources

I am writing to clarify and restate our policy regarding the total ban on accepting gifts from any company, organization, or individual that we do business with.

Gifts include anything of value, meals, sporting or theater tickets, or articles of clothing. This includes employees at work, on the road, as well as any interactions you may have off the job.

We do this to avoid any appearance of partiality toward customers or suppliers.

The full details of this policy are spelled out in the employee manual. Please discuss any questions about this policy with your supervisor or the human resources department.

Violations of the policy are cause for suspension or termination.

Informing employees of policy regarding gratuities

To All Employees,

It is the policy of the Rolling Meadow Historical Association that gratuities are not to be solicited or accepted for services rendered at the museum. Our guests pay an entrance fee or an annual membership, and all services within our walls are included.

For visitors insisting on offering a token of thanks, please ask them to visit the front desk where they can make a donation to the museum.

If you have any questions about this policy, please contact me to discuss them. Violations of any element of the employee handbook are grounds for discipline or dismissal.

William Hadwen, Director

Notice of dress code

To All Employees,

In recent weeks we have noticed a lack of attention to company guidelines regarding appropriate attire among employees.

I want to remind you that the employee handbook includes details of what we consider appropriate attire for those working on the sales floor, in the executive offices, and in the warehouse.

We do not mean to restrict anyone's freedom of expression, but it is our belief that sales professionals and support personnel should always be dressed in a professional way. Our customers have come to rely on our store as a cut above the discount retailers in quality of merchandise and level of service, and we intend to keep to that model.

Among articles of clothing not permitted are T-shirts, shorts, jeans, and clothing with political, commercial, or suggestive phrases. Workers in the warehouse and delivery departments have additional requirements regarding uniforms and safety shoes.

Please consult the manual or check with us in the human resources office if you have any questions about the dress code. Employees who are improperly attired can be sent home for the day, and repeated violation of the code can lead to termination.

Mary Grace, Personnel Manager

Reminder to department heads about summer dress code

To: All Department Heads
From: Human Resources

With the arrival of summer weather, we want to remind all department heads of company policy regarding our dress code.

It is our expectation that all employees maintain a professional appearance and adhere to all safety codes. That includes a ban on sandals and flip-flops and a requirement that all clothing be appropriate for both our workplace and our customers.

Our employee manual spells out what is appropriate and inappropriate to wear to the office and when visiting our customers or suppliers. Please contact HR with any questions.

Policy on bereavement leave

To All Employees,

Effective immediately, we have made changes to our policies on bereavement leave so that we are able to grant additional time off when necessary.

In addition to the existing policies that are detailed in the employee manual, we are adding the following,

- Any full-time employee may take one day off, with pay, to attend the funeral of a close friend or acquaintance who is not a family member. Requests for such bereavement leaves must be made in writing to the human resources department, and the company may require verification of the details of the request. No more than three such requests will be approved in each calendar year.
- Part-time employees are permitted to request as many as three days off, without pay, to make funeral arrangements or to attend a funeral for a member of their immediate family. Part-time employees may also take one day off, without pay, to attend the funeral of a close friend or acquaintance who is not a family member. A request for a bereavement leave must be made in writing to the human resources department, and the company may require verification of the details of the request.

The company may, at its discretion, grant additional unpaid time off for any employee who needs to travel a great distance or who has a reasonable exceptional need. Application for additional bereavement leave must be made in writing to the human resources department and must also be approved by the employee's supervisor.

Policy on holiday schedule

Memorandum from Human Resources Department

To All Department Heads and Employees,

As the end of the year and holiday season approaches, we want to remind all employees at Rolling Meadow Lumber about our corporate policy regarding observances of religious holidays.

We celebrate the diversity of our workers, and we want everyone to enjoy their own culture and respect that of others. Therefore, we instruct all employees not to decorate their offices or common areas with any religious symbols or statements.

Our annual holiday party will be held on December 20; details will be announced in a forthcoming memo. At that observance we will ask all members of the Rolling Meadow Lumber family to join in offering best wishes for the holidays and the New Year, in common cause and respect for each other.

If you have any questions about this policy, please contact the human resources department.

Policy on religious observances

To All Department Heads and Employees,

Here at Rolling Meadow Lumber we want to reinforce our commitment to honoring all religious and personal beliefs of our employees and our intention to follow the full scope of all federal and state laws in this area.

It is our policy that there be no discrimination of any kind in hiring, promotion, or other employment matters.

We also ask all employees to separate their religious beliefs and practices from the performance of their jobs in the workplace and at the premises of any of our suppliers and customers.

Please reread the employment manual for details of policies that are drawn from federal law and court decisions supporting the company's right to discipline or dismiss an employee or manager who discriminates against, harasses, or demeans another individual's religious beliefs.

If you have any questions about this policy, please contact the human resources department.

Policy on display of political material

To All Employees,

In this political season, it is very important that all employees understand company policy regarding the display of any kind of political material in the workplace.

Rolling Meadow Lumber respects the opinions and beliefs of all of our employees, suppliers, and customers. For that reason, we do not allow the display of political posters or banners or the wearing of buttons or other campaign items anywhere on company property. The same policy applies when sales, purchasing, or installation personnel visit suppliers or clients.

We encourage all employees to become involved in political campaigns and to exercise their right to vote. At the same time, we also remind staffers that the use of company telephones, computers, copying machines, and other equipment for political purposes is not permitted.

If you have any questions about this policy, please contact the human resources department.

Policy on office relationships

To All Employees,

The purpose of this memo is to advise all employees of a newly expanded section of the employee handbook regarding relationships between any manager and a staffer under his or her supervision.

Effective immediately, any person in a supervisory position who has a personal relationship with any staff member is advised to notify their department head or senior executive as soon as it is practical.

The reason for this policy is our commitment to protect the rights of all employees, both at the supervisory and staff levels. We seek to avoid any situation where a supervisory relationship could lead to harassment or special favors in the workplace. If necessary, the human resources department may choose to reassign employees to situations where such conflicts could not occur.

If you have any questions about this policy, or have any concerns about possible or actual harassment or favoritism in the workplace, please immediately contact the human resources department.

Objecting to party on company time

Stephanie Berman (e-mail)
Anderson Textile Company

Stephanie,

I just received your e-mail inviting me to the baby shower for Julie Vigneau on March 6.

I certainly wish Julie well, and I would like to help her celebrate her upcoming motherhood.

But I wonder if you want to rethink the timing for the party. It is set for 3 P.M. on a workday, something that is clearly not in keeping with company policy for personal events.

I know that there was a problem about a year ago with a similar party; we all received a memorandum from human resources reminding us of the need to schedule this sort of event outside of working hours and also the requirement that a department head give approval.

I would hate for anyone to get in trouble over this very special time for Julie.

Cindy Mason

Directive from executive to change party time

Stephanie Berman (e-mail)

Stephanie,

I have been made aware of your plans for a baby shower for Julie Vigneau on March 6 at 3 P.M. in Conference Room A.

While I join everyone in wishing Julie the best, as your supervisor I must inform you that the scheduling violates company policy. We do not permit personal parties during ordinary working hours.

I must ask that you reschedule the party for after 5 P.M., or on the weekend in a location not on company property. I will be speaking directly to Julie to make certain she understands we are only seeking that the party not take away from the performance of our jobs.

Mark Nichols

Advisory to employees about flu outbreak

To All Employees,
From Shelia Davis, health services

As you all know, there is a significant outbreak of influenza in our region, and we have already seen some illness among our work force.

The good news is that this season's flu appears to be relatively mild and not all that dangerous to people who do not have other underlying medical conditions. However, it is very contagious and can cause absences from work of about a week for those affected.

217

I am writing to advise you of our company policy regarding this illness. Our most important concern is for the health and well-being of our employees and their families. Secondly, we want to do everything we can to be able to continue our operations as near to normal as possible.

According to medical sources, the most common first stage of this particular strain is high fever and general pain; later stages progress to chest congestion and a persistent cough.

Please follow these guidelines,

- If you fell ill at home, please do not come to work. Call your personal physician and follow his or her instructions for treatment and recovery. Contact our office to advise us of your status so that we can track the health of all of our staff.
- If you become ill at work, please immediately leave your work area and come to the health center. We will evaluate all cases and make a determination about whether you should be sent home to recover or whether immediate treatment is required.
- Wash your hands frequently. We are also distributing hand sanitizers throughout our facility and ask you use them.
- If you cough or sneeze, cover your mouth and nose and then wash your hands.

Please feel free to call me at any time with questions. We all hope we can get past this outbreak without major impact on our personal lives and the success of the company.

Notification of smoking ban

To Department Heads and Employees,

Effective May 1, it will be against Rolling Meadow Lumber policy to smoke tobacco anywhere on company property and in company-owned vehicles.

We believe that the use of tobacco is a significant contributor to health care costs, a major expense for the company. And open flames and cigarette ash also present a fire threat in the workplace.

Any employee found smoking on company property, including outdoor areas, will be subject to disciplinary action; violations may result in suspension or termination of employment.

To assist employees, the company medical office will provide counseling on tobacco-cessation techniques and programs. In cooperation with our health insurance carrier, we will offer a one-time subsidy of as much as $500 per employee toward the documented cost of participation in any preapproved antismoking program.

Total ban on tobacco use by employees

To All Employees,

Effective immediately, the use of tobacco in any form is banned on company property as well as at the workplaces of our suppliers and customers.

It is our intention to maintain a safe and healthy environment for all employees. It is our judgment that the use of tobacco is a significant contributor to health care costs and also a danger in the workplace.

Smoking is not permitted anywhere on company property or in company-owned or operated vehicles.

Effective immediately, applicants for employment must agree not to smoke tobacco at the workplace or at home, and agree to random testing for the presence of nicotine in their system. Refusal to submit to a test, or a test result positive for tobacco use, will be grounds for dismissal.

Effective 90 days from today, all current employees of Consolidated Intergalactic must agree not to smoke tobacco at the workplace or at home, and agree to random testing for the presence of nicotine in their system. Refusal to submit to a test, or a test result positive for tobacco use, will be grounds for dismissal.

To assist our employees in meeting these new requirements, the company medical office will provide counseling on tobacco-cessation techniques and will offer subsidies for approved programs.

Advisory on updates to alcohol and drug possession policy

To All Employees,

We ask all staff to read the attached update to the company policy regarding the total ban on alcohol and illegal drugs in the workplace and in any location related to our operations and those of our suppliers and customers.

It is prohibited to:

- Use, possess, buy, or sell any narcotic or controlled substances.
- Use, possess, or buy medications without a valid prescription, or to sell such medications to others.
- Use, possess, buy, or sell alcohol.
- The purpose of our policy is to protect the health and safety of all employees in the performance of their duties.

The new section of our company policy adds the following:

- Any employee who is prescribed a drug that might in any way affect his or her ability to drive or operate machinery must notify the company's medical office. We reserve the right to temporarily or permanently reassign an employee whose performance may be affected in this way. If you have any questions about whether a particular medication may come under this policy, please consult with the medical office; all medical records will continue to be kept confidential.
- Any employee or part-time worker who is found in possession of alcohol, narcotics, or other controlled substances, or who misuses prescription drugs in any situation on or off company property, may be terminated if it is determined that this adversely affects the organization's reputation or standing in the community.

Policy on cell phone usage in workplace

To: Employees of Rolling Meadow Gas and Electric Company
From: Human Resources Department

Effective immediately, it is company policy that all employees are to turn off and not use any personal cell phone or other personal electronic device while on the job or in a company vehicle or workplace.

This policy is intended to help prevent dangerous distractions on the job, and especially in working areas and vehicles.

Violation of this policy will be considered sufficient cause for suspension from duty or termination.

All company vehicles and workplaces will continue to be supplied with officially authorized communication devices. These phones, radios, and computers are to be used only for official business and only when they can be operated in a safe manner.

Ban on personal music players

To All Employees,

Employees are not to use personal music players, including cell phones with music capabilities, in the workplace.

We consider these devices to be a safety hazard, interfering with the ability to communicate with others and distracting employees and others who are operating machinery.

Supervisors are asked to instruct employees not to use such devices. Subsequent violations of this policy should be reported to the human resources department for possible disciplinary action including termination of employment.

Asking clarification of liability coverage

To Lester Jones, Executive Director

As you know, we had an incident last week where a visitor to the company slipped and fell in the entrance lobby.

The man suffered a cut, which we helped treat with items from the first-aid kit. He declined transportation to the hospital.

After the incident, though, several of us who are part-time employees realized that we are not certain as to whether we are covered under the company's liability insurance policy. We certainly want to be able to help in any medical emergency, but we feel we need to know whether we are exposing ourselves to any legal risk in doing so.

I am writing to ask that the company issue a written policy regarding liability and other issues as they affect part-time employees. I look forward to hearing from you on this matter.

Response to question about liability

To Staff,

After a recent incident in which a customer was injured in the store, several staffers have asked for clarification as to their personal liability when coming to someone's assistance.

If an employee responds with reasonable efforts to assist a customer or another employee, our general liability insurance coverage will be extended to protect against personal liability.

Please understand that in the event of any serious injury or medical problem, employees should immediately summon an ambulance for emergency care.

Ending company support for holiday party

To All Employees
From Human Resources Department

At the suggestion of many employees, we have made a change in our policy for the annual holiday party that will save money in these difficult economic times.

The company will allocate all of the funds that would have been spent on the party to salaries and benefits; it is estimated this will help avoid the equivalent of two full-time layoffs.

Employees and their families who want to gather for a party will be allowed to use the company cafeteria for a potluck dinner that will be organized by a volunteer committee. Details will be forthcoming.

Although we realize this change in policy may disappoint some employees, we hope you will all join us in appreciating the fact we are able to redirect funds toward jobs.

Change in policy regarding snacks for night staff

To All Staff,

For many years, we have shown our appreciation to the staffers who work overtime hours late into the evening during the holiday season by providing a dinner buffet in the employee break room.

This has become a bit of a tradition here at the store, but I am afraid the dinners have become more and more elaborate—and costly—in recent years.

In this difficult year, we have consistently looked for ways to reduce costs without being forced to lay off employees. For that reason, we have decided to end the free buffet at least for this upcoming holiday season.

I hope there is no misunderstanding here about our commitment to our employees. This year we had to decide between free pizza or two fewer members of staff working overtime hours during the holiday.

Sincerely,
Patrick Curtis

Asking timely delivery of meeting minutes

To: Janice Miller, Sales Department
From: Tim Martin, Executive Vice President for Sales

As you know, I was away from the office last Tuesday and missed our monthly sales meeting. Although I try to attend all meetings, there are some schedule conflicts I am unable to avoid.

For the third consecutive time, the minutes of that meeting were not prepared and distributed for more than a week.

Please make an effort to prepare those minutes and distribute them by e-mail to all participants and interested parties within one day after each meeting. That is our standard policy for all departments.

There is a reason for this policy: it allows all of us, whether we are able to attend the meeting or not, to be up to date on all announcements, new programs, and policy changes.

If you have a problem accomplishing this important part of your job description, please contact me immediately so that we can discuss the matter.

Suggesting tighter agenda for staff meetings

To: Jennifer Abbott, Marketing Director
From: Phil Tyler, Executive Vice President for Marketing

Re: Weekly staff meeting

I am a firm believer in the value of staff meetings as a way to share important news, changes in policies, and to solicit the input of everyone in the department.

Unfortunately, I am afraid we have gone off the rails recently. At the last two meetings I attended, there was little or no planned agenda. It was closer to a social gathering than a business meeting. As much as I appreciate parties, I would really be unhappy to have to justify the hourly cost of the meeting based on the salaries of all involved.

Can I suggest the following? As the director of the department, you should draw up an agenda of topics to be discussed and send it to all attendees two or three days ahead of the meeting. You could also solicit suggestions from others at the same time.

The meeting itself should be held to the agenda, with perhaps ten minutes reserved at the end of the session for off-agenda questions.

I don't think you will have any difficulty coming up with topics for meetings, but if we do reach the point where there is nothing important to discuss, I would suggest canceling the meeting for that week. As you know, all of us are being asked to find ways to cut costs and improve productivity; these meetings should be part of that process.

CHAPTER 29

Workday Matters

QUESTIONING ITEM ON EXPENSE REPORT ➤ 224

DENYING EXPENSE ON TRAVEL REIMBURSEMENT FORM ➤ 224

ASKING RESUBMISSION OF TRAVEL EXPENSE FORM ➤ 224

DISAPPROVING ATTENDANCE AT CONFERENCE ➤ 225

DECLINING REQUEST FOR TIME OFF ➤ 225

DENYING VACATION TIME REQUEST ➤ 225

VIOLATION OF SICK DAY POLICY ➤ 225

DECLINING TO GRANT PAID DAY OFF ➤ 226

MEMO ABOUT EXCESSIVE LATENESS ➤ 226

NOTIFICATION ABOUT ABSENCE FROM TRAINING SESSIONS ➤ 226

REPRIMAND FOR REFUSING OVERTIME ➤ 227

FAILURE TO MEET DEADLINES ➤ 227

REASSIGNING EMPLOYEE ➤ 227

REDUCING HOURS FROM FULL TIME TO PART TIME ➤ 228

REQUESTING RETURN OF COMPANY EQUIPMENT ➤ 228

DISCREPANCY ON HOURLY RATE ➤ 228

Questioning item on expense report

To: Shelia Reynolds
From: Accounting

We are in receipt of your July expense report and receipts.

According to the employee travel policy, all car rentals must be made through one of the companies listed in the manual and using our corporate discount rate. Exceptions must document a reason for using an unauthorized company and must be approved by a supervisor.

On your form you ask reimbursement for a three-day rental of a motorcycle from a local dealer in Smith Point. We are withholding payment for that claimed expense and await further explanation and approval.

Please consult with your department head or contact the accounting department with any questions.

Denying expense on travel reimbursement form

To: John Martin, Sales and Marketing
From: Accounting Department

We have received your travel reimbursement request for April, including expenses related to your trip to Atlanta to attend the International Lumber Forum.

It is not company policy to pay the expenses of a spouse or traveling companion unless a department head has specifically requested such travel and has received preapproval from the accounting department.

Please consult your employee manual for full details of the company's guidelines regarding travel and reimbursement.

Please resubmit the form, listing only those expenses directly related to your own travel, and also excluding certain nonreimbursable expenses including entertainment, dry cleaning, and spa services.

Asking resubmission of travel expense form

To: Janice Timmons
From: Beverly Miller, Payroll Department

I am in receipt of your receipts for reimbursement for expenses incurred in travel to a seminar in Atlanta in April. We have received authorization from your department head to pay expenses related to that seminar.

The receipts you submitted show an additional flight, from Atlanta to Miami, plus a flight from Miami back to Rolling Meadow. I have checked with your supervisor and he has informed me that you took a week's vacation at the end of the seminar.

Please submit an accounting to us that shows the additional cost, if any, between a roundtrip from Rolling Meadow to Atlanta and the three flights you took. According to company travel policies, we will reimburse an amount equal to the cost of travel to and from the seminar and not any additional expenses related to your vacation.

Disapproving attendance at conference

To: Sandra Martin
From: Jim Hastings, Marketing Director

After reviewing the information you provided about next June's trade show in Venice, Italy, I have determined that this is not a good use of company funds.

I am thus not approving your request for travel to the conference. I am pleased that you want to broaden your knowledge of the field and encourage you to look for other ways to accomplish this.

Declining request for time off

To: Thomas Sullivan
From: Jan Dablook, Sales Director

I have received your request for vacation leave for the week of July 10 through July 16.

I am sorry to have to deny the request.

In May, all employees were notified that because of the imminent launch of our new line of security doors no requests for vacation or nonemergency personal days would be accepted until after August 1. We are all very busy with final production, promotion, and sales projects, and this is a time when we feel we need all staff fully involved.

I hope you are able to find a time for vacation that does not conflict with company needs. Please feel free to contact me to discuss any policy, including those dealing with vacation and personal leaves.

Denying vacation time request

To: Thomas Carter
From: Benefits Office

We have received your request for seven days of paid vacation time this July.

Based on the policies detailed in the employee manual, as of July you will have accrued a total of four days vacation time.

Company policy does allow an employee to "borrow" one day of vacation time from any that may be accrued in the three months that follow requested days. Therefore, we would be able to grant five days of paid leave if you make a request for that amount.

Please adjust your request and resubmit it.

If you have any further questions, please contact this office.

Violation of sick day policy

To Employee,

As we discussed this morning, we have determined that you have not followed company policy regarding the use of sick days.

We have noted a recurring pattern of "sick" days that occur on the day before or day after a holiday or a holiday weekend.

As stated in the employee manual, sick days may only be used for actual medical problems or appointments and may not be used to extend vacation or holiday periods. We have the right to request documentation of illness or medical treatment.

Your department head has been asked to closely monitor your attendance record. We hope we will not see further instances of inappropriate absences.

If we determine that sick days have been improperly used, we will seek your termination from employment.

We consider you a talented and capable worker, and we hope you will make a successful career with the company.

Declining to grant paid day off

To: Nancy Thomas
From: Human Resources

I have received your request for time off on May 16.

You are requesting the day to accompany one of your children on a school trip.

According to the employee handbook, this does not qualify as a reason for a paid leave. You are free to use one of your personal or vacation days for this purpose, with the approval of your departmental supervisor.

Please advise me of your plans as soon as possible.

Memo about excessive lateness

To: Rick Perry, Sales Associate
From: Dennis Sylvia, Sales Director

It has been brought to my attention that for the past month you have been consistently coming to work well past your scheduled starting time of 8:30 A.M.

As your supervisor, I would like to know if there is something that is preventing you from being at your desk at your scheduled start time. Within reason, we are willing to consider adjustment of working hours because of personal situations or difficulties in commuting schedules.

However, I must advise you that any further unexcused latenesses may result in disciplinary action, as outlined in the employee manual.

Please contact me immediately to discuss this matter.

Notification about absence from training sessions

To: Brian Cannon
From: Leslie Oliver, Sales Director

You were absent from an important sales training session yesterday, the second session you have missed in the past month.

Attendance at sales training meetings is an essential part of your job. Employees have been asked to build their schedules around the weekly sessions and to contact their supervisor if unforeseen circumstances prevent their attendance.

Please make an appointment to see me immediately. I will want to discuss this matter with you and then make arrangements for you to meet with marketing personnel to go over the materials presented at the session.

I expect you to attend future training meetings as scheduled.

Reprimand for refusing overtime

To: David Ellis
From: Director of Sales

According to your department supervisor, you have refused three requests for overtime work in the past month.

The sales department is involved in a major program requiring all salaried and commissioned employees to be available as needed. As outlined in the company manual, requests for overtime hours cannot be unreasonably refused.

All employees affected by this program were made aware of its urgency three months ago and were told to make appropriate plans so that they would be available for overtime hours when asked.

With this letter, I am asking that you be prepared to work overtime hours when requested.

Future problems of this nature will be considered as grounds for disciplinary action or termination of employment.

If you have any questions about company policy, please consult with the human resources department.

Failure to meet deadlines

Dear Fred,

I am writing to put on the record our discussion today about your repeated failure to meet reasonable deadlines in the performance of your job.

We are not in any way questioning your commitment to your job or to the company as a whole. You are a dedicated worker, and we appreciate your efforts.

However, we cannot continue to tolerate repeated instances of failure to meet deadlines for assignments. Your work in marketing is one link in the chain that leads from product development to sales and shipping; a delay at any point can have a serious impact on the company's ability to meet its financial goals.

We have arranged for training from a consultant who specializes in helping workers become more organized in the performance of their duties. The sessions will begin within the next two weeks.

It is our hope that you will be able to meet all of our expectations and make a career here at Rolling Meadow Lumber Company.

Please feel free to contact me at any time with questions about this letter or the general performance of the duties of your job.

Reassigning employee

To: Kathy Steele
From: Liz Herbert, Manager, Burk's Department Store

Effective immediately, we are changing your job description from sales clerk to inventory assistant. Your hourly wage will remain the same, although you will not be eligible for sales-related bonuses in your new position.

As we discussed in our meeting earlier today, we are doing so because of a sustained pattern of discrepancies in the accounting for your cash register. At this time we believe you do not have the attention to detail and other skills we require for the sales clerk position.

We do hope you will stay with the company and add new responsibilities as you gain experience.

Please report immediately to Saul Rabin, department head in the warehouse division. He will give you instructions for your new position and be available to answer further questions about the assignment.

Reducing hours from full time to part time

John Singer

Dear John,

I regret to inform you that, effective April 1, we will be forced to reduce your working hours from your present typical schedule of about thirty-five hours to about twenty hours per week.

We have no choice but to make this change because of severe reductions in state funding and donations.

You have been an excellent member of our staff for nearly a year, and this change is in no way meant to express any dissatisfaction with your work. We would not be making this change for any reason other than lack of funds.

I will be placing a copy of this memo in your file as a commendation of your services to the organization.

Please meet with me at your first opportunity to discuss your new schedule.

Requesting return of company equipment

To Departing Employee,

According to our records, you were issued a laptop computer to be used when on company-approved travel.

Please return the laptop computer, along with all power cords, cables, software, carrying cases, and other accessories to the office services department at least two business days before your last day of employment. You will be issued a receipt for the items, which we ask that you immediately deliver to the payroll department.

As outlined in the employee manual, your final paycheck will be withheld until all loaned equipment is returned.

Discrepancy on hourly rate

Margaret Reeves
Margaret's Cleaning Services

Dear Ms. Reeves,

I recently engaged your company to clean my house, and I have been generally satisfied with the work done and the professionalism of your staff.

When I agreed to use your service, the terms were that your workers would be at my home on Tuesday mornings, working for no more than three hours and paid at a rate of $18 per hour.

When I returned home on Tuesday, I saw that the invoice left on my kitchen was for five hours at $20 per hour.

If I am to continue using your company's services, I must insist that it be under the terms we agreed. Please advise.

Sincerely,
Gloria Abbott

CHAPTER 30

Firings, Layoffs, and Cutbacks

ANNUAL LETTER TO EMPLOYEES IN
DIFFICULT YEAR ➴ 231

ADDRESSING RUMOR OF LAYOFFS ➴ 231

ANNOUNCING CLOSING OF OFFICE ➴ 231

ASKING SUPERVISORS TO
CURTAIL OVERTIME ➴ 232

CUTTING SALARIES ACROSS
THE BOARD ➴ 232

NOTIFICATION OF LAYOFF ➴ 232

ADVISING OF COMPANY-WIDE
LAYOFFS ➴ 233

NOTICE OF SALARY FREEZE ➴ 233

REDUCING WORK WEEK
FOR EMPLOYEE ➴ 234

CANCELING BONUSES ➴ 234

NOTIFYING EMPLOYEE OF ELIMINATION
OF JOB ➴ 234

NOTICE OF TERMINATION ➴ 235

ASKING FOR RESIGNATION ➴ 235

ADDING FEE FOR CHILDCARE
BENEFIT ➴ 235

DISCONTINUING VISION
CARE BENEFIT ➴ 236

ANNOUNCING INCREASE IN HEALTH
INSURANCE COST ➴ 236

SUSPENDING TUITION
REIMBURSEMENT PROGRAM ➴ 236

ANNOUNCING CLOSURE
OF BUSINESS ➴ 237

SEEKING ALTERNATIVE TO LETTER
OF RESIGNATION ➴ 237

Annual letter to employees in difficult year

To: Employees of Rolling Meadow Lumber Company
From: Jonathan Neal, President

As this difficult year comes to a close, I want to take this opportunity to thank all of you for the dedication and hard work you have given to Rolling Meadow Lumber Company.

It has not been an easy year for our company, and I am sure all of you have experienced personal difficulties. It is no secret that sales are down and we experienced our first operational loss in company history.

The good news is that we have all pulled together to find ways to reduce our costs without having to lay off employees.

I know you will all join with me in looking for ways to make our way through the coming year in expectation of a return to more normal financial conditions.

Please accept my best wishes for a healthy and prosperous new year.

Addressing rumor of layoffs

To: Employees of Rolling Meadow Lumber Company
From: Jonathan Neal, President

In this time of economic difficulty, I would like to address some widespread—and incorrect—rumors that are circulating throughout the company.

At this time, there are no plans for reorganization or layoffs at our Rolling Meadow factory. It is our hope that the cost reductions and production efficiencies already in effect will allow us to keep our company and family of employees intact.

As I stated in our recent annual meeting, if the economy and our sales continues to decline we will seek to find ways to reduce working hours across the company rather than lay off employees. We hope we are not forced to do that, but we feel this would be in keeping with our core values.

I promise to keep all of you informed of any major changes in our situation, and I welcome suggestions from anyone in the company about ways to weather this economic storm.

Announcing closing of office

To: Employees of Rolling Meadow Lumber Company
From: Jonathan Neal, President

We are announcing today that our satellite shipping center in Waterford will be closed effective March 15.

We have determined that we can make significant cost savings by incorporating that small office into our main facility in Rolling Meadow.

All employees currently working at the Waterford office will be offered jobs performing the same duties at our main plant. Our human resources department is meeting with all affected staffers today.

I want to reiterate to all of our family of employees that it will always be our goal to seek budget savings in operational costs before considering layoffs or reduction in working hours.

Asking supervisors to curtail overtime

To: All Supervisors
From: Ed Miller, Director of Operations

Effective immediately, all overtime hours must be approved in advance by department heads.

In these difficult times, it is our goal to avoid layoffs among full-time staffers; one way to do this is to sharply curtail or eliminate overtime pay.

In general, overtime will only be approved in the event of emergencies or to fulfill unanticipated customer orders.

Please feel free to contact me to discuss this matter or any other payroll issue.

Cutting salaries across the board

To All Salaried Employees,

It is with regret that I must inform you that, effective January 1, we will be reducing all salaries and hourly wages by 5 to 10 percent.

We do not take such an action lightly; we realize this will be difficult for all our valued employees.

This reduction will save the company about $2 million per quarter; it will also allow us to stay at full employment. Without the reduction in salary and wages, we estimate we would have had to lay off about 100 people, and that is something we will always seek to avoid.

Your department head will meet with each of you individually in the coming days to discuss this matter. The amount of the salary reduction will be on a sliding scale with those in the highest wage bracket seeing the largest reduction.

It is our hope that the economy will begin to recover soon, and it is our promise that once we return to profitability we will begin to return salaries and wages to their previous levels and to progress from there.

And for the record, members of the executive committee are also affected by this reduction, including me.

Kevin Jeffers, President

Notification of layoff

C. John Kent, shipping department

Dear Mr. Kent,

It is with regret that we must inform you that your full time employment will end effective March 1.

As you were informed by your supervisor, economic conditions force us to reduce our work force by 10 percent; with the exception of certain employees determined to be essential to operations, we have made layoffs beginning with those most recently hired.

Although we cannot make any promises at this time, it is our intention that when conditions permit us to resume hiring we will first offer jobs to former employees.

Your supervisor has asked you to contact the human resources department by the end of the day to schedule an appointment to review your available benefits, eligibility for severance pay, accrued vacation time, and information about unemployment payments.

In addition, the company will be working in cooperation with the Rolling Meadow Chamber of Commerce to establish a local web-based job bank listing available positions in the area.

Again, on behalf of all of us, please accept our apologies for this unfortunate situation.

Advising of company-wide layoffs

To All Employees,

I am afraid it should come as no surprise that Wilson Textiles did not meet its financial goals for the past year. We expect that the coming year will not be quite as bad, but we are already in a hole.

I have always promised to be truthful and upfront with all of our employees, and I wanted you all to hear the whole story from me instead of from the rumor mill.

It is our intention to continue to look for ways to trim as much from our spending as possible and to hold on to as many of our employees as we possibly can. At this point, I expect that we will have to lay off about 100 of our staff, a decision that pains all of us greatly.

In keeping with company policy, job cuts will be made based on seniority; this means we will have to lay off some of our most promising young staffers. The only exceptions will be in positions that we deem to be essential and for which we do not have a more experienced employee.

Although we must—in fairness—call this a layoff, it is our hope that it will be more of a furlough for many of those affected. We promise to offer jobs to those laid off before any outside applicants are considered.

Anyone laid off will be entitled to all company benefits as promised in the employee handbook as well as any state unemployment payments.

We expect we will have a plan ready to announce in about two weeks.

I wish the news was better. I hope everyone here at Wilson understands that this action is in no way a reflection on the fine work and dedication that all of you have shown.

Marylou Arnott, President

Notice of salary freeze

To All Employees,

The final budget for the next fiscal year has been approved by the Board of Directors.

Your department heads will be advising you of various changes to our budgets that will affect marketing, promotion, capital expenditures, and office supplies. We welcome suggestions from any employee on additional ways to save money.

It is our belief that our family of workers is our greatest asset and needs to be protected. It has been our goal all through this difficult year to find ways to trim our operating costs and expenses while avoiding layoffs.

Effective immediately, all salaries and hourly wages will be frozen at their present level. We hope that better results in the coming year will permit us to lift this freeze.

Thank you.

Marylou Arnott, President

Reducing work week for employee

Peter Hall
Rolling Meadow

Dear Peter,

I regret to inform you that, effective May 1, we will be reducing your work schedule from thirty hours per week to twenty-four hours per week.

This change is in no way a reflection on the quality of your work. You are an excellent worker with a great attitude and a commitment to the team.

As you know, in this poor economy our sales have fallen off dramatically. We hope for a change in the coming months, and we will certainly try to give you more hours when we can.

We understand that this will present difficulties to you. Please discuss with me the best schedule for your reduced hours; we would fully understand it if you were to seek a second job elsewhere, and we will do everything we can to accommodate your needs.

Sincerely,
Greg Wilson

Canceling bonuses

To All Employees,

As we reach the end of this difficult year, I want first of all to thank everyone for their dedication and hard work all through the year.

Sadly, though, I must report that we will not be able to give bonuses this year. The numbers are just not there to support it; we ended the year with a loss.

We had to choose between paying bonuses and laying off staff, and I'm sure you will agree with me in our decision. As always, the staff at Curtis Department Store is like family to each other, and that will always be our goal.

The good news is that we will enter the New Year with our present work force intact and with high hopes for better results.

My very best to you and your family; keep up your excellent work and thank you again.

Sincerely,
Patrick Curtis
President, Curtis Department Store

Notifying employee of elimination of job

Dear Sarah,

I am sorry to inform you that your position as assistant cashier will be eliminated effective March 31.

We are forced to take this action because of a sharp decline in business; your job is one of about twenty positions we have had to remove from our budget.

We were extremely pleased with the quality of your work and are very sorry to lose you. When economic conditions improve, we would hope to be able to offer you a job.

Please don't hesitate to use my name as a reference for other jobs you might seek.

You are entitled to certain benefits and accrued vacation pay. Please make an appointment to see Mary Mulligan in human resources as soon as possible.

Notice of termination

Jim Boehner, receiving department

Your employment with Rolling Meadow Lumber Company has been terminated, effective immediately.

As stated in the employee manual, any member of the staff may be terminated for any lawful reason at any time.

Your department head will escort you to the human resources department immediately to discuss arrangements for issuance of your final paycheck and any benefits for which you may be eligible.

You will be expected to clear your desk and remove any personal effects and leave the building immediately after your appointment at human resources.

Asking for resignation

To Charlotte Flannigan,

As you are aware, your employment at Consolidated Manufacturing will terminate on May 16. We have already discussed the reasons for this decision by the company.

As your immediate supervisor, I am giving you the opportunity to voluntarily resign your position before that date. By exiting in this way, your employment record will not indicate that you have been terminated for cause.

This may help you find a job that is a better fit for you. I would suggest you meet with human resources to discuss this option, including its effects—if any—on your benefits.

Adding fee for childcare benefit

To All Employees,

We have been pleased to be able to offer on-site childcare to full-time employees for the past ten years. We are very proud of our facility and intend to maintain it at the highest level.

However, in this economy, we find it necessary to impose a daily fee to partially defray the cost of operations of the childcare center. Although we realize this may cause some difficulty for employees who make use of this benefit, in fairness we feel that users should bear some of the cost.

Effective March 1, we will deduct from paychecks fees for use of the facility. The charges will be on a sliding scale, based on the pay rate of each employee and the number of children in care.

Please read the enclosed rate schedule. For further information or to ask questions about this policy, please contact the benefits office.

Discontinuing vision care benefit

To All Employees,

We regret to inform you that, effective April 15, we will be discontinuing the vision care benefit included in the health care package offered to all full-time employees.

The costs of health care continue to rise sharply, and we are determined to find ways to reduce our expenditures in all departments in order to avoid layoffs.

The savings to the company realized by discontinuing the vision care option will be applied to the overall cost of the health care benefit.

Please consult the benefits office if you are interested in purchasing a vision care add-on to your company-provided health care plan.

Announcing increase in health insurance cost

To All Employees,

Effective March 1, the employee contribution to the cost of company-supported health insurance will increase between 5 and 7 percent. Rates will vary based on the number of dependents covered and any options you may have selected.

As you know, medical costs continue to increase rapidly. Rolling Meadow Lumber Company is committed to providing our employees with the best possible package of benefits, and we will continue to subsidize the health insurance plan.

We apologize for having to pass along the increase in costs. Once again, we are in a situation where we must either reduce costs or consider layoffs of staff.

Please contact the benefits office if you have any questions about the new rates or if you want to find out about alternative plans that may be less costly. Please note, though, that lower-cost plans may require higher copays or deductibles.

Suspending tuition reimbursement program

Dear Valued Employees,

I am sorry to inform you that we have decided to suspend our tuition reimbursement program, effective immediately. Any employee currently enrolled in an authorized course will continue to receive payments through the end of the class.

Although we very much want to support our employees in furtherance of their education and training, we have decided to apply the money in this account to salaries for the coming year. In this way we expect to avoid or reduce any possible layoffs.

It is our hope to resume this program and others recently ended as soon as possible.

Thank you for your understanding.

Bill Princup, President

Announcing closure of business

To Our Valued Patrons,

The Bartlett family has been honored to be a part of the Rolling Meadow community for the past twenty-three years.

Running the Tavern on the Square has been a labor of love for three generations of our family.

It is with regret, though, that we must announce that we will be closing our doors on May 31. We have found we can no longer compete financially against the many chain restaurants that have come to town. We believe we offered the best food at the best possible prices, but this battle was one we could not win.

All of us will be working for the next two months. We hope that our customers—many of whom have become like part of our extended family—will come by for a few more meals before the kitchen closes.

Sincerely,
Tom Bartlett

Seeking alternative to letter of resignation

Dear Helen,

I was sorry to receive your letter of resignation from the position of sales supervisor in our sales and marketing department.

Before I accept it, I would like to see if there is some way we can address your concerns and persuade you to stay.

As your supervisor, I feel that you have performed quite well in your brief time with the company; your departure would be a big loss to us all.

In your letter you make reference to personal conflicts you have had with some of the others in our department. With your permission, I would like to ask the human resources department to become involved and to look for a way to improve the working environment.

Please advise me by the end of the day whether you would like to explore this opportunity. I hope you will allow us to try to keep a valued employee.

Shelia Kelly, Sales and Marketing Director

Index

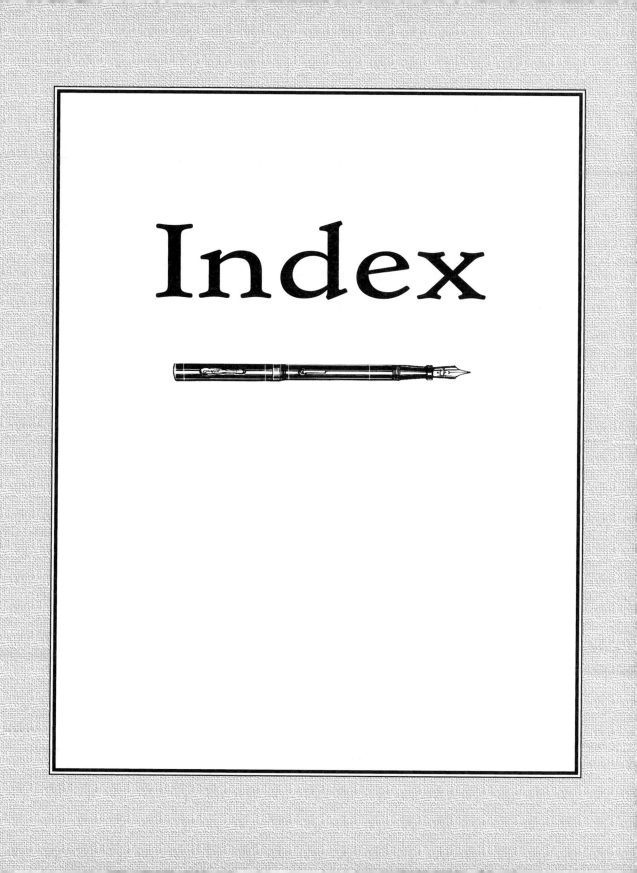

Adult party, 26
Advanced placement course, 161
Airline issues, 119–20
Alcohol possession policy, 219
Allergies, 58, 64
Anniversaries, 63, 65
Apartment
  damage to, 127
  rental issues, 121–29
  rent reduction, 122–23
  repair requests, 123, 124
Appointment, missing, 101
Arguments, 24–25, 38
Attorney, power of, 12
Attorney advice, seeking, 97
Auto rental loss, 82
Auto repair complaint, 98
Awkward situations, 25

Babysitter issues, 61
Bad mood apology, 54
Baggage insurance, 82
Bereavement leave, 215
Bills
  clarifying, 86
  disputing, 87, 88, 92, 94, 105
  itemizing, 86
  justifying, 80
  reviewing, 77, 101
Bonuses, canceling, 234
Book donations, 143–44
Boss, letters to, 184–88

Business
  closing, 199, 237
  letters regarding, 183–237
  personal business, 71–129
  reducing hours for, 113
Bus route complaint, 180
Bus stop change, 162

Cable company bills, 77, 101
Campaign involvement, declining, 171
Candidate support, declining, 171
Caregiver complaints, 98–99
Caretaking services, 76
Car pool arrangements, 151
Caterer costs, 76–77
Cell phone issues, 31, 219
Chairmanship, declining, 134
Child
  allergies of, 58
  death of, 4, 16
  transporting, 57
Childcare benefit fee, 235
Childcare needs, 99
Children
  and adult party, 26
  caring for, 61
  child support for, 32–33
  controlling, 58
  and divorce, 32–33
  issues regarding, 56–61
  and school, 153–64
  teasing/bullying, 160–61
  visits from, 59–60, 67

Church
  changing, 166–67
  construction plans for, 167
  funding goals, 167
  matters regarding, 165–68
  member thanks, 166
  and politics, 168
  sermon objections, 167–68
Civic club invitation, 133
Classes, canceling, 88, 202
Classroom disruptions, 156–57
Class trip supervision, 154–55
Club events, 64, 132–40
Club resignation, 135
Coaches, seeking, 151
Coaching request, declining, 158
Coffee club rules, 191
Collections notice, 195
College aid request, 164
College grades, 23
Committee dedication, 138
Committee withdrawal, 136
Community organizations, 131–68
Community pool cleanliness, 177
Community service, ending, 178
Company equipment, returning, 228
Company investment, 80
Complaints, 84–90, 93–120.
  See also specific complaints

Condolences and sympathy, 3–7

Conference attendance, 225

Conflict of interest issues, 177

Consultation fees, 78–79

Contracts, 74–75

Contribution request, declining, 148–49

Contributions, seeking, 143

Corporate support, withdrawing, 149

Course fees, 164

Credit cards
late fees for, 87–88
protecting, 81–83
returns on, 81
and warranty issues, 81

Customer loyalty card, 201

Customer service, 200–204

Cutbacks and layoffs, 230–37

Damages, 43–44, 60, 127

Daycare issues, 154

Deadlines, meeting, 227

Death, announcing, 16

Default notice, 85

Delivery, discontinuing, 204

Delivery charges, adding, 203

Difficult year letter, 231

Dinner club policies, 64

Dinner group, 65

Dinner guests, 64, 68–69

Dinner invitation, declining, 64

Discount, asking for, 110

Discount, denying, 195

Discount programs, 201, 202

Disputes, 54, 84–90. *See also specific disputes*

Divorce matters, 32–33, 50–52, 159–60

Doctors, 10–11, 17

Dogs. *See also* Pets
complaints about, 38–40, 126
dog-sitting, 40–41
license for, 181
supervising, 38–39
teasing, 40

Donations
accepting, 144
complaint about, 150
declining, 144
issues regarding, 141–52
listing amounts of, 146–47
returning, 145
seeking, 143–44

Dress code notice, 214–15

Driving issues, 57

Drug possession policy, 219

Elders, assisting, 28–30

Election issues, 171–72, 182

Employee
annual letter to, 231
death of, 7
hiring, 205–12
matters regarding, 189–92, 205–37
policies for, 213–22
reassigning, 227–28

Endowment allocation, 150

Equipment, returning, 228

Equipment, sharing, 38

Estate item purchase, 34

Estrangement, family, 23

Estrangement, friend, 48

Event, missing, 63

Eviction notice, 126

Executive, death of, 6, 7

Family affairs, 21–34

Family argument apologies, 38

Family estrangement, 23

Family involvement, 28–29

Family matters, 22–26, 32

Family member loan, 32

Final arrangements, 15–20

Financial support, ending, 31

Fire victims, helping, 166

Firings, 234–35. *See also* Layoffs

Florist bill complaint, 105

Flu outbreak advisory, 217–18

Food allergies, 58, 64

Food quality complaint, 107

Friends
concern about, 48–49
disputes with, 54
estrangement with, 48
former friend, 5
in grave health, 13
helping, 47–55
inquiring about, 12–13
intervention for, 55
memorial for, 4–5

Friends—*continued*
  moving away from, 55
  and neighbors, 35–69
  sympathy for, 4
  thanking, 49
Fundraising
  complaints about, 146–47
  matters regarding, 141–52
  objections to, 146–47
  phone bank for, 142
  withdrawing funds, 149
Funeral arrangements, 17–19

Gift-acceptance policies, 214
Gift card complaint, 108
Gift-giving issues, 23, 25, 65,
  177, 190
Goodbye, saying, 6, 55
Government affairs, 176–82
Gratuities policy, 214
Guests, 64, 68–69

Handicapped parking, 181–82
Handling charge complaint,
  108
Health insurance matters, 73,
  236
Health issues, 8–14
Helping friends, 47–55
Hiring employees, 205–12
Hiring relatives/friends, 209,
  210
Holidays
  assistance with, 24

parties during, 24, 220–21
  schedule for, 215–16
  trip costs for, 159
Home, donating, 20
Home, selling, 20, 28, 128–29
Home care service complaints,
  98–99
Home repair complaint, 100
Hospital payment plan, 74
Hospital release, 6
Hotel
  complaints about, 116–20
  condition of, 117
  noise in, 118
  rate adjustment for, 118–19
  reservations for, 116–17
Hourly rate discrepancy,
  228–29
House-sitting, 41
Hurt feelings, 53

Illness. See also Health issues
  announcing, 16
  and breaking lease, 127–28
  of former friend, 5
  of spouse, 13
  support during, 9
Inappropriate words, 55
Ingredient substitution
  complaint, 106
Insufficient funds, 85
Insurance policy cancellation,
  73
Internet use, 59, 101
Internship, declining, 188

Intervention for friend, 55
Investment, declining, 80
Invitation, declining, 64
Invoice payment requests,
  194–95
Invoice questions, 196
Item
  on display, 145–46
  refusing, 113
  removing, 46
  replacing, 43
  returning, 33, 42–44, 57,
    105, 111–13

Job
  applying for, 206–7
  eliminating, 234–35
  leaving, 185
  loss of, 50
  searching for, 211
  terminating, 235
  training for, 208
  unavailability of, 208–10
Job interviews, 206, 208
Job offers, 209–10
Job opportunities, 185
Job references, 211–12

Landlord concerns, 121–29
Landscaping costs, 37, 76,
  94–96, 202–3
Layoffs, 190, 232–33
Lease issues, 124–28
Legal advice, seeking, 97

Legal bill dispute, 87
Liability coverage, 220
Library concerns, 152, 179
Linen rental complaint, 94
Loan
    clarifying, 145
    declining, 80
    extension for, 80
    to family member, 32
    of item, 42–45
    renegotiation of, 73
    repaying, 85–86
    of vehicle, 44–45
Loud parties, 41
Loyalty card, 201

Mailing lists, 90
Manufacturer complaint, 104
Medical issues, 8–14
Medical records, 11
Meetings, 135–36, 221–22
Membership cancellation, 75
Membership matters, 132–40
Memorial donation, 143–44
Memorial for friend, 4–5
Memorial service invitation, 17
Money
    issues regarding, 72–83
    and possessions, 27–34
    requests for, 29–32
    and work matters, 193–99
Motor vehicles department, 179
Mourning, 5, 14

Moving assistance, 41–42
Moving away, 55
Music players, 220

Neighbor
    cutting tree, 37
    dog of, 38–39
    and friends, 35–69
    helping, 12
    introducing, 37
    issues regarding, 36–46
New relationship, 52
Newspaper coverage request, 139–40
Newspaper errors, 140
Nomination acceptance, 133
Nursing home, 14

Office concerns, 216–17, 231. See also Work
Overbearing guests, 68–69
Overtime, 227, 232
Ownership of display items, 145–46
Ownership transfer, 128

Parental care, 28–29
Parent teachers association, 155
Partisanship objections, 182
Part-time employment, 188, 228
Party
    adult party, 26

on company time, 217
    complaints about, 41
    holiday party, 24, 220–21
    missing, 63
    retirement party, 191
Payment assistance, 74
Payment plans, 73–74
Payment requests, 194–95
Personal business, 71–129
Personal life difficulties, 14
Person to person matters, 1–20
Pets, 5, 68. See also Dogs
Pet-sitting, 40–41
Photograph issues, 88, 106
Political actions, objecting to, 138–39
Political mail, stopping, 174
Political matters, 170–75
Political organization sponsorship, 174–75
Politicians, 172–73
Politics and church, 168
Politics and work, 216
Pool supervision, 60
Possessions and money, 27–34
Power of attorney, 12
Prepaid funeral arrangements, 18–19
Preschool, withdrawing from, 154
Price reduction, 83
Products
    complaints about, 103–8
    deceptive packaging, 106–7
    restocking, 105–6, 111
    seeking, 110–11

Products—*continued*
substituting, 83
unavailability of, 204
Project
postponing, 78
reducing size of, 77–78
suggestions for, 134
Property, selling, 20, 28,
128–29
Public facility concerns, 168,
173–74, 177–79
Purchases, 81–83. *See also* Bills

Real estate matters, 121–29
Reckless driving, 57
Recycling fee objections,
180–81
Refund request, 75, 83, 112
Relationship, new, 52
Religion and work, 216
Religious observances, 216
Remarriage, 52–53
Rent in trade, 122–23
Rent reduction request, 122
Repairs
complaints about, 96–98,
100, 107–8
cost of, 79
refund for, 97
by relatives, 32
request for, 123, 124
Resignation
alternative to, 237
asking for, 235
as club president, 135

from community board,
135
from community group,
134
due to advancement,
185–86
due to family, 186, 187
due to illness, 136, 186
explanation for, 185–87
of politician, 173
as volunteer, 137
without explanation, 185
Restaurant bill reduction, 92
Restaurant service complaint,
93, 102
Restocking fee complaint,
105–6
Restocking product, 111
Resume issues, 207
Retirement notification, 187
Retirement party invitation,
191
Reunions, 65–66
Roommate possessions, 46

Safety complaint, 124
Salary issues, 232, 233
Satisfaction guaranteed return,
105
Scholarship bequest, 143
Scholarship payment, 89
School
events at, 159–61
expansion plans for, 172
fees for, 162–64

lunch menu for, 158
matters regarding, 153–64
teasing/bullying at, 160–61
withdrawing child from,
154
Security deposit return, 122
Sermon objections, 167–68
Service
canceling, 75
issues regarding, 91–102
not using, 92
reducing cost of, 76
Service company
choosing, 196–97
contract changes by, 198
dismissing, 198
Service fees
adding, 204
overcharging for, 87
renegotiating, 198–99
Service person complaint, 95
Service provider agreement,
199
Shipping delay, 201
Short-term contracts, 74–75
Sick day policy violation,
225–26
Single parents, 159–60
Smoking ban notice, 218
Snow removal request, 123
Social engagements, 62–69
Soda complaint, 104
Speakers, 137–38
Special-event room complaint,
102
Special-needs family, 10